MW01383726

Customs Broker Exam Study Guide & How to Start Your Own CHB Business
Thru Apr. 2014 Exam Edition

Jon K Sasaki, LCB

CHB Solutions

Published 2010, 2011, 2012, 2013, 2014 by CHB Solutions, A division of Attaché Books
Vancouver, Washington, U.S.A.

CHB Solutions

Manufactured in the United States of America

10   9   8   7   6   5   4   3   2   1

Library of Congress Cataloging-in-Publication Data

Sasaki, Jon K.
    Customs Broker Exam Study Guide & How to Start Your Own CHB Business: Thru Apr. 2014
    Exam Edition / Jon K Sasaki, LCB.

Business & Economics, Exports & Imports

ISBN-13: 978-0692241219
ISBN-10: 0692241213

The internet web addresses in this book were confirmed to be valid and correct at the time of the book's publication but may be subject to change.

Disclaimer:

This book is designed to provide expert guidance regarding the subject matter covered. This information is given with the understanding that neither the author nor the publisher is engaged in rendering legal, accounting, or other professional advice. Since the details of your situation are fact dependent, you should also seek the advice of a competent professional.

Contents at a Glance

————Book 1————
Customs Broker Exam Study Guide

1.	Introduction	1
2.	Getting Started	2
3.	Nature of the Exam	3
4.	How to Use this Book	4
5.	HTS Classification Tips	6
6.	GRI's in Exam Examples	16
7.	Most Commonly Tested	36
8.	All Sections Appearing on Exams	70
9.	Exam with Commentary (Apr. 2014)	85

Contents at a Glance

----------Book 2----------
How to Start Your Own CHB Business

1. **Introduction**   167

2. **Necessary Links**   168

3. **Start with Customs**   169
    Customs broker license   169
    To operate under a trade name   169
    District permit request   171
    Filer code request   173

4. **Type of Organization**   175
    Legal designation   175
    Taxes   176

5. **Marketing your CHB Business**   177
    Customs website   177
    Port website   177
    Other marketing advice   177

6   **ABI Vendor**   178
    Selecting an ABI vendor   178
    Reproducing customs forms   179
    Letter of intent   179
    VPN ISA   181

7. **Selecting a Surety Company**   182

9. **Running Your CHB Business**   183
    Power of attorney   183
    ACH payment   186
    Accounting software   186
    Pricing   186
    Truckers   186
    Necessary office equipment   187
    Recordkeeping   187
    Working with customs   187

Contents at a Glance

----------Book 3----------

Import & Export Documentation Simplified: A Handbook of Samples, Templates, & Tips

1.	Introduction (in Brief)	188
2.	Air Waybill (AWB)	189
3.	Arrival Notice (A/N)	193
4.	Bill of Lading (BL)	197
5.	Booking Request	201
6.	Cargo Insurance Certificate (COI)	205
7.	Certificate of Origin (COO)	209
8.	Commercial Invoice (CI)	213
9.	Declaration for Free Entry of Returned U.S. Goods (USGR)	217
10.	Declaration of No Wood Packing Material (WPM)	221
11.	Declaration of Non-Coniferous Wood Packing Material (WPM)	225
12.	Entry Summary (Customs Form 7501)	229
13.	Importer Security Filing Form (ISF)	233
14.	Importer's Blanket Statement of Non-Reimbursement of Anti-Dumping Duties (AD/CVD)	237
15.	Letter of Credit Application (L/C)	241
16.	Packing List (PL)	245
17.	Power of Attorney (POA)	249
18.	Pre-Shipment Inspection Certificate (PSIC)	253
19.	Pro Forma Invoice	257
20.	Purchase Order (PO)	261
21.	Sales Order (SO)	265
22.	Shipping Instructions (SI)	269
23.	Telex Release Request (TLX)	273
24.	Toxic Substances Control Act Statement (TSCA)	277

━━━━━━━━1━━━━━━━━

Book 1 Introduction
Customs Broker Exam Study Guide

"Sabermetrics". The echoes of this word reverberate in my mind when I sit down to work on our study guide. And it is a sabermetrics-related analogy that I feel best communicates the spirit of this book, though I admit, the book is related to the odd term in spirit only.

So what is "sabermetrics"? It is the empirical analysis of baseball, namely of baseball statistics (empirical data). An example of the practice of sabermetrics is for a baseball team to put (relatively) more stock in a baseball player's slugging percentage and on-base percentage in order to measure a player's true effectiveness and potential, and do so based on historical data. While in contrast, almost dogmatically, baseball teams have traditionally largely emphasized statistics such as batting average and stolen bases as a barometer for ability.

The concept of sabermetrics truly revolutionized the world of major league baseball. They even made a movie about one of its major advocates and the subject, starring Brad Pitt, based on Michael Lewis' book "Moneyball". Sabermetrics is now widely recognized as an objective and proven system for finding overlooked talent, and at a deep discount. For nearly half a century it lingered in obscurity. Now it is most likely adopted, in at least some shape or form, by all MLB teams.

What's the correlation between the sabermetrics phenomenon and the passing of the customs broker exam? Maybe someone could apply the similar principles to the game of basketball. Or to football? Or to the customs broker exam?

This study guide does its best to dissuade the examinee from studying, in-depth, ALL of the exam reference material, as traditionally may have been the case for customs brokers past. Instead, this study guide helps the student target his or her finite study time by isolating the most frequent and trending aspects of the exam, working large to small, and based on empirical data (i.e. observations from previous exams). Visualize yourself and your studies as a laser guided missile amongst a sea of shotguns.

 $ Money Saving Tip $ The 19 CFR and HTS publications are quite significant investments (approx. $175/ea.). You may save money on these items by buying used and/or older versions of each. The difference in content from issue to issue and year to year isn't really that significant.

---------**2**---------

Getting Started

FOR...
- *past customs broker exams and exam keys*
- *additional exam references such as directives, etc.*
- *application for customs broker license examination (CBP Form 3124E)*
  - ***GO TO...***
    - US Customs' (CBP) website:
      - **http://www.cbp.gov/document/publications/past-customs-broker-license-examinations-answer-keys**

      - **http://www.cbp.gov/trade/broker/exam/announcement**

      - **http://www.cbp.gov/newsroom/publications/forms**

FOR...
- *Code of Federal Regulations (CFR) "online version"*
  - ***GO TO...***
    - US Government Printing Office (GPO) website:
      - **www.eCFR.gov**

FOR...
- *Harmonized Tariff Schedule of the United States (HTSUS) "online version"*
  - ***GO TO...***
    - United States International Trade Commission (ITC) website:
      - **http://www.usitc.gov/tata/HTS/index.htm**

FOR...
- *"hardcopies" of HTS and CFR Title 19 for sale*
  - ***GO TO...***
    - Boskage Commerce Publications **and/or** U.S. Government Bookstore websites:
      - **http://www.boskage.com**

      - **http://bookstore.gpo.gov**
      - (and search "Code of Federal Regulations Title 19" **and** "Harmonized Tariff Schedule of the United States")

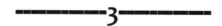

Nature of the Exam

In order to become a customs broker there are a few requirements. Anyone is eligible to apply to become a customs broker as long as they're at least 21 years of age, a US citizen, and not a federal employee. Second, and the aim of this book, is the requirement of passing the customs broker exam—a four hour open-book test consisting of 80 multiple choice questions and requiring a 75% to pass. As you may already be aware, the exam is administered twice a year, once on the first Wednesday of each April, and on the first Wednesday of each October. Applications for the exam are to be submitted to the nearest service port (or the location where you would like to sit for the exam) within at least about a month prior to the test. A list of ports, sorted by state can be found on Customs' website at **http://www.cbp.gov/xp/cgov/toolbox/contacts/ports/**. The exam application and further instructions are found at Customs' website as well. And, ultimately, upon passing the exam, the applicant is to submit their official application to become a customs broker to US Customs.

It is said that the average passing rate for the exam, which, by the way, varies remarkably from year-to-year, is as low as 5 to 10%. Regardless of these statistics, your experience will be entirely unique, based primarily on your preparation and mindset.

What about my experience with the exam? When I made my mind up to start studying for my first attempt at the exam, I began by just reviewing a few of the previous exams. And in the process I realized a significant pattern. A majority of the questions were being drawn directly from the 19 CFR (as opposed to the HTSUS, etc.), AND many of the same subjects and questions were being repeated from one exam to the next. So, I made note of which 19 CFR Parts, Section, and Paragraphs were a part of this pattern. I then removed the "unnecessary" parts of my newly purchased 19 CFR, and did my best to focus on the items that would most likely appear on the exam (as I will further outline for you in this book). With this newly conceived strategy of mine, and a commitment to study at least a little each day up to the date of the next exam, the goal was in sight and I felt a surge of confidence. And what was the result? On my first stab at the exam, I surprised myself by scoring a passing grade.

Notated immediately below this paragraph is a quick snapshot of each of the major sources of exam reference material, and the approximate percentages of each occurring over the last 10 exams (thru the April 2014 exam).

Title 19 CFR: 56% of the questions *(vs. 51% thru Oct. 2013 exam)*
HTSUS: 36% of the questions *(vs. 40% thru Oct. 2013 exam)*
Instructions for Preparation of CBP Form 7501: 3% of the questions *(vs. 4% thru Oct. 2013 exam)*
Directive(s): 3% of the questions *(vs. 4% thru Oct. 2013 exam)*
Customs & Trade Automated Interface Requirements (CATAIR): 1% *(vs. 1% thru Oct. 2013 exam)*

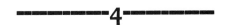

How to Use This Book

This book, by itself, will not guarantee your success on the customs broker exam. It is, however, one of several tools that will best prepare you for the big day. "Preparation" is the key word and preparedness in context of the customs broker exam means studying as efficiently as possible and on a daily basis. As the personal finance icon and pragmatist, Dave Ramsey says, "get gazelle intense!" Act as if you didn't want to take the test more than once. Listed below is a sort of checklist of things you should do before getting too far into your studies.

√ First, go to the following link to Customs' website.

http://www.cbp.gov/trade/broker/exam/announcement

Here, you will find links to all the references and material (HTSUS, 19 CFR, 7501 instructions etc.) that Customs says it may draw from for the exam. You are allowed and encouraged to bring all of these references to the actual exam.

√ Print out all of the reference materials except for the Title 19 Code of Federal Regulations (19 CFR) and the Harmonized Tariff Schedule (HTS). These two items contain too many pages to print. Instead, ask to borrow these items from work or a friend, or purchase from one of the resources listed in the section of this book marked "Getting Started".

√ Make yourself familiar with the reference material you have just printed (except for the HTS and 19 CFR, which require more involved study and I will further explain here in a bit). Just be aware and prepared to look something up on these printouts during the actual exam, but I wouldn't recommend trying to memorize too much here. The CATAIR, for example, is over 70 pages, yet has only historically appeared on 1% of the exam.

√ Next, begin printing out a few of the old exams and exam keys, starting with the most recent exams. Take your time just perusing through these exams and try to get a feeling of what kinds of questions are being asked, and how they are presented, etc. Once you get a little more familiar with everything, you will want to take mock exams utilizing these old exams to improve on your skills and gauge your progress.

√ Once you have a Title 19 CFR available to use, go to the section of this book marked "All Sections Appearing on Exams". In this section of the study guide is a table, which lists in order by CFR Part, Section, Paragraph, etc., all of the 19 CFR-related material tested in the last 10 exams. With a highlighter, begin notating directly into your 19 CFR, these Parts, Sections, and Paragraphs that most frequently appear on exams as indicated on this table. Not only will this process improve your familiarity with the 19 CFR and these various entries, it will make these items more easily stand out when you are searching for answers during your mock tests and during the actual day of the exam.

√ Once you have an HTS at your disposal, you will want to affix sticky tabs for all chapters (on the side) and for all sections (on top) for the purpose of simplified navigation through the HTSUS text. Undoubtedly, the best training method for strengthening your HTS classification skills is to simply go through the old exams and try to classify all the different sorts of merchandise described throughout the previous exams. This process will expose you to a wide variety of products and materials. It will also help to get you used to the kinds of HTS-based questions appearing in exams that require you to check chapter notes, section notes, general notes, and consider the general rules of interpretation (GRI) before deciding on the most appropriate classification and answer. This book also includes an "HTS Classification Tips" section, which explains the fundamentals of classification, and dissects a few classification questions derived directly from old exams.

√ Next to last, this study guide includes a section called "Most Commonly Tested". This part of the book isolates and quotes the specific "Sections" and "Paragraphs" of the 19 CFR that have most often appeared within exam questions during the last ten customs broker exams. It is, for the sake of prioritizing study time and for ease of navigation, arranged by frequency of appearances in the past ten exams and then numerically by CFR Part, Section, and then by Paragraph. Attempt to memorize as much as you can of this section. The reason for this is that the more you are able to answer exam questions from memory and on the fly, then the more time you will have to focus on the more time-consuming parts, namely HTS classification.

√ Finally, this study guide also includes the most recent exam with answers and commentary. The commentary will provide you with explanations in proportion to the complexity of each particular exam question. Direct excerpts from the HTSUS, 19 CFR, etc. are also included as supporting points of reference for each answer.

———————5———————

HTS Classification Tips

What is an HTSUS number?

All items imported into the United States must be assigned an HTSUS (also commonly referred to as the "HTS") number. Among having other purposes, the HTSUS number determines the duty rate of an imported item. Depending on the product, the process of selecting the correct HTSUS can be either a trek up Mount Everest or a trip down the bunny hill.

So, let's use "cross-country skis" as an example. The structure and terminology of the HTSUS Number is as follows:

95	06.	11.20	00
Chapter	Heading	Subheading	Statistical

Just note that there is a certain hierarchical and logical structure.

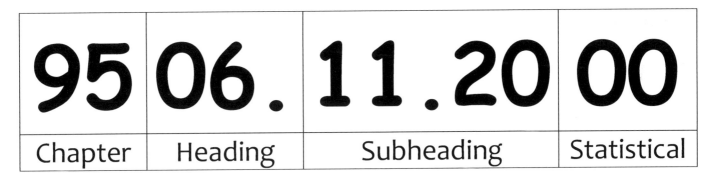

Heading/ Subheading	Stat. Suf- fix	Article Description	Unit of Quantity	Rates of Duty		
				1		2
				General	Special	
9506		Articles and equipment for general physical exercise, gymnastics, athletics, other sports (including table-tennis) or outdoor games, not specified or included elsewhere in this chapter; swimming pools and wading pools; parts and accessories thereof:				
		Snow-skis and other snow-ski equipment; parts and accessories thereof:				
9506.11		Skis and parts and accessories thereof, except ski poles:				
9506.11.20	00	Cross-country skis	prs.	Free		33 1/3%
9506.11.40		Other skis.		2.6%	Free (A,AU,BH,CA, CL,CO,E,IL,JO, KR,MA,MX,OM, P,PA,PE,SG)	33 1/3%

Which chapters do I study?

The exam may produce HTS classification-based questions pulled anywhere from Chapter 1 thru Chapter 99 of the HTS. I guess one could say that for the last ten exams, Customs has pretty evenly spread out the use of the various chapters throughout. However, there are definitely some outliers. Several chapters have, historically speaking, never appeared, and yet others are almost sure to appear on each exam. For example, chapter 61 (knitted apparel) has appeared over 20 times over the last 10 exams, whereas chapters 10 thru 14 (cereals, fats, etc.) haven't appeared one time. See the following page for statistical data in terms of which chapters of the HTSUS have appeared during the last 10 exams, and the frequency of occurrence for each.

Do the classifications last?

The HTS classification portion of the exam can easily end up taking up the lion's share of the test taker's time. Therefore, my first recommendation for those taking the exam, and especially for those whose strong point isn't in classification, is to budget sufficient time for, and do the classification part of the test last. Have a plan when you enter the test room, and do your best to implement that plan accordingly.

What are your options?

When you take on the classification portion of the exam try this. After you read through the question and have made mental notes on what you guess to be the key points, quickly scan over the five multiple choice answers and take stock of which chapters of the HTS are give to you as an options. You may ask yourself the following types of questions. Which chapters are overrepresented? Are there any seemingly dead giveaways or tells? Which classifications can be disregarded right of the back? Should I skip the question for now and revisit it later?

HTSUS Chapter Frequency for last 10 exams (Note: chapters omitted have not appeared).

HTS Chapter	Occurrences	HTS Chapter	Occurrences
General Notes	50	58	2
1	1	59	1
2	2	60	1
3	1	61	21
4	3	62	12
5	2	63	4
7	6	64	4
8	3	65	1
9	1	66	1
16	4	67	2
17	6	68	3
18	2	69	7
20	8	70	7
21	4	71	6
22	4	72	5
25	1	73	5
28	1	74	2
29	3	75	1
30	1	76	1
31	3	82	2
33	1	83	2
38	3	84	11
39	5	85	10
40	3	87	6
42	8	88	2
44	6	90	2
46	1	92	3
48	2	94	4
50	1	95	4
51	3	96	1
52	2	97	3
53	1	98	20
54	1	99	4
55	1		

The principles and procedure for correctly classifying imported products and materials is based on the GRI's (General Rules of Interpretation). There are six GRI's. GRI 1 thru GRI 4 are to be applied in sequential order. As is true with many other disciplines, as a person gains more experience in HTS classification, these "rules" eventually almost become 2nd nature, and the act of classification becomes a mostly automatic process.

Let's Get to Know the GRI's

To remember the GRI's, try remembering the following acronym **"HUM SELMA"**

H Headings and any relative Section & Chapter Notes determine the HTS#. GRI 1

U Unfinished items are classified as if finished (if unfinished item has essential character of finished). GRI 2(a)

M Mixtures may be implied (unless otherwise prohibited in the headings or notes). GRI 2(b)

S Specific HTS description preferred (over more general descriptions). GRI 3(a)

E Essential character of item determines HTS#. GRI 3(b)

L Last in order HTS# shall be used (if item cannot be classified by 3(a) or by 3(b)). GRI 3(c)

M Most akin item's HTS# to be used (if not classifiable by the above rules). GRI 4

A Article-specific cases, and packaging are classified with item (unless they are "the item"). GRI 5(a) & (b)

In brief, The General Rules of Interpretation can be broken-down per the following...

GRI 1: Headings and any relative Section & Chapter Notes determine the HTS#.

Most items are classifiable based on GRI 1. The titles of sections & chapters, the HTSUS alphabetical index, etc. are for reference purposes only. To classify, use the headings (i.e. HTS Article Description) and Section & Chapter Notes. An example of this would be the classification of chocolate-covered peanuts. Although Chapter 20 is named "PREPARATIONS OF VEGETABLES, FRUIT, NUTS OR OTHER PARTS OF PLANTS", this Chapter 20 Note 2 states that heading 2008 does not apply to "chocolate confectionery (heading 1806)". So, instead, the chocolate-covered peanuts would be classified in Chapter 18 (cocoa and cocoa preparations) as per the Chapter Notes.

Quoting GRI 1 directly from the HTSUS General Rules of Interpretation...

1.   The table of contents, alphabetical index, and titles of sections, chapters and sub-chapters are provided for ease of reference only; for legal purposes, classification shall be determined according to the terms of the headings and any relative section or chapter notes and, provided such headings or notes do not otherwise require, according to the following provisions:

GRI 2(a): Unfinished items are classified as if finished (if unfinished item has essential character of finished).

Any reference in an HTS heading to an article shall apply to the same article even if the said article is incomplete or unfinished. An example of this would be a pair of basketball shoes imported without its laces. Though not completely functional or ready for use in their imported state, these shoes are still essentially basketball shoes, even without laces.

Quoting GRI 2(a) directly from the HTSUS General Rules of Interpretation...

2.   (a)   Any reference in a heading to an article shall be taken to include a reference to that article incomplete or unfinished, provided that, as entered, the incomplete or unfinished article has the essential character of the complete or finished article. It shall also include a reference to that article complete or finished (or falling to be classified as complete or finished by virtue of this rule), entered unassembled or disassembled.

GRI 2(b): Mixtures may be implied (unless otherwise prohibited in the headings or notes).

This rule is, in a way, the flipside of GRI 2(a). GRI 2(b) says that an item may be classifiable under a single heading/classification even if the item is combined with other substances. In other words, mixtures may be implied (unless otherwise prohibited in the section notes, chapter notes, and headings). An example of this could be a chrome-plated steel wire garment hanger (clothes hanger). "Garment hangers" are specifically provided for in the HTSUS and classified under 7326.20.0020 following the sub-heading of "Articles of iron or steel wire". No Section Note, no Chapter Note, and no Classification Heading advise otherwise. Therefore, ultimately, the presence of the chrome plating in this instance does not preclude the classification of the item as a "steel" wire garment hanger.

Quoting GRI 2(b) directly from the HTSUS General Rules of Interpretation...

(b)   Any reference in a heading to a material or substance shall be taken to include a reference to mixtures or combinations of that material or substance with other materials or substances. Any reference to goods of a given material or substance shall be taken to include a reference to goods consisting wholly or partly of such material or substance. The classification of goods consisting of more than one material or substance shall be according to the principles of rule 3.

GRI 3(a): When goods are classifiable under two or more different headings, then... Specific HTS description preferred (over more general descriptions).

This rule says that, in general, the HTS heading that best describes the product should be used. For example, which of the two following classifications more specifically describes a keyboard for a desktop computer?

A) 8471.60.2000   Automatic data processing machines and units thereof... >>Input or output units... >>Other>>Keyboards

Or

B) 8537.10.9070   Boards, panels, consoles... equipped with two or more apparatus of heading 8535 or 8536, for electric control... >>For a voltage not exceeding 1,000V>>Other>>Other>>Other

"A" is a more specific description than "B". The word "keyboards" is explicitly part of the description (though Customs' word for "computer" is "Automatic Data Processing Machines"). "B" is a commonly used classification for control units in general.

Quoting GRI 3(a) directly from the HTSUS General Rules of Interpretation...

3.   When, by application of rule 2(b) or for any other reason, goods are, *prima facie*, classifiable under two or more headings, classification shall be effected as follows:

   (a)   The heading which provides the most specific description shall be preferred to headings providing a more general description. However, when two or more headings each refer to part only of the materials or substances contained in mixed or composite goods or to part only of the items in a set put up for retail sale, those headings are to be regarded as equally specific in relation to those goods, even if one of them gives a more complete or precise description of the goods.

GRI 3(b): When goods are classifiable under two or more different headings, then... Essential character of item determines HTS#.

This rule says that for products consisting of multiple materials or components, or sets shall be classified under the material which gives the product its essential character. For example, a nice leather baseball glove for an adult, which has been packaged with a gratuitous baseball and small bottle of glove oil, would just be classified as a baseball glove (4203.21.4000), as this item clearly gives the set its essential character.

Quoting GRI 3(b) directly from the HTSUS General Rules of Interpretation...

3.   When, by application of rule 2(b) or for any other reason, goods are, *prima facie*, classifiable under two or more headings, classification shall be effected as follows:

   (b)   Mixtures, composite goods consisting of different materials or made up of different components, and goods put up in sets for retail sale, which cannot be classified by reference to 3(a), shall be classified as if they consisted of the material or component which gives them their essential character, insofar as this criterion is applicable.

GRI 3(c): When goods are classifiable under two or more different headings, then... Last in order HTS# shall be used (if item cannot be classified by 3(a) or by 3(b).

This rule says that if neither of the previous rules worked, the largest (numerically speaking) classification prevails. For example, if an item is classifiable in both chapter 84 and chapter 85, then choose the classification in chapter 85, as this classification occurs later in the HTSUS than does the chapter 84 item.

Quoting GRI 3(c) directly from the HTSUS General Rules of Interpretation...

3.   When, by application of rule 2(b) or for any other reason, goods are, *prima facie*, classifiable under two or more headings, classification shall be effected as follows:

(c)   When goods cannot be classified by reference to 3(a) or 3(b), they shall be classified under the heading which occurs last in numerical order among those which equally merit consideration.

GRI 4: Most akin item's HTS# to be used (if not classifiable by the other rules).

This rule concedes that goods still unclassifiable per the previously mentioned rules shall be classified under the heading for goods that are most similar in character. For example, a "computer monitor magnifier" (accessory attached to front of monitor to magnify items on screen) is classifiable as 9013.80.2000. The article description of which is "Hand magnifiers, magnifying glasses, loupes, thread counters and similar apparatus", most of which could be considered akin to the computer monitor magnifier.

Quoting GRI 4 directly from the HTSUS General Rules of Interpretation...

4.   Goods which cannot be classified in accordance with the above rules shall be classified under the heading appropriate to the goods to which they are most akin.

GRI 5(a) & (b): Article-specific cases, and packaging are classified with item (unless they are "the item").

These rules deal with cases and packaging, and are fairly self-explanatory.

Example of 5(a): A diamond encrusted case for reading glasses would not be classified with the glasses for which it contains.

Example of 5(b): Styrofoam peanuts used to pack delicate electronic goods would not be classified by themselves.

Quoting GRI 5(a) & (b) directly from the HTSUS General Rules of Interpretation...

5.   In addition to the foregoing provisions, the following rules shall apply in respect of the goods referred to therein:

   (a)   Camera cases, musical instrument cases, gun cases, drawing instrument cases, necklace cases and similar containers, specially shaped or fitted to contain a specific article or set of articles, suitable for long-term use and entered with the articles for which they are intended, shall be classified with such articles when of a kind normally sold therewith. This rule does not, however, apply to containers which give the whole its essential character;

   (b)   Subject to the provisions of rule 5(a) above, packing materials and packing containers entered with the goods therein shall be classified with the goods if they are of a kind normally used for packing such goods. However, this provision is not binding when such packing materials or packing containers are clearly suitable for repetitive use.

GRI 6: Apply the GRI's to the headings, then the sub-headings, then ...

This means the logic and cadence of the GRI's are repeated from one level to the next lower level. In my humble opinion, this rule does not have much of a practical application. Further, it was decided to omit this GRI from the afore-mentioned acronym H.U.M. S.E.L.M.A. to keep things as simple as possible.

Quoting GRI 6 directly from the HTSUS General Rules of Interpretation...

6. For legal purposes, the classification of goods in the subheadings of a heading shall be determined according to the terms of those subheadings and any related subheading notes and, *mutatis mutandis*, to the above rules, on the understanding that only subheadings at the same level are comparable. For the purposes of this rule, the relative section, chapter and subchapter notes also apply, unless the context otherwise requires.

Additional U.S. Rules of Interpretation:

Also worth noting, but omitted from the acronym are the "Additional U.S. Rules of Interpretation". Particularly, Addl. Rule 1(c), which says that (in general) "parts and accessories" may be classified as "parts", UNLESS the part in question happens to be specifically provided for in the HTSUS. A good example of this is the question of where to classify a "glass fuse" manufactured for an automobile. Many might just classify as "a part" for an automobile (Chapter 87). However, since a "glass fuse" is specifically provided for in Chapter 85 with other electronics, the fuse if classifiable accordingly in Chapter 85.

Quoting Additional U.S. Rules of Interpretation from the HTSUS General Rules of Interpretation...

1. In the absence of special language or context which otherwise requires--

   (a) a tariff classification controlled by use (other than actual use) is to be determined in accordance with the use in the United States at, or immediately prior to, the date of importation, of goods of that class or kind to which the imported goods belong, and the controlling use is the principal use;

   (b) a tariff classification controlled by the actual use to which the imported goods are put in the United States is satisfied only if such use is intended at the time of importation, the goods are so used and proof thereof is furnished within 3 years after the date the goods are entered;

   (c) a provision for parts of an article covers products solely or principally used as a part of such articles but a provision for "parts" or "parts and accessories" shall not prevail over a specific provision for such part or accessory; and

   (d) the principles of section XI regarding mixtures of two or more textile materials shall apply to the classification of goods in any provision in which a textile material is named.

In their entirety, the General Rules of Interpretation as presented on page 1 of the HTSUS:

GENERAL RULES OF INTERPRETATION

Classification of goods in the tariff schedule shall be governed by the following principles:

1. The table of contents, alphabetical index, and titles of sections, chapters and sub-chapters are provided for ease of reference only; for legal purposes, classification shall be determined according to the terms of the headings and any relative section or chapter notes and, provided such headings or notes do not otherwise require, according to the following provisions:

2. (a) Any reference in a heading to an article shall be taken to include a reference to that article incomplete or unfinished, provided that, as entered, the incomplete or unfinished article has the essential character of the complete or finished article. It shall also include a reference to that article complete or finished (or falling to be classified as complete or finished by virtue of this rule), entered unassembled or disassembled.

    (b) Any reference in a heading to a material or substance shall be taken to include a reference to mixtures or combinations of that material or substance with other materials or substances. Any reference to goods of a given material or substance shall be taken to include a reference to goods consisting wholly or partly of such material or substance. The classification of goods consisting of more than one material or substance shall be according to the principles of rule 3.

3. When, by application of rule 2(b) or for any other reason, goods are, *prima facie*, classifiable under two or more headings, classification shall be effected as follows:

    (a) The heading which provides the most specific description shall be preferred to headings providing a more general description. However, when two or more headings each refer to part only of the materials or substances contained in mixed or composite goods or to part only of the items in a set put up for retail sale, those headings are to be regarded as equally specific in relation to those goods, even if one of them gives a more complete or precise description of the goods.

    (b) Mixtures, composite goods consisting of different materials or made up of different components, and goods put up in sets for retail sale, which cannot be classified by reference to 3(a), shall be classified as if they consisted of the material or component which gives them their essential character, insofar as this criterion is applicable.

    (c) When goods cannot be classified by reference to 3(a) or 3(b), they shall be classified under the heading which occurs last in numerical order among those which equally merit consideration.

4. Goods which cannot be classified in accordance with the above rules shall be classified under the heading appropriate to the goods to which they are most akin.

5. In addition to the foregoing provisions, the following rules shall apply in respect of the goods referred to therein:

    (a) Camera cases, musical instrument cases, gun cases, drawing instrument cases, necklace cases and similar containers, specially shaped or fitted to contain a specific article or set of articles, suitable for long-term use and entered with the articles for which they are intended, shall be classified with such articles when of a kind normally sold therewith. This rule does not, however, apply to containers which give the whole its essential character;

    (b) Subject to the provisions of rule 5(a) above, packing materials and packing containers entered with the goods therein shall be classified with the goods if they are of a kind normally used for packing such goods. However, this provision is not binding when such packing materials or packing containers are clearly suitable for repetitive use.

6. For legal purposes, the classification of goods in the subheadings of a heading shall be determined according to the terms of those subheadings and any related subheading notes and, *mutatis mutandis*, to the above rules, on the understanding that only subheadings at the same level are comparable. For the purposes of this rule, the relative section, chapter and subchapter notes also apply, unless the context otherwise requires.

—————6—————

GRI's in Exam Examples

Exam Example of GRI 1

"Headings and any relative Section & Chapter Notes determine the HTS#."

What is the classification for a removable 1-gigabyte flash memory card with EEPROM memory and controller integrated circuits that is used to download sound or video images from a personal computer and play them on a cell phone, DVD player, CD player, video game or a laptop computer?

A. 8473.30.1140   Parts and accessories (other than covers, carrying cases and the like) suitable for use solely or principally with machines of 8469 to 8472>>Parts and accessories of the machines of heading 8471>>Not incorporating a cathode ray tube>>Printed circuit assemblies>>Memory modules suitable for use solely or principally with machines of heading 8471.

B. 8523.51.0000   Discs, tapes, solid-state non-volatile storage devices…>>Semiconductor media>>Solid-state non-volatile storage devices

C. 8542.32.0050   Electronic integrated circuits; parts thereof>>Electronic integrated circuits>>Memories>>Electrically erasable programmable read-only memory (EEPROM).

D. 8543.90.8880   Electrical machines and apparatus, having individual functions, not specified or included elsewhere in this chapter; parts thereof>>Parts>>Other>>Other>>Other>>Other

E. 9504.50.0000   Video game consoles and machines…parts and accessories thereof>>Video game consoles and machines… and parts and accessories thereof

After reading through the question, and noting what you anticipate to be the significant details presented therein, you are given 5 choices as possible answers: One option from Chapter 84, three options from Chapter 85, and one option from Chapter 95.

Basically, the question asks for the classification for a removable flash memory card. Though this technology is arguably not common knowledge to the general public, you may have been exposed to the synonymous term "sold-state drive", and examples of this include SD cards, Micro SD cards, CF cards, etc.

Regarding your multiple choices, "A" (8473.30.1140) is essentially parts and accessories for machines 8469 to 8472, which among a few other devices, this range of headings (8469 to 8472) most significantly includes personal computers (heading 8471 refers to personal computers as Automatic Data Processing Machines). Though a "flash memory card" may at first glance be considered to be an accessory for a personally computer, note that per Section XVI (chapters 84 & 85 of the HTSUS) Note 2 (a) has the following to say on the subject:

2. Subject to note 1 to this section, note 1 to chapter 84 and to note 1 to chapter 85, parts of machines (not being parts of the articles of heading 8484, 8544, 8545, 8546 or 8547) are to be classified according to the following rules:

   (a) Parts which are goods included in any of the headings of chapter 84 or 85 (other than headings 8409, 8431, 8448, 8466, 8473, 8487, 8503, 8522, 8529, 8538 and 8548) are in all cases to be classified in their respective headings;

This means that the item in question, a removable flash memory card, should not be automatically classified as a part or accessory of a computer (8473.30.1140) if a flash memory card is described anywhere within chapters 84 or 85.

Multiple choice "B" appears to suitably describe the item in question. As describe by Chapter 85 Note 4 (a):

4. For the purposes of heading 8523 :

   (a) "Solid-state non-volatile storage devices" (for example, "flash memory cards" or "flash electronic storage cards") are storage devices with a connecting socket, comprising in the same housing one or more flash memories (for example, "FLASH E²PROM") in the form of integrated circuits mounted on a printed circuit board. They may include a controller in the form of an integrated circuit and discrete passive components, such as capacitors and resistors;

Multiple choice "C" does specifically state "EEPROM", which referred to in the exam question's description of the product. However, this describes only part of the item's character and only part of the item's function.

Multiple choice "D" is somewhat of a last resort used to classify parts of electrical machines not included in chapter 85, etc., and will not be considered if that is the case.

Multiple choice "E" describes parts of video game consoles. As per Chapter 95 Note 1 (m): "This chapter does not cover sold-sate non-volatile devices (a.k.a. flash memory cards), thus eliminating "E" as an option.

(m) Pumps for liquids (heading 8413), filtering or purifying machinery and apparatus for liquids or gases (heading 8421), electric motors (heading 8501), electric transformers (heading 8504), discs, tapes, solid-state non-volatile storage devices, "smart cards" and other media for the recording of sound or of other phenomena, whether or not recorded (heading 8523), radio remote control apparatus (heading 8526) or cordless infrared remote control devices (heading 8543);

Through the process of referring to the Section and Chapter notes, and also through the process of elimination, the examinee can deduce that "B" is the correct answer. Admittedly, scanning the Section and Chapter notes for these classification guidelines does seem a tedious endeavor. Repetitive classification work does, however, progressively train the eyes to look out for and locate these notes scattered throughout.

Heading/ Subheading	Stat. Suffix	Article Description	Unit of Quantity	Rates of Duty		
				1		2
				General	Special	
8523 (con.)		Discs. tapes, solid-state non-volatile storage devices, "smart cards" and other media for the recording of sound or of other phenomena, whether or not recorded, including matrices and masters for the production of discs, but excluding products of Chapter 37 (con.):				
		Optical media:				
8523.41.00	00	Unrecorded........................	X........	Free		80%
8523.49		Other:				
8523.49.20		For reproducing phenomena other than sound or image....................	....	Free		86.1¢/m^2 of recording surface
	10	Prepackaged software for automatic data processing machines, of a kind sold at retail............................	No. m^2			
	20	Other........................	No. m^2			
8523.49.30	00	For reproducing sound only.	No. m^2	Free		86.1¢/m^2 of recording surface
		Other:				
8523.49.40	00	For reproducing representations of instructions, data, sound, and image, recorded in a machine readable binary form, and capable of being manipulated or providing interactivity to a user, by means of an automatic data processing machine; proprietary format recorded discs.........	No......	Free		80%
8523.49.50	00	Other...................	No......	2.7%	Free (A,AU,BH, CA,CL,CO,E,IL, JO,KR,MA,MX. OM,P,PA,PE,SG)	80%
		Semiconductor media:				
8523.51.00	00	Solid-state non-volatile storage devices.	No......	Free		80%
8523.52.00		"Smart cards".....................	....	Free		35%
	10	Unrecorded.....................	No.			
	90	Other.......................	No.			
8523.59.00	00	Other...................	X......	Free		35%
8523.80		Other:				
8523.80.10	00	Phonograph records.................	No......	1.8%	Free (A,AU,BH, CA,CL,CO,E,IL, JO,KR,MA,MX. OM,P,PA,PE,SG)	30%
8523.80.20	00	Other...................	X......	Free		80%

Exam Example of GRI 2(a)
"Unfinished items are classified as if finished (if unfinished item has essential character of finished)."

What is the CLASSIFICATION for a belt made of woven hemp from Ecuador? The belt is imported with punched holes, of which are fitted with bronze eyelets. The belt is not imported with the buckle closure apparatus. The belt is 2 inches in length and 35 inches in length.

A. 5609.00.2000   Articles of yarn, strip or the like of heading 5404 or 5405, twine cordage, rope or cables, not elsewhere specified or included>>Of vegetable fibers, except cotton

B. 6217.10.9530   Other made up clothing accessories; parts of garments or of clothing accessories, other than those of heading 6212>>Accessories>>Other>>Other>>Of man-made fibers

C. 6217.10.9550   Other made up clothing accessories; parts of garments or of clothing accessories, other than those of heading 6212>>Accessories>>Other>>Other>>Other

D. 6217.90.9070   Other made up clothing accessories; parts of garments or of clothing accessories, other than those of heading 6212>>Parts>>Other>>Of trousers and breeches>>Other

E. 6217.90.9095   Other made up clothing accessories; parts of garments or of clothing accessories, other than those of heading 6212>>Parts>>Other>>Other>>Other

The first question the examinee asks himself or herself is "is this unfinished item classified as a belt or not?" Per GRI 2(a),

> "Any reference in a heading to an article shall be taken to include a reference to that article incomplete or unfinished, provided that, as entered, the incomplete or unfinished article has the essential character of the complete or finished article. It shall also include a reference to that article complete or finished (or failing to be classified as complete or finished by virtue of this rule) entered unassembled or disassembled".

Translated, if the incomplete item still manages to maintain the essential character (in name and in general) of the item as if it were finished, then it should be classified just as the complete article would. So, in terms of the belt in question, although the belt is without a buckle closure apparatus, it is still referred to as, and universally considered to be a belt. Therefore, the applicable classification for the item is 6217.10.9550 ("C").

Note: Customs includes hemp within the category of "vegetable fibers".

Heading/ Subheading	Stat. Suf- fix	Article Description	Unit of Quantity	Rates of Duty		
				1		2
				General	Special	
6217		Other made up clothing accessories; parts of garments or of clothing accessories, other than those of heading 6212:				
6217.10		Accessories:				
6217.10.10		Containing 70 percent or more by weight of silk or silk waste..................................		2.3%	Free (AU,BH,CA, CL,CO,E,IL,JO, KR,MA,MX,OM, P,PA,PE,SG)	90%
	10	Headbands, ponytail holders and similar articles................................	doz. kg			
	90	Other (759).........................	doz. kg			
		Other:				
6217.10.85	00	Headbands, ponytail holders and similar articles................................	doz. kg	14.6%	Free (A,AU,BH, CA,CL,CO,E*,IL, JO,KR,MA, MX,OM,P,PA, PE,SG)	90%
6217.10.95		Other............................		14.6%	Free (AU,BH,CA, CL,CO,E*,IL,JO, KR,MA,MX,OM, P,PA,PE,SG)	90%
	10	Of cotton (359).....................	doz. kg			
	20	Of wool or fine animal hair (459).........	doz. kg			
	30	Of man-made fibers (659)..............	doz. kg			
	50	Other (859)........................	doz. kg			
6217.90		Parts:				
6217.90.10		Containing 70 percent or more by weight of silk or silk waste..................................		2.3%	Free (AU,BH,CA, CL,CO,E,IL,JO, KR,MA,MX,OM, P,PA,PE,SG)	90%
	10	Of blouses and shirts (741)...............	doz. kg			
	20	Of coats and jackets (735)...............	doz. kg			
	30	Of trousers and breeches (748)............	doz. kg			
	60	Other (759)........................	doz. kg			

Exam Example of GRI 2(b)
"Mixtures may be implied (unless otherwise prohibited in the headings or notes)"

What is the CLASSIFICATION for dried and prepared seaweed from Korea? The edible food is made from raw kelp-type seaweed that is filtered for impurities, pressed, formed into square sheets, dried, and finally roasted and seasoned with sesame oil, salt, MSG, and soy sauce.

A. 1212.21.0000   Locust beans, seaweeds and other algae ... of a kind used primarily for human consumption, not elsewhere specified or included>>Seaweeds and other algae>>Fit for human consumption

B. 1212.29.0000   Locust beans, seaweeds and other algae ... of a kind used primarily for human consumption, not elsewhere specified or included>>Seaweeds and other algae>>Other

C. 2008.99.6100   Fruit, nuts and other edible parts of plants, otherwise prepared or preserved, whether or not containing added sugar or other sweetening matter or spirit, not elsewhere specified or included>>Other>>Other>>Soybeans

D. 2008.99.9090   Fruit, nuts and other edible parts of plants, otherwise prepared or preserved, whether or not containing added sugar or other sweetening matter or spirit, not elsewhere specified or included>>Other>>Other>>Other>>Other>>Other

E. 2103.10.0000   Sauces and preparations therefore: mixed condiments and mixed seasonings; mustard flour and meal and prepared mustard>>Soy sauce

GRI 2(b) says that an item may be classifiable under a single heading/classification even if the item is combined with other substances. In other words, mixtures may be implied (unless otherwise prohibited in the section notes, chapter notes, and headings). Multiple choice "D" is the correct classification for edible seaweed. However this dried seaweed snack contains, in addition to seaweed) a multitude of other substances (i.e. impurities, sesame oil, salt, MSG, and soy sauce), so can it also be classified as such? Per the before mentioned GRI 2(b), it is a given that these other substances are inconsequential to the nature of the item, and thus the correct answer is "D".

The other multiple choices may be addressed as per the following. Both "A" and "B" are located within the heading 1212, which does include "seaweed primarily for human consumption", however the item in question is more suitably classified under heading 2008, which includes "prepared" (i.e. processed) plant food items. Multiple choices "C" and "E" are the classifications for prepared soybeans and soy sauce, respectively.

Heading/ Subheading	Stat. Suffix	Article Description	Unit of Quantity	Rates of Duty		
				1		2
				General	Special	
2008 (con.)		Fruit, nuts and other edible parts of plants, otherwise prepared or preserved, whether or not containing added sugar or other sweetening matter or spirit, not elsewhere specified or included (con.): Other, including mixtures other than those of sub-heading 2008.19 (con.):				
2008.99 (con.)		Other (con.):				
2008.99.40	00	Mangoes...................	kg......	1.5¢/kg	Free (A,AU,BH,CA, CL,CO,E,IL,JO, KR,MA,MX,OM,P, PA,PE,SG)	33¢/kg
		Papayas:				
2008.99.45	00	Pulp.................	kg......	14%	Free (A,AU,BH,CA, CL,CO,E,IL,JO, MA,MX,OM,P,PA, PE,SG) 5.6% (KR)	35%
2008.99.50	00	Other..................	kg......	1.8%	Free (A,AU,BH,CA, CL,CO,E,IL,JO. KR,MA,MX,OM,P, PA,PE,SG)	35%
2008.99.60	00	Plums (including prune plums and sloes)................	kg......	11.2%	Free (A+,AU,BH, CA,CL,CO,D,E, IL,JO,KR,MX, OM,P,PA.PE,SG) 1.1% (MA)	35%
2008.99.61	00	Soybeans.....................	kg......	3.8%	Free (A,AU,BH,CA, CL,CO,E,IL,JO, KR,MA,MX,OM,P, PA,PE,SG)	35%
2008.99.63	00	Sweet ginger..................	kg......	4.4%	Free (A,AU,BH,CA, CL,CO,E,IL,JO, KR,MA,MX,OM,P, PA,PE,SG)	35%
2008.99.65	00	Cassava (manioc).................	kg......	7.9%	Free (A,AU,BH,CA, CL,CO,E,IL,JO, MA,MX,OM,P,PA, PE,SG) 3.1% (KR)	35%
		Chinese water chestnuts:				
2008.99.70	00	Frozen................	kg......	11.2%	Free (A+,AU,BH, CA,CL,CO,D,E, IL,JO,MX,OM,P, PA,PE,SG) 1.1% (MA) 6.4% (KR)	35%
2008.99.71		Other................		Free		35%
	10	Sliced.............	kg			
	20	Whole.............	kg			
		Other:				
2008.99.80	00	Pulp.................	kg......	9.6%	Free (A*,AU,BH, CA,CL,CO,E,IL, JO,KR,MA,MX, OM,P,PA,PE,SG)	35%
2008.99.90		Other................		6%	Free (A,AU,BH,CA. CL,CO,E,IL,JO, KR,MA,MX,OM,P. PA,PE,SG)	35%
	10	Bean cake, bean stick, miso and similar products..................	kg			
	90	Other....................	kg			

Exam Example of GRI 3(a)
"Specific HTS description preferred (over more general description)."

What is the CLASSIFICATION for a submersible pump o-ring? The o-ring is made of vulcanized rubber and for use within a saltwater submersible pump.

A. 4016.93.1010   Other articles of vulcanized rubber other than hard rubber>>Other>>Gaskets, washers, and other seals>>Of a kind used in the automotive goods of chapter 87>>O-rings

B. 4016.93.5010   Other articles of vulcanized rubber other than hard rubber>>Other>>Gaskets, washers, and other seals>>Other>>O-rings

C. 4016.93.5050   Other articles of vulcanized rubber other than hard rubber>>Other>>Gaskets, washers, and other seals>>Other>>Other

D. 8413.70.2004   Pumps for liquids, whether or not fitted with a measuring device; liquid elevators; part thereof>>Other centrifugal pumps>>Other>>Submersible pumps

E. 8413.91.9080   Pumps for liquids, whether or not fitted with a measuring device; liquid elevators; part thereof>>Parts>>Of pumps>>Other>>Other

The item in question, an o-ring for use with a submersible pump, certainly may be considered as being classifiable under more than one heading. The HTSUS does indeed provide a specific description and classification for O-rings within subheading 4016.93. The HTSUS also provides a specific description of Submersible Pumps, as well as a more general classification for Parts of pumps.

Per GRI 3(a), "The heading which provides the most specific description shall be preferred to headings providing a more general description." This simply means that the classification description that is most descriptive in terms of describing the item in question should be used.

Accordingly, the description of "O-rings" (of vulcanized rubber) is more descriptive than "Parts of pumps". Multiple choice "B" is preferred over "E". "B" is the correct answer.

Heading/ Subheading	Stat. Suf- fix	Article Description	Unit of Quantity	Rates of Duty General	Rates of Duty Special	2
4016 4016.10.00	00	Other articles of vulcanized rubber other than hard rubber: Of cellular rubber. Other:	X	Free		25%
4016.91.00	00	Floor coverings and mats.	X	2.7% 1/	Free (A,AU,BH,B, CA,CL,CO,E,IL, JO,KR,MA, MX,OM,P, PA,PE,SG)	40%
4016.92.00	00	Erasers.	X	4.2% 2/	Free (A,AU,BH. CA,CL,CO,E,IL, JO,KR,MA, MX,OM,P, PA,PE,SG)	35%
4016.93 4016.93.10		Gaskets, washers and other seals: Of a kind used in the automotive goods of chapter 87.		2.5%	Free (A,AU,BH,B, CA,CL,CO,E,IL, JO,KR,MA, MX,OM,P. PA,PE,SG)	25%
	10	O-Rings.	kg			
	20	Oil seals.	No. kg			
	50	Other.	kg			
4016.93.50		Other.		2.5%	Free (A,AU,BH,C, CA,CL,CO,E,IL, JO,KR,MA, MX,OM,P. PA,PE,SG)	25%
	10	O-Rings.	kg			
	20	Oil seals.	No. kg			
	50	Other.	kg			
4016.94.00	00	Boat or dock fenders, whether or not inflatable.	X	4.2%	Free (A,AU,BH. CA,CL,CO,E,IL, JO,KR,MA, MX,OM,P. PA,PE,SG)	80%
4016.95.00	00	Other inflatable articles.	X	4.2%	Free (A,AU,BH, CA,CL,CO,E,IL, JO,KR,MA, MX,OM,P. PA,PE,SG)	25%

Exam **Example of GRI 3(b)**
"Essential character of item determines HTS#."

What is the CLASSIFICATION for a Digital Multifunction Printer from China? The Multifunction Printing Device, advertised by the manufacturer as an "All-In-One Printer", performs as a printer, copier, and scanner. The printer and copier functions are performed by a black & white laser type printer, capable of producing up to 21 pages per minute. The scanner function of the unit is performed by an optical scanner and automatic document feeder. The All-In-One is capable of being connected to an automatic data processing machine and/or to a network and its dimensions are 16 x 16 x 14 inches.

A. 8443.31.0000   Printing machinery used for printing by means of plates, cylinders and other printing components of heading 8442; other printers, copying machines and facsimile machines, whether or not combined; parts and accessories thereof>>Other printers, copying machines and facsimile machines, whether or not combined>>Machines which perform two or more of the functions of printing, copying or facsimile transmission, capable of connecting to an automatic data processing machine or to a network.

B. 8443.32.1010   Printing machinery used for printing by means of plates, cylinders and other printing components of heading 8442; other printers, copying machines and facsimile machines, whether or not combined; parts and accessories thereof>>Other printers, copying machines and facsimile machines, whether or not combined>>Other, capable of connecting to an automatic data processing machine or to a network>>Printer units>>Laser>>Capable of producing more than 20 pages per minute

C. 8443.32.1020   Printing machinery used for printing by means of plates, cylinders and other printing components of heading 8442; other printers, copying machines and facsimile machines, whether or not combined; parts and accessories thereof>>Other printers, copying machines and facsimile machines, whether or not combined>>Other, capable of connecting to an automatic data processing machine or to a network>>Printer units>>Laser>>Other

D. 8543.90.8880   Printing machinery used for printing by means of plates, cylinders and other printing components of heading 8442; other printers, copying machines and facsimile machines, whether or not combined; parts and accessories thereof>>Other printers, copying machines and facsimile machines, whether or not combined>>Other, capable of connecting to an automatic data processing machine or to a network>>Other

E. 8471.60.8000   Automatic data processing machines and units thereof: magnetic or optical readers, machines for transcribing data onto data media in coded form and machines for processing such data, not elsewhere specified or included>>Input or output units, whether or not containing storage units in the same housing>>Other>>Optical scanners and magnetic ink recognition devices

The question behind the question is, "is this device classified as a printer, a copier, a scanner, all of the above, or none of the above?" One could reasonably assume that since the item is being marketed as a "multifunction printer", and that its name implies that the primary purpose is for most, that of a printer, then accordingly the device's essential character is that of a printer. Then based on this logic multiple choices "D" (copier, capable of connecting to an ADP or to a network) and "E" (scanner) may be disregarded.

Next, based on the remaining multiple choice classification descriptions, both "A" and "B" appear to be the most suitable. Multiple choice "B" does, in deed, describe in detail the specifics of the printer. However, the description for "B" does not provide for the inclusion of the copier function of the device. Multiple choice "A" does, and thus "8443.31.0000" is the most appropriate classification.

Note: Customs refers to personal computers as "Automatic Data Processing (ADP) Machines".

(This Page Intentionally Left Blank)

Heading/ Subheading	Stat. Suf- fix	Article Description	Unit of Quantity	Rates of Duty		
				1		2
				General	Special	
8443		Printing machinery used for printing by means of plates, cylinders and other printing components of heading 8442; other printers, copying machines and facsimile machines, whether or not combined; parts and accessories thereof:				
		Printing machinery used for printing by means of plates, cylinders and other printing components of heading 8442 :				
8443.11		Offset printing machinery, reel-fed:				
8443.11.10	00	Double-width newspaper printing presses......	No.......	3.3%	Free (A,AU,BH, CA,CL,CO,E,IL, JO,KR,MA,MX, OM,P,PA,PE,SG)	25%
8443.11.50	00	Other........	No......	Free		25%
8443.12.00	00	Offset printing machinery, sheet-fed, office type (using sheets with one side not exceeding 22 cm and the other side not exceeding 36 cm in the unfolded state)........	No......	Free		25%
8443.13.00	00	Other offset printing machinery:............	No......	Free		25%
8443.14.00	00	Letterpress printing machinery, reel fed, excluding flexographic printing............	No......	2.2%	Free (A,AU,BH, CA,CL,CO,E,IL, JO,KR,MA,MX, OM,P,PA,PE.SG)	25%
8443.15.00	00	Letterpress printing machinery, other than reel fed, excluding flexographic printing............	No......	Free		25%
8443.16.00	00	Flexographic printing machinery............	No......	2.2%	Free (A,AU,BH, CA,CL,CO,E,IL, JO,KR,MA,MX, OM,P,PA,PE,SG)	25%
8443.17.00	00	Gravure printing machinery............	No......	2.2%	Free (A,AU,BH, CA,CL,CO,E,IL, JO,KR,MA,MX, OM,P,PA,PE,SG)	25%
8443.19		Other:				
8443.19.20	00	Textile printing machinery............	X.......	2.6% 1/	Free (A,AU,BH, CA,CL,CO,E,IL, JO,KR,MA,MX, OM,P,PA,PE,SG)	40%
8443.19.30	00	Other............	X.......	Free		25%
		Other printers, copying machines and facsimile machines, whether or not combined :				
8443.31.00	00	Machines which perform two or more of the functions of printing, copying or facsimile transmission, capable of connecting to an automatic data processing machine or to a network............	No......	Free		35%
8443.32		Other, capable of connecting to an automatic data processing machine or to a network:				
8443.32.10		Printer units:............		Free		35%
		Laser:				
	10	Capable of producing more than 20 pages per minute............	No.			
	20	Other............	No.			
	30	Light bar electronic type............	No.			
	40	Ink jet............	No.			
	50	Thermal transfer............	No.			
	60	Ionographic............	No.			
	70	Daisy wheel............	No.			
	80	Dot matrix............	No.			
	90	Other............	No.			
8443.32.50	00	Other............	X.......	Free		35%

Exam Example of GRI 3(c)
"Last in order HTS# shall be used (if item cannot be classified by 3(a) or by 3(b))."

What is the CLASSIFICATION for a high-end youth fishing combo set composed of 1 fishing rod, 1 fishing reel, and 1 snelled fish hook? All three articles are packaged together, though they are not attached within the clear plastic packaging, and are all made in Japan. The fishing set is intended for freshwater use and is marketed as a "set" by the manufacturer. The value of the rod is $50 USD. The value of the reel is $50 USD. The value of the hook is $1 USD.

A. 9507.10.0040   Fishing rods, fish hooks and other line fishing tackle; ...; parts and accessories thereof>>Fishing rods and parts and accessories thereof>>Fishing rods

B. 9507.20.4000   Fishing rods, fish hooks and other line fishing tackle; ...; parts and accessories thereof>>Fishing rods and parts and accessories thereof>>Parts and accessories

C. 9507.20.4000   Fishing rods, fish hooks and other line fishing tackle; ...; parts and accessories thereof>>Fish hooks, whether or not snelled>>Snelled hooks

D. 9507.30.6000   Fishing rods, fish hooks and other line fishing tackle; ...; parts and accessories thereof>>Fishing reels and parts and accessories thereof>>Fishing reels>>Valued over $8.45 each

E. 9507.90.8000   Fishing rods, fish hooks and other line fishing tackle; ...; parts and accessories thereof>>Other>>Other, including parts and accessories>>Other, including parts and accessories

The item in question is "Prima Facie" (classifiable under two or more different headings). There are three distinct items (rod, reel, & hook) within the fishing combo set, and represented by multiple choices "A", "D", and "C", respectively.

Each has its own unique classification description within the HTSUS, none of which is any more specific than the other. Thus, the set cannot be classified under GRI 3(a). GRI 3(b) then says to classify based on the component that gives the set its essential character. In the case of the fishing rod compared to the fishing reel, neither value nor functionality would lead an impartial party to logically deduce that one trumps the other in imparting essential character. However, the fish hook may be reasonably eliminated as a candidate for imparting essential character. Subsequently we proceed to GRI 3(c), which says to classify based on the classification that (numerically) occurs last. Accordingly, 9507.30.6000 (the reel) occurs in order after 9507.10.0040, and thus "A" is the correct answer.

Heading/ Subheading	Stat. Suffix	Article Description	Unit of Quantity	Rates of Duty		
				1		2
				General	Special	
9507		Fishing rods, fish hooks and other line fishing tackle; fish landing nets, butterfly nets and similar nets; decoy "birds" (other than those of heading 9208 or 9705) and similar hunting or shooting equipment; parts and accessories thereof:				
9507.10.00		Fishing rods and parts and accessories thereof.........		6%	Free (A+,AU,BH, CA,CL,CO,D,E,IL, JO,KR,MA,MX, OM,P,PA,PE,SG)	55%
	40	Fishing rods.	No.			
	80	Parts and accessories..................	X			
9507.20		Fish hooks, whether or not snelled:				
9507.20.40	00	Snelled hooks................	X.......	4%	Free (A,AU,BH,CA, CL,CO,E,IL,JO, KR,MA,MX,OM, P,PA,PE,SG)	55%
9507.20.80	00	Other....................	X.......	4.8%	Free (A,AU,BH,CA, CL,CO,E,IL,JO, KR,MA,MX,OM, P,PA,PE,SG)	45%
9507.30		Fishing reels and parts and accessories thereof: Fishing reels:				
9507.30.20	00	Valued not over $2.70 each.	No......	9.2%	Free (A+,AU,BH, CA,CL,CO,D,E,IL, JO,KR,MA,MX, OM,P,PA,PE,SG)	55%
9507.30.40	00	Valued over $2.70 but not over $8.45 each.....	No......	24¢ each	Free (A+,AU,BH, CA,CL,CO,D,E,IL, JO,KR,MA,MX, OM,P,PA,PE,SG)	55%
9507.30.60	00	Valued over $8.45 each........	No......	3.9%	Free (A,AU,BH,CA, CL,CO,E,IL,JO, KR,MA,MX,OM, P,PA,PE,SG)	55%
9507.30.80	00	Parts and accessories........................	X.......	5.4%	Free (A,AU,BH,CA, CL,CO,E,IL,JO, KR,MA,MX,OM, P,PA,PE,SG)	55%
9507.90		Other:				
9507.90.20	00	Fishing line put up and packaged for retail sale.....	X.......	3.7%	Free (A,AU,BH,CA, CL,CO,E,IL,JO, KR,MA,MX,OM, P,PA,PE,SG)	65%
9507.90.40	00	Fishing casts or leaders.	doz.....	5.6%	Free (A,AU,BH,CA, CL,CO,E,,IL, JO,KR,MA,MX, OM,P,PA,PE,SG)	55%
9507.90.60	00	Fish landing nets, butterfly nets and similar nets....	No.......	5%	Free (A,AU,BH,CA, CL,CO,E,IL,JO, KR,MA,MX,OM, P,PA,PE,SG)	40%
		Other, including parts and accessories:				
9507.90.70	00	Artificial baits and flies	doz.....	9%	Free (A+,AU,BH, CA,CL,CO,D,E,IL, JO,KR,MA,MX, OM,P,PA,PE,SG)	55%
9507.90.80	00	Other, including parts and accessories........	X.......	9%	Free (A,AU,BH,CA, CL,CO,E,IL,JO, KR,MA,MX,OM, P,PA,PE,SG)	55%
9508		Merry-go-rounds, boat-swings, shooting galleries and other fairground amusements; traveling circuses and traveling menageries; traveling theaters; parts and accessories thereof:				
9508.10.00	00	Traveling circuses and traveling menageries; parts and accessories.	X.......	Free		35%
9508.90.00	00	Other	X.......	Free		35%

30

Exam Example of GRI 4
"Most akin item's HTS# to be used (if not classifiable by the previous rules)."

What is the CLASSIFICATION for a "dummy launcher"? The dummy launcher is a stationary device that uses a .22 caliber blank to launch a bird dummy (not included with item) in the air from the ground for the purpose of training hunting dogs.

A. 9303.90.4000   Other firearms and similar devices which operate by the firing of an explosive charge (for example, sporting shotguns and rifles, ..., pistols and revolvers for firing blank ammunition, ...)>>Other>>Pistols and revolvers designed to fire only blank cartridges or blank ammunition

B. 9303.90.8000   Other firearms and similar devices which operate by the firing of an explosive charge (for example, sporting shotguns and rifles, ..., pistols and revolvers for firing blank ammunition, ...)>>Other>>Other

C. 9304.00.4000   Other arms (for example, spring, air or gas guns and pistols, truncheons), excluding those of heading 9307>>Pistols, rifles and other guns which eject missiles by release of compressed air or gas, or by the release of a spring mechanism or rubber held under tension>>Other

D. 9503.00.0090   Tricycles, scooters, pedal cars and similar wheeled toys; dolls' carriages; dolls, other toys; reduced-scale ("scale") models and similar recreational models, working or not; puzzles of all kinds; parts and accessories thereof>>Other

E. 9506.99.6080   Articles and equipment for general physical exercise, gymnastics, athletics, other sports (including table-tennis) or outdoor games, not specified or included elsewhere in this chapter, swimming pools and wading pools; parts and accessories thereof>>Other>>Other>>Other>>Other

Based on the multiple choice selection, the "dummy launcher" in question does not appear to be described (in name or function) in any of the HTSUS headings or subheadings. The item is not a gun (pistol, revolver, etc.), nor does it include a bird dummy (to be considered a toy doll), nor is the complete product a "part or accessory" for an outdoor game, etc.

So, assuming that the item is not classifiable by GRI's 1 thru 3, we subsequently apply GRI 4 (utilize most akin item's HTS#). Let's disregard "D" and "E" for the above-mentioned reasons. "C" may be excluded as there is no spring or rubber mechanism at work here. "A" describes an item that fires "only" blanks, so the relatively more inclusive "B" is preferred above all. Or at least a reasonable argument as such could be made that "B" is the correct answer.

Heading/ Subheading	Stat. Suf- fix	Article Description	Unit of Quantity	Rates of Duty		
				1		2
				General	Special	
9303		Other firearms and similar devices which operate by the firing of an explosive charge (for example, sporting shot- guns and rifles, muzzle-loading firearms, Very pistols and other devices designed to project only signal flares, pistols and revolvers for firing blank ammunition, captive-bolt humane killers, line-throwing guns):				
9303.10.00	00	Muzzle-loading firearms............................	No......	Free		Free
9303.20.00		Other sporting, hunting or target-shooting shotguns, including combination shotgun-rifles....................		2.6%	Free (A,AU,BH,CA, CL,CO,E,IL,JO, KR,MA,MX,OM, P,PA,PE,SG)	65%
		Shotguns:				
	20	Autoloading............................	No.			
	30	Pump action.	No.			
	40	Over and under........................	No.			
	65	Other..................................	No.			
	80	Combination shotgun-rifles....................	No.			
9303.30		Other sporting, hunting or target-shooting rifles:				
9303.30.40		Valued over $25 but not over $50 each.		3.8% on the value of the rifle + 10% on the value of the telescopic sight, if any	Free (A,AU,BH,CA, CL,CO,E,IL,JO, KR,MA,MX,OM, P,PA,PE,SG)	65%
	10	Telescopic sights imported with rifles..........	No. 1/			
		Rifles:				
	20	Centerfire.	No. 1/			
	30	Rimfire.	No. 1/			
9303.30.80		Other.		3.1% on the value of the rifle + 13% on the value of the telescopic sight, if any	Free (A,AU,BH,CA, CL,CO,E,IL,JO, KR,MA,MX,OM, P,PA,PE,SG)	65%
	05	Telescopic sights imported with rifles..........	No. 1/			
		Rifles:				
		Centerfire:				
	10	Autoloading......................	No. 1/			
		Bolt action:				
	12	Single shot...................	No. 1/			
	17	Other.	No. 1/			
	25	Other..........................	No. 1/			
	30	Rimfire.	No. 1/			
9303.90		Other:				
9303.90.40	00	Pistols and revolvers designed to fire only blank cartridges or blank ammunition.................	No......	4.2%	Free (A,AU,BH,CA, CL,CO,E,IL,JO, KR,MA,MX,OM, P,PA,PE,SG)	105%
9303.90.80	00	Other...............................	No......	Free		27.5%

Exam Example of GRI 5 (a)
"Article-specific cases are classified with item (unless they are 'the item')"

What is (are) the classification(s) of a clarinet and its fitted case, with an outer surface of plastic sheeting, imported together from China?

A. 9205.90.4020   **Wind musical instruments (for example, keyboard pipe organs, accordions, clarinets, trumpets, bagpipes), other than fairground organs and mechanical street organs>>Other>>Woodwind instruments>>Other>>Clarinets**

AND 9209.99.4040   **Parts (for example, mechanisms for music boxes) and accessories (for example, cards, discs and rolls for mechanical instruments) of musical instruments; metronomes, tuning forks and pitch pipes of all kinds>>Other>>Other>>Other>>For other woodwind and brass wind musical instruments>>For woodwind musical instruments**

B. 9205.90.4020   **Wind musical instruments (for example, keyboard pipe organs, accordions, clarinets, trumpets, bagpipes), other than fairground organs and mechanical street organs>>Other>>Woodwind instruments>>Other>>Clarinets**

AND 9209.99.4080   **Parts (for example, mechanisms for music boxes) and accessories (for example, cards, discs and rolls for mechanical instruments) of musical instruments; metronomes, tuning forks and pitch pipes of all kinds>>Other>>Other>>Other>>For other woodwind and brass wind musical instruments>>Other**

C. 9205.90.4020 ONLY

D. 9205.90.4020   **Wind musical instruments (for example, keyboard pipe organs, accordions, clarinets, trumpets, bagpipes), other than fairground organs and mechanical street organs>>Other>>Woodwind instruments>>Other>>Clarinets**

AND 4202.92.5000   **Trunks, suitcases, vanity cases, attaché cases, …, musical instrument cases, …, and similar containers, of leather or of composition leather, of sheeting of plastics, of textile materials, of vulcanized fiber or of paperboard, or wholly or mainly covered with such materials or with paper>>Other>>With outer surface of sheeting of plastic or textile materials>>Musical instrument cases**

E. 4202.92.5000 ONLY

GRI 5(a) states that cases (including musical cases) fitted to contain a specific article shall be classified with such articles, except when such containers give the whole its essential character. Such is exactly the case for the fitted, yet nondescript case for the clarinet. The correct classification for the clarinet is 9205.90.4020. The clarinet case will be classified with the clarinet under the same classification and on the same Entry Summary line. "C" is the correct answer.

Heading/ Subheading	Stat. Suf- fix	Article Description	Unit of Quantity	Rates of Duty		
				1		2
				General	Special	
9205		Wind musical instruments (for example, keyboard pipe organs, accordions, clarinets, trumpets, bagpipes), other than fairground organs and mechanical street organs:				
9205.10.00		Brass-wind instruments............................		2.9%	Free (A,AU,BH,CA, CL,CO,E,IL,JO, KR,MA,MX,OM, P,PA,PE,SG)	40%
	40	Valued not over $10 each.....................	No.			
	80	Valued over $10 each......................	No.			
9205.90		Other:				
		Keyboard pipe organs; harmoniums and similar keyboard instruments with free metal reeds:				
9205.90.12	00	Keyboard pipe organs.....................	No.	Free		35%
9205.90.14	00	Other..........................	No.	2.7%	Free (A,AU,BH,CA, CL,CO,E,IL.JO, KR,MA,MX,OM,P, PA,PE,SG)	40%
		Accordions and similar instruments; mouth organs:				
		Accordions and similar instruments:				
9205.90.15	00	Piano accordions......................	No.	Free		40%
9205.90.18	00	Other..........................	No.	2.6%	Free (A,AU,BH,CA, CL,CO,E,IL.JO, KR,MA,MX,OM, P,PA,PE,SG)	40%
9205.90.19	00	Mouth organs...........................	doz.	Free		40%
		Woodwind instruments:				
9205.90.20	00	Bagpipes...........................	No.	Free		40%
9205.90.40		Other..........................		4.9%	Free (A,AU,BH,CA, CL,CO,E,IL.JO, KR,MA,MX,OM, P,PA,PE,SG)	40%
	20	Clarinets...........................	No.			
	40	Saxophones...........................	No.			
	60	Flutes and piccolos (except bamboo).......	No.			
	80	Other..........................	No.			
9205.90.60	00	Other..........................	No.	Free		40%
9206.00		Percussion musical instruments (for example, drums, xylophones, cymbals, castanets, maracas):				
9206.00.20	00	Drums..........................	No.	4.8%	Free (A,AU,BH,CA, CL,CO,E,IL.JO, KR,MA,MX,OM, P,PA,PE,SG)	40%
9206.00.40	00	Cymbals............................	No.	Free		40%
9206.00.60	00	Sets of tuned bells known as chimes, peals or carillons........................	No.	Free		50%
9206.00.80	00	Other..........................	No.	5.3%	Free (A,AU,BH,CA, CL,CO,E,IL.JO, KR,MA,MX,OM, P,PA,PE,SG)	40%

Exam Example of GRI 5 (b)
"Packaging is classified with item (unless they are 'the item')"

An importer in the U.S. receives 500 single action economy stopwatches shipped by air from Munich, Germany. The stopwatches are individually packaged in plastic blister packaging for retail sale. Which statement regarding the plastic blister packaging is TRUE?

     A.   The packaging is classified with the stopwatches
     B.   The packaging is classified separately as articles of plastic
     C.   The packaging costs are deducted from the entered value
     D.   The importer's name must be on the packaging
     E.   The manufacturer's name must be on the packaging

Paraphrasing GRI 5(b), normally used packaging is to be classified with the goods therein. "A" is the correct answer.

Most Commonly Tested
TITLE 19 CFR

This section points out parts, sections, and paragraphs of the 19 CFR that have most often appeared as questions over the last ten exams. It is arranged by frequency of appearances from the past ten exams, and then numerically by CFR Part, Section, and then by Paragraph. Attempt to memorize as much as you can of the major points of this section of the study guide. The reason for this is that the more you are able to answer exam questions "on the fly" (without having to refer to your 19 CFR, HTS, directives, etc.), then the more time you will have to focus on the more time-consuming parts of the exam, especially HTS classification.

Most Commonly Tested
TITLE 19 CFR

Part 152.103(a)

CLASSIFICATION AND APPRAISEMENT OF MERCHANDISE>>Valuation of Merchandise>>Transaction value>>Price actually paid or payable

Number of times appearing in last 10 exams: 12
Last appeared in exam: April 2014

The gist of it...

     This paragraph explains that the price actually paid or payable is to be used when determining transaction value, which may be derived by means of additions to or deductions (e.g. deducting freight charges from invoice value, etc.). Several examples are provided as reference.

Excerpt from 19 CFR...

(a) Price actually paid or payable—(1) General. In determining transaction value, the price actually paid or payable will be considered without regard to its method of derivation. It may be the result of discounts, increases, or negotiations, or may be arrived at by the application of a formula, such as the price in effect on the date of export in the London Commodity Market. The word "payable" refers to a situation in which the price has been agreed upon, but actual payment has not been made at the time of importation. Payment may be made by letters of credit or negotiable instruments and may be made directly or indirectly.

Example 1. In a transaction with foreign Company X, a U.S. firm pays Company X $10,000 for a shipment of meat products, packed ready for shipment to the United States. No selling commission, assist, royalty, or license fee is involved. Company X is not related to the U.S. purchaser and imposes no condition or limitation on the buyer.

The customs value of the imported meat products is $10,000—the transaction value of the imported merchandise.

Example 2. A foreign shipper sold merchandise at $100 per unit to a U.S. importer. Subsequently, the foreign shipper increased its price to $110 per unit. The merchandise was exported after the effective date of the price increase. The invoice price of $100 was the price originally agreed upon and the price the U.S. importer actually paid for the merchandise.

How should the merchandise be appraised?

Actual transaction value of $100 per unit based on the price actually paid or payable.

Example 3. A foreign shipper sells to U.S. wholesalers at one price and to U.S. retailers at a higher price. The shipment undergoing appraisement is a shipment to a U.S. retailer. There are continuing shipments of identical and similar merchandise to U.S. wholesalers.

How should the merchandise be appraised?

Actual transaction value based on the price actually paid or payable by the retailer.

Example 4. Company X in the United States pay $2,000 to Y Toy Factory abroad for a shipment of toys. The $2,000 consists of $1,850 for the toys and $150 for ocean freight and insurance. Y Toy Factory would have charged Company X $2,200 for the toys; however, because Y owed Company X $350, Y charged only $1,850 for the toys. What is the transaction value?

The transaction value of the imported merchandise is $2,200, that is, the sum of the $1,850 plus the $350 indirect payment. Because the transaction value excludes C.I.F. charges, the $150 ocean freight and insurance charge is excluded.

Example 5. A seller offers merchandise at $100, less a 2% discount for cash. A buyer remits $98 cash, taking advantage of the cash discount.

The transaction value is $98, the price actually paid or payable.

(2) Indirect payment. An indirect payment would include the settlement by the buyer, in whole or in part, of a debt owed by the seller, or where the buyer receives a price reduction on a current importation as a means of settling a debt owed him by the seller. Activities such as advertising, undertaken by the buyer on his own account, other than those for which an adjustment is provided in §152.103(b), will not be considered an indirect payment to the seller though they may benefit the seller. The costs of those activities will not be added to the price actually paid or payable in determining the customs value of the imported merchandise.

(3) Assembled merchandise. The price actually paid or payable may represent an amount for the assembly of imported merchandise in which the seller has no interest other than as the assembler. The price actually paid or payable in that case will be calculated by the addition of the value of the components and required adjustments to form the basis for the transaction value.

Example 1. The importer previously has supplied an unrelated foreign assembler with fabricated components ready for assembly having a value or cost at the assembler's plant of $1.00 per unit. The importer pays the assembler 50¢ per unit for the assembly. The transaction value for the assembled unit is $1.50.

Example 2. Same facts as Example 1 above except the U.S. importer furnishes to the foreign assembler a tooling assist consisting of a tool acquired by the importer at $1,000. The transportation expenses to the foreign assembler's plant for the tooling assist equal $100. The transaction value for the assembled unit would be $1.50 per unit plus a pro rata share of the tooling assist valued at $1,100.

(4) Rebate. Any rebate of, or other decrease in, the price actually paid or payable made or otherwise effected between the buyer and seller after the date of importation of the merchandise will be disregarded in determining the transaction value under §152.103(b).

(5) Foreign inland freight and other inland charges incident to the international shipment of merchandise—(i) Ex-factory sales. If the price actually paid or payable by the buyer to the seller for the imported merchandise does not include a charge for foreign inland freight and other charges for services incident to the international shipment of merchandise (an ex-factory price), those charges will not be added to the price.

(ii) Sales other than ex-factory. As a general rule, in those situations where the price actually paid or payable for imported merchandise includes a charge for foreign inland freight, whether or not itemized separately on the invoices or other commercial documents, that charge will be part of the transaction value to the extent included in the price. However, charges for foreign inland freight and other services incident to the shipment of the merchandise to the United States may be considered incident to the international shipment of that merchandise within the meaning of §152.102(f) if they are identified

separately and they occur after the merchandise has been sold for export to the United States and placed with a carrier for through shipment to the United States.

(iii) Evidence of sale for export and placement for through shipment. A sale for export and placement for through shipment to the United States under paragraph (a)(5)(ii) of this section shall be established by means of a through bill of lading to be presented to the port director. Only in those situations where it clearly would be impossible to ship merchandise on a through bill of lading (e.g., shipments via the seller's own conveyance) will other documentation satisfactory to the port director showing a sale for export to the United States and placement for through shipment to the United States be accepted in lieu of a through bill of lading.

(iv) Erroneous and false information. This regulation shall not be construed as prohibiting Customs from making appropriate additions to the dutiable value of merchandise in instances where verification reveals that foreign inland freight charges or other charges for services incident to the international shipment of merchandise have been overstated.

Most Commonly Tested
TITLE 19 CFR

Part 141.89
ENTRY OF MERCHANDISE>>Invoices>>Additional information for certain classes of merchandise

Number of times appearing in last 10 exams: 8
Last appeared in exam: April 2014

The gist of it...
    For some imported items, Customs requires additional information to be provided with the entry. Some chemicals, for example, require a Chemical Abstracts Service (CAS) number(s) to be provided as part of the customs entry.

Excerpt from 19 CFR...

(a) Invoices for the following classes of merchandise, classifiable under the Harmonized Tariff Schedule of the United States (HTSUS), shall set forth the additional information specified: [75-42, 75-239, 78-53, 83-251, 84-149.]

Aluminum and alloys of aluminum classifiable under subheadings 7601.10.60, 7601.20.60, 7601.20.90, or 7602.00.00, HTSUS (T.D. 53092, 55977, 56143)—Statement of the percentages by weight of any metallic element contained in the article.

Articles manufactured of textile materials, Coated or laminated with plastics or rubber, classifiable in Chapter(s) 39, 40, and 42—Include a description indicating whether the fabric is coated or laminated on both sides, on the exterior surface or on the interior surface.

Bags manufactured of plastic sheeting and not of a reinforced or laminated construction, classified in Chapter 39 or in heading 4202—Indicate the gauge of the plastic sheeting.

Ball or roller bearings classifiable under subheading 8482.10.50 through 8482.80.00, HTSUS (T.D. 68-306)—(1) Type of bearing (i.e., whether a ball or roller bearing); (2) If a roller bearing, whether a spherical, tapered, cylindrical, needled or other type; (3) Whether a combination bearing (i.e., a bearing containing both ball and roller bearings, etc.); and (4) If a ball bearing (not including ball bearing with integral shafts or parts of ball bearings), whether or not radial, the following: (a) outside diameter of each bearing; and (b) whether or not a radial bearing (the definition of radial bearing is, for Customs purposes, an antifriction bearing primarily designed to support a load perpendicular to shaft axis).

Beads (T.D. 50088, 55977)—(1) The length of the string, if strung; (2) The size of the beads expressed in millimeters; (3) The material of which the beads are composed, i.e., ivory, glass, imitation pearl, etc.

Bed linen and Bedspreads—Statement as to whether or not the article contains any embroidery, lace, braid, edging, trimming, piping or applique work.

Chemicals—Furnish the use and Chemical Abstracts Service number of chemical compounds classified in Chapters 27, 28 and 29, HTSUS.

......

Most Commonly Tested
TITLE 19 CFR

Part 152.103(j)
CLASSIFICATION AND APPRAISEMENT OF MERCHANDISE>>Valuation of Merchandise>>Transaction value>>Limitations on use of transaction value

Number of times appearing in last 10 exams: 8
Last appeared in exam: October 2013

The gist of it...

This paragraph lists the types of import transactions that will preclude the importer or broker from using the preferred method of appraisement, that of the transaction value.

Excerpt from 19 CFR...

(j) Limitations on use of transaction value—(1) In general. The transaction value of imported merchandise will be the appraised value only if:

(i) There are no restrictions on the disposition or use of the imported merchandise by the buyer, other than restrictions which are imposed or required by law, limit the geographical area in which the merchandise may be resold, or do not affect substantially the value of the merchandise;

(ii) The sale of, or the price actually paid or payable for, the imported merchandise is not subject to any condition or consideration for which a value cannot be determined;

(iii) No part of the proceeds of any subsequent resale, disposal, or use of the imported merchandise by the buyer will accrue directly or indirectly to the seller, unless an appropriate adjustment can be made under paragraph (b)(1)(v) of this section; and

(iv) The buyer and seller are not related, or the buyer and seller are related but the transaction value is acceptable.

(2) Related person transactions. (i) The transaction value between a related buyer and seller is acceptable if an examination of the circumstances of sale indicates that their relationship did not influence the price actually paid or payable, or if the transaction value of the imported merchandise closely approximates:

(A) The transaction value of identical merchandise; or of similar merchandise, in sales to unrelated buyers in the United States; or

(B) The deductive value or computed value of identical merchandise, or of similar merchandise; and

(C) Each value referred to in paragraph (j)(2)(i) (A) and (B) of this section that is used for comparison relates to merchandise that was exported to the United States at or about the same time as the imported merchandise.

(ii) In applying the values used for comparison, differences with respect to the sales involved will be taken into account if based on sufficient information supplied by the buyer or otherwise available to Customs and if the differences relate to:

... ...

Most Commonly Tested
TITLE 19 CFR

Part 111.1
CUSTOMS BROKERS>>General Provisions>>Definitions

Number of times appearing in last 10 exams: 7
Last appeared in exam: April 2014

The gist of it...
     This list of definitions include the meanings of terms such as "customs business" and "responsible supervision and control" as defined by CBP.

Excerpt from 19 CFR...

When used in this part, the following terms have the meanings indicated:

Assistant Commissioner. "Assistant Commissioner" means the Assistant Commissioner, Office of International Trade, U.S. Customs and Border Protection, Washington, DC.

Broker. "Broker" means a customs broker.

Corporate compliance activity. "Corporate compliance activity" means activity performed by a business entity to ensure that documents for a related business entity or entities are prepared and filed with CBP using "reasonable care", but such activity does not extend to the actual preparation or filing of the documents or their electronic equivalents. For purposes of this definition, a "business entity" is an entity that is registered or otherwise on record with an appropriate governmental authority for business licensing, taxation, or other legal purposes, and the term "related business entity or entities" encompasses a business entity that has more than a 50 percent ownership interest in another business entity, a business entity in which another business entity has more than a 50 percent ownership interest, and two or more business entities in which the same business entity has more than a 50 percent ownership interest.

Customs broker. "Customs broker" means a person who is licensed under this part to transact customs business on behalf of others.

Customs business. "Customs business" means those activities involving transactions with CBP concerning the entry and admissibility of merchandise, its classification and valuation, the payment of duties, taxes, or other charges assessed or collected by CBP on merchandise by reason of its importation, and the refund, rebate, or drawback of those duties, taxes, or other charges. "Customs business" also includes the preparation, and activities relating to the preparation, of documents in any format and the electronic transmission of documents and parts of documents intended to be filed with CBP in furtherance of any other customs business activity, whether or not signed or filed by the preparer. However, "customs business" does not include the mere electronic transmission of data received for transmission to CBP and does not include a corporate compliance activity.

District. "District" means the geographic area covered by a customs broker permit other than a national permit. A listing of each district, and the ports thereunder, will be published periodically.

Employee. "Employee" means a person who meets the common law definition of employee and is in the service of a customs broker.

Freight forwarder. "Freight forwarder" means a person engaged in the business of dispatching shipments in foreign commerce between the United States, its territories or possessions, and foreign countries, and handling the formalities incident to such shipments, on behalf of other persons.

Officer. "Officer", when used in the context of an association or corporation, means a person who has been elected, appointed, or designated as an officer of an association or corporation in accordance with statute and the articles of incorporation, articles of agreement, charter, or bylaws of the association or corporation.

Permit. "Permit" means any permit issued to a broker under §111.19.

Person. "Person" includes individuals, partnerships, associations, and corporations.

Records. "Records" means documents, data and information referred to in, and required to be made or maintained under, this part and any other records, as defined in §163.1(a) of this chapter, that are required to be maintained by a broker under part 163 of this chapter.

Region. "Region" means the geographic area covered by a waiver issued pursuant to §111.19(d).

Responsible supervision and control. "Responsible supervision and control" means that degree of supervision and control necessary to ensure the proper transaction of the customs business of a broker, including actions necessary to ensure that an employee of a broker provides substantially the same quality of service in handling customs transactions that the broker is required to provide. While the determination of what is necessary to perform and maintain responsible supervision and control will vary depending upon the circumstances in each instance, factors which CBP will consider include, but are not limited to: The training required of employees of the broker; the issuance of written instructions and guidelines to employees of the broker; the volume and type of business of the broker; the reject rate for the various customs transactions; the maintenance of current editions of CBP Regulations, the Harmonized Tariff Schedule of the United States, and CBP issuances; the availability of an individually licensed broker for necessary consultation with employees of the broker; the frequency of supervisory visits of an individually licensed broker to another office of the broker that does not have a resident individually licensed broker; the frequency of audits and reviews by an individually licensed broker of the customs transactions handled by employees of the broker; the extent to which the individually licensed broker who qualifies the district permit is involved in the operation of the brokerage; and any circumstance which indicates that an individually licensed broker has a real interest in the operations of a broker.

Department of Homeland Security or any representative of the Department of Homeland Security. "Department of Homeland Security or any representative of the Department of Homeland Security" means any office, officer, or employee of the U.S. Department of Homeland Security, wherever located.

Most Commonly Tested

TITLE 19 CFR

Part 111.19
CUSTOMS BROKERS>>Procedure to Obtain License or Permit>>Permits

Number of times appearing in last 10 exams: 7
Last appeared in exam: October 2011

The gist of it...
    This section outlines the procedure and fees due for district and national permits.

Excerpt from 19 CFR...

(a) General. Each person granted a broker's license under this part will be concurrently issued a permit for the district in which the port through which the license was delivered to the licensee (see §111.15) is located and without the payment of the $100 fee required by §111.96(b), if it is shown to the satisfaction of the port director that the person intends to transact customs business within that district and the person otherwise complies with the requirements of this part.

(b) Submission of application for initial or additional district permit. A broker who intends to conduct customs business at a port within another district for which he does not have a permit, or a broker who was not concurrently granted a permit with the broker's license under paragraph (a) of this section, and except as otherwise provided in paragraph (f) of this section, must submit an application for a permit in a letter to the director of the port at which he intends to conduct customs business. Each application for a permit must set forth or attach the following:

... ...

(c) Fees. Each application for a district permit under paragraph (b) of this section must be accompanied by the $100 and $138 fees specified in §§111.96(b) and (c). In the case of an application for a national permit under paragraph (f) of this section, the $100 fee specified in §111.96(b) and the $138 fee specified in §111.96(c) must be paid at the port through which the applicant's license was delivered (see §111.15) prior to submission of the application. The $138 fee specified in §111.96(c) also must be paid in connection with the issuance of an initial district permit concurrently with the issuance of a license under paragraph (a) of this section.

Most Commonly Tested
TITLE 19 CFR

Part 111.28

CUSTOMS BROKERS>>Duties and Responsibilities of Customs Brokers>>Responsible supervision

Number of times appearing in last 10 exams: 7
Last appeared in exam: April 2014

The gist of it...

     This section describes what is expected from the customs broker in regards to the "responsible supervision" of their customs brokerage operations, including the submittal of a list of all of their current and new employees.

Excerpt from 19 CFR...

(a) General. Every individual broker operating as a sole proprietor and every licensed member of a partnership that is a broker and every licensed officer of an association or corporation that is a broker must exercise responsible supervision and control (see §111.1) over the transaction of the customs business of the sole proprietorship, partnership, association, or corporation.

(b) Employee information—(1) Current employees—(i) General. Each broker must submit, in writing, to the director of each port at which the broker intends to transact customs business, a list of the names of persons currently employed by the broker at that port. The list of employees must be submitted upon issuance of a permit for an additional district under §111.19, or upon the opening of an office at a port within a district for which the broker already has a permit, and before the broker begins to transact customs business as a broker at the port. For each employee, the broker also must provide the social security number, date and place of birth, current home address, last prior home address, and, if the employee has been employed by the broker for less than 3 years, the name and address of each former employer and dates of employment for the 3-year period preceding current employment with the broker. After the initial submission, an updated list, setting forth the name, social security number, date and place of birth, and current home address of each current employee, must be submitted with the status report required by §111.30(d).

... ...

Most Commonly Tested
TITLE 19 CFR

Part 152.103(b)

CLASSIFICATION AND APPRAISEMENT OF MERCHANDISE>>Valuation of Merchandise>>Transaction value>>Additions to price actually paid or payable

Number of times appearing in last 10 exams: 7
Last appeared in exam: October 2013

The gist of it...

This paragraph states that packing costs, selling commissions, assists, royalties, and proceeds to seller are to be added to the transaction value, in order to arrive at the entered value. Remember the acronym "C.R.A.P.P." (Commissions, Royalties, Assists, Packaging, Proceeds).

Excerpt from 19 CFR...

(b) Additions to price actually paid or payable. (1) The transaction value of imported merchandise is the price actually paid or payable for the merchandise when sold for exportation to the United States, plus amounts equal to:

(i) The packing costs incurred by the buyer with respect to the imported merchandise;

(ii) Any selling commission incurred by the buyer with respect to the imported merchandise;

(iii) The value, apportioned as appropriate, of any assist;

(iv) Any royalty or license fee related to the imported merchandise that the buyer is required to pay, directly or indirectly, as a condition of the sale of the imported merchandise for exportation to the United States; and

(v) The proceeds of any subsequent resale, disposal, or use of the imported merchandise that accrue, directly or indirectly, to the seller.

(2) The price actually paid or payable for imported merchandise will be increased by the amounts attributable to the items (and no others) described in paragraphs (b)(1) (i) through (v) of this section to the extent that each amount is not otherwise included within the price actually paid or payable, and is based on sufficient information. If sufficient information is not available, for any reason, with respect to any amount referred to in this section, the transaction value will be treated as one that cannot be determined.

(3) Interpretative note. A royalty is paid on the basis of the price in a sale in the United States of a gallon of a particular product imported by the pound and transformed into a solution after importation. If the royalty is based partially on the imported merchandise and partially on other factors which have nothing to do with the imported merchandise (such as if the imported merchandise is mixed with domestic ingredients and is no longer separately identifiable, or if the royalty cannot be distinguished from special financial arrangements between the buyer and the seller), it would be inappropriate to attempt to make an addition for the royalty. However, if the amount of this royalty is based only on the imported merchandise and can be readily quantified, an addition to the price actually paid or payable will be made.

Most Commonly Tested
TITLE 19 CFR

Part 101.1
GENERAL PROVISIONS>>Definitions

Number of times appearing in last 10 exams: 6
Last appeared in exam: April 2014

The gist of it...

Here, regularly used Customs terms are given their definition for the sake of clarity in the regulations.

Excerpt from 19 CFR...

As used in this chapter, the following terms shall have the meanings indicated unless either the context in which they are used requires a different meaning or a different definition is prescribed for a particular part or portion thereof:

Business day. A "business day" means a weekday (Monday through Friday), excluding national holidays as specified in §101.6(a).

Customs station. A "Customs station" is any place, other than a port of entry, at which Customs officers or employees are stationed, under the authority contained in article IX of the President's Message of March 3, 1913 (T.D. 33249), to enter and clear vessels, accept entries of merchandise, collect duties, and enforce the various provisions of the Customs and navigation laws of the United States.

Customs territory of the United States. "Customs territory of the United States" includes only the States, the District of Columbia, and Puerto Rico.

Date of entry. The "date of entry" or "time of entry" of imported merchandise shall be the effective time of entry of such merchandise, as defined in §141.68 of this chapter.

Date of exportation. "Date of exportation" or "time of exportation" shall be as defined in §152.1(c) of this chapter.

Date of importation. "Date of importation" means, in the case of merchandise imported otherwise than by vessel, the date on which the merchandise arrives within the Customs territory of the United States. In the case of merchandise imported by vessel, "date of importation" means the date on which the vessel arrives within the limits of a port in the United States with intent then and there to unlade such merchandise.

Duties. "Duties" means Customs duties and any internal revenue taxes which attach upon importation.

Entry or withdrawal for consumption. "Entry or withdrawal for consumption" means entry for consumption or withdrawal from warehouse for consumption.

Exportation. "Exportation" means a severance of goods from the mass of things belonging to this country with the intention of uniting them to the mass of things belonging to some foreign country. The shipment of merchandise abroad with the intention of returning it to the United States with a design to circumvent provisions of restriction or limitation in the tariff laws or to secure a benefit accruing to imported merchandise is not an exportation. Merchandise of foreign origin returned from abroad under these circumstances is dutiable according to its nature, weight, and value at the time of its original arrival in this country.

Importer. "Importer" means the person primarily liable for the payment of any duties on the merchandise, or an authorized agent acting on his behalf. The importer may be:

(1) The consignee, or

(2) The importer of record, or

(3) The actual owner of the merchandise, if an actual owner's declaration and superseding bond has been filed in accordance with §141.20 of this chapter, or

(4) The transferee of the merchandise, if the right to withdraw merchandise in a bonded warehouse has been transferred in accordance with subpart C of part 144 of this chapter.

Port and port of entry. The terms "port" and "port of entry" refer to any place designated by Executive Order of the President, by order of the Secretary of the Treasury, or by Act of Congress, at which a Customs officer is authorized to accept entries of merchandise to collect duties, and to enforce the various provisions of the Customs and navigation laws. The terms "port" and "port of entry" incorporate the geographical area under the jurisdiction of a port director. (The Customs ports in the Virgin Islands, although under the jurisdiction of the Secretary of the Treasury, have their own Customs laws (48 U.S.C. 1406(i)). These ports, therefore, are outside the Customs territory of the United States and the ports thereof are not "ports of entry" within the meaning of these regulations).

Principal field officer. A "principal field officer" is an officer in the field service whose immediate supervisor is located at Customs Service Headquarters.

Service port. The term "service port" refers to a Customs location having a full range of cargo processing functions, including inspections, entry, collections, and verification.

Shipment. "Shipment" means the merchandise described on the bill of lading or other document used to file or support entry, or in the oral declaration when applicable.

Most Commonly Tested
TITLE 19 CFR

Part 111.23
CUSTOMS BROKERS>>Duties and Responsibilities of Customs Brokers>>Retention of records

Number of times appearing in last 10 exams: 6
Last appeared in exam: October 2013

The gist of it...
This section describes the requirements, including length of time (5 years), for customs brokers' record keeping.

Excerpt from 19 CFR...

(a) Place of retention. A licensed customs broker may retain records relating to its customs transactions at any location within the customs territory of the United States in accordance with the provisions of this part and part 163 of this chapter. Upon request by CBP to examine records, the designated recordkeeping contact identified in the broker's applicable permit application, in accordance with §111.19(b)(6) of this chapter, must make all records available to CBP within 30 calendar days, or such longer time as specified by CBP, at the broker district that covers the CBP port to which the records relate.

(b) Period of retention. The records described in this section, other than powers of attorney, must be retained for at least 5 years after the date of entry. Powers of attorney must be retained until revoked, and revoked powers of attorney and letters of revocation must be retained for 5 years after the date of revocation or for 5 years after the date the client ceases to be an "active client" as defined in §111.29(b)(2)(ii), whichever period is later. When merchandise is withdrawn from a bonded warehouse, records relating to the withdrawal must be retained for 5 years from the date of withdrawal of the last merchandise withdrawn under the entry.

Most Commonly Tested
TITLE 19 CFR

Part 159.32

LIQUIDATION OF DUTIES>>Conversion of Foreign Currency>>Date of exportation

Number of times appearing in last 10 exams: 6
Last appeared in exam: October 2013

The gist of it...

Here customs states that that the currency conversion rate to be used to convert commercial invoice values stated in foreign currency amounts is to be based on the date of exportation.

Excerpt from 19 CFR...

§159.32 Date of exportation.

The date of exportation for currency conversion shall be fixed in accordance with §152.1(c) of this chapter.

§152.1 Definitions.

The following are general definitions for the purposes of part 152:

(a)-(b) [Reserved]

(c) Date of exportation. "Date of exportation," or the "time of exportation" referred to in section 402, Tariff Act of 1930, as amended (19 U.S.C. 1401a), means the actual date the merchandise finally leaves the country of exportation for the United States. If no positive evidence is at hand as to the actual date of exportation, the port director shall ascertain or estimate the date of exportation by all reasonable ways and means in his power, and in so doing may consider dates on bills of lading, invoices, and other information available to him.

Most Commonly Tested
TITLE 19 CFR

Part 181.22

NAFTA>>Import Requirements>>Maintenance of records and submission of Certificate by importer

Number of times appearing in last 10 exams: 6
Last appeared in exam: October 2012

The gist of it...

Customs states that NAFTA-related records must be kept for 5 years and explains the acceptable form of the certificate of origin.

Excerpt from 19 CFR...

(a) Maintenance of records. Each importer claiming preferential tariff treatment for a good imported into the United States shall maintain in the United States, for five years after the date of entry of the good, all documentation relating to the importation of the good. Such documentation shall include a copy of the Certificate of Origin and any other relevant records as specified in §163.1(a) of this chapter.

(b) Submission of Certificate. An importer who claims preferential tariff treatment on a good under §181.21 of this part shall provide, at the request of the port director, a copy of each Certificate of Origin pertaining to the good which is in the possession of the importer. A Certificate of Origin submitted to CBP under this paragraph or under §181.32(b)(3) of this part:

(1) Shall be on CBP Form 434, including privately-printed copies thereof, or on such other form as approved by the Canadian or Mexican customs administration, or, as an alternative to CBP Form 434 or such other approved form, in an approved computerized format or such other medium or format as is approved by the Office of International Trade, U.S. Customs and Border Protection, Washington, DC 20229. An alternative format must contain the same information and certification set forth on CBP Form 434;

(2) Shall be signed by the exporter or by the exporter's authorized agent having knowledge of the relevant facts;

(3) Shall be completed either in the English language or in the language of the country from which the good is exported. If the Certificate is completed in a language other than English, the importer shall also provide to the port director, upon request, a written English translation thereof;

(4) Shall be accepted by CBP for four years after the date on which the Certificate was signed by the exporter or producer; and

(5) May be applicable to:

(i) A single importation of a good into the United States, including a single shipment that results in the filing of one or more entries and a series of shipments that results in the filing of one entry; or

(ii) Multiple importations of identical goods into the United States that occur within a specified period, not exceeding 12 months, set out therein by the exporter or producer. ... ...

Most Commonly Tested
TITLE 19 CFR

Part 111.11

CUSTOMS BROKERS>>Procedure to Obtain License or Permit>>Basic requirements for a license

Number of times appearing in last 10 exams: 5
Last appeared in exam: April 2014

The gist of it...

This section specifies the minimum requirements for obtaining a broker's license for individuals, for partnerships, and for corporations.

Excerpt from 19 CFR...

(a) Individual. In order to obtain a broker's license, an individual must:

(1) Be a citizen of the United States on the date of submission of the application referred to in §111.12(a) and not an officer or employee of the United States Government;

(2) Attain the age of 21 prior to the date of submission of the application referred to in §111.12(a);

(3) Be of good moral character; and

(4) Have established, by attaining a passing (75 percent or higher) grade on a written examination taken within the 3-year period before submission of the application referred to in §111.12(a), that he has sufficient knowledge of customs and related laws, regulations and procedures, bookkeeping, accounting, and all other appropriate matters to render valuable service to importers and exporters.

(b) Partnership. In order to qualify for a broker's license, a partnership must have at least one member of the partnership who is a broker.

(c) Association or corporation. In order to qualify for a broker's license, an association or corporation must:

(1) Be empowered under its articles of association or articles of incorporation to transact customs business as a broker; and

(2) Have at least one officer who is a broker.

Most Commonly Tested
TITLE 19 CFR

Part 111.29(a)
CUSTOMS BROKERS>>Duties and Responsibilities of Customs Brokers>>Diligence in correspondence and paying monies>>Due diligence by broker

Number of times appearing in last 10 exams: 5
Last appeared in exam: October 2013

The gist of it...

     This paragraph states the responsibilities of the customs broker in making payments to Customs on behalf of their customers.

Excerpt from 19 CFR...

(a) Due diligence by broker. Each broker must exercise due diligence in making financial settlements, in answering correspondence, and in preparing or assisting in the preparation and filing of records relating to any customs business matter handled by him as a broker. Payment of duty, tax, or other debt or obligation owing to the Government for which the broker is responsible, or for which the broker has received payment from a client, must be made to the Government on or before the date that payment is due. Payments received by a broker from a client after the due date must be transmitted to the Government within 5 working days from receipt by the broker. Each broker must provide a written statement to a client accounting for funds received for the client from the Government, or received from a client where no payment to the Government has been made, or received from a client in excess of the Governmental or other charges properly payable as part of the client's customs business, within 60 calendar days of receipt. No written statement is required if there is actual payment of the funds by a broker.

Most Commonly Tested
TITLE 19 CFR

Part 111.30(d)
CUSTOMS BROKERS>>Duties and Responsibilities of Customs Brokers>>Notification of change of business address, organization name, or location of business records; status report; termination of brokerage business>>Status Report

Number of times appearing in last 10 exams: 5
Last appeared in exam: April 2014

The gist of it...
　　　　This paragraph provides instructions on the customs broker triennial status report. The next status reports are due in Feb. 2015 and then in Feb. 2018.

Excerpt from 19 CFR...

(d) Status report—(1) General. Each broker must file a written status report with Customs on February 1, 1985, and on February 1 of each third year after that date. The report must be accompanied by the fee prescribed in §111.96(d) and must be addressed to the director of the port through which the license was delivered to the licensee (see §111.15). A report received during the month of February will be considered filed timely. No form or particular format is required.

(2) Individual. Each individual broker must state in the report required under paragraph (d)(1) of this section whether he is actively engaged in transacting business as a broker. If he is so actively engaged, he must also:

(i) State the name under which, and the address at which, his business is conducted if he is a sole proprietor;

(ii) State the name and address of his employer if he is employed by another broker, unless his employer is a partnership, association or corporation broker for which he is a qualifying member or officer for purposes of §111.11(b) or (c)(2); and

(iii) State whether or not he still meets the applicable requirements of §111.11 and §111.19 and has not engaged in any conduct that could constitute grounds for suspension or revocation under §111.53.

(3) Partnership, association or corporation. Each corporation, partnership or association broker must state in the report required under paragraph (d)(1) of this section the name under which its business as a broker is being transacted, its business address, the name and address of each licensed member of the partnership or licensed officer of the association or corporation who qualifies it for a license under §111.11(b) or (c)(2), and whether it is actively engaged in transacting business as a broker, and the report must be signed by a licensed member or officer.

(4) Failure to file timely. If a broker fails to file the report required under paragraph (d)(1) of this section by March 1 of the reporting year, the broker's license is suspended by operation of law on that date. By March 31 of the reporting year, the port director will transmit written notice of the suspension to the broker by certified mail, return receipt requested, at the address reflected in Customs records. If the broker files the required report and pays the required fee within 60 calendar days of the date of the notice of suspension, the license will be reinstated. If the broker does not file the required report within that 60-day period, the broker's license is revoked by operation of law without prejudice to the filing of an application for a new license. Notice of the revocation will be published in the Customs Bulletin.

Most Commonly Tested
TITLE 19 CFR

Part 111.53
CUSTOMS BROKERS>>Cancellation, Suspension, or Revocation of License or Permit, and Monetary Penalty in Lieu of Suspension or Revocation>>Grounds for suspension or revocation of license or permit

Number of times appearing in last 10 exams: 5
Last appeared in exam: October 2013

The gist of it...

     This part of the regulations lists the instances that may result in the suspension or revocation of the broker's license or permit.

Excerpt from 19 CFR...

The appropriate Customs officer may initiate proceedings for the suspension, for a specific period of time, or revocation of the license or permit of any broker for any of the following reasons:

(a) The broker has made or caused to be made in any application for any license or permit under this part, or report filed with Customs, any statement which was, at the time and in light of the circumstances under which it was made, false or misleading with respect to any material fact, or has omitted to state in any application or report any material fact which was required;

(b) The broker has been convicted, at any time after the filing of an application for a license under §111.12, of any felony or misdemeanor which:

(1) Involved the importation or exportation of merchandise;

(2) Arose out of the conduct of customs business; or

(3) Involved larceny, theft, robbery, extortion, forgery, counterfeiting, fraudulent concealment, embezzlement, fraudulent conversion, or misappropriation of funds;

(c) The broker has violated any provision of any law enforced by Customs or the rules or regulations issued under any provision of any law enforced by Customs;

(d) The broker has counseled, commanded, induced, procured, or knowingly aided or abetted the violations by any other person of any provision of any law enforced by Customs or the rules or regulations issued under any provision of any law enforced by Customs;

(e) The broker has knowingly employed, or continues to employ, any person who has been convicted of a felony, without written approval of that employment from the Assistant Commissioner;

(f) The broker has, in the course of customs business, with intent to defraud, in any manner willfully and knowingly deceived, misled or threatened any client or prospective client; or

(g) The broker no longer meets the applicable requirements of §§111.11 and 111.19.

Most Commonly Tested
TITLE 19 CFR

Part 152.103(d)
CLASSIFICATION AND APPRAISEMENT OF MERCHANDISE>>Valuation of Merchandise>>Transaction Value>>Assist

Number of times appearing in last 10 exams: 5
Last appeared in exam: April 2014

The gist of it...
This paragraph explains methods for assessing the value for assists, including examples.

Excerpt from 19 CFR...

(d) Assist. If the value of an assist is to be added to the price actually paid or payable, or to be used as a component of computed value, the port director shall determine the value of the assist and apportion that value to the price of the imported merchandise in the following manner:

(1) If the assist consist of materials, components, parts, or similar items incorporated in the imported merchandise, or items consumed in the production of the imported merchandise, acquired by the buyer from an unrelated seller, the value of the assist is the cost of its acquisition. If the assist were produced by the buyer or a person related to the buyer, its value would be the cost of its production. In either case, the value of the assist would include transportation costs to the place of production.

(2) If the assist consists of tools, dies, molds, or similar items used in the production of the imported merchandise, acquired by the buyer from an unrelated seller, the value of the assist is the cost of its acquisition. If the assist were produced by the buyer or a person related to the buyer, its value would be cost of its production. If the assist has been used previously by the buyer, regardless of whether it had been acquired or produced by him, the original cost of acquisition or production would be adjusted downward to reflect its use before its value could be determined. If the assist were leased by the buyer from an unrelated seller, the value of the assist would be the cost of the lease. In either case, the value of the assist would include transportation costs to the place of production. Repairs or modifications to an assist may increase its value.

Example 1. A U.S. importer supplied detailed designs to the foreign producer. These designs were necessary to manufacture the merchandise. The U.S. importer bought the designs from an engineering company in the U.S. for submission to his foreign supplier.

Should the appraised value of the merchandise include the value of the assist?

No, design work undertaken in the U.S. may not be added to the price actually paid or payable.

Example 2. A U.S. importer supplied molds free of charge to the foreign shipper. The molds were necessary to manufacture merchandise for the U.S. importer. The U.S. importer had some of the molds manufactured by a U.S. company and others manufactured in a third country.

Should the appraised value of the merchandise include the value of the molds?

Yes. It is an addition required to be made to transaction value.

Most Commonly Tested
TITLE 19 CFR

Part 24.3
CUSTOMS FINANCIAL AND ACCOUNTING PROCEDURES>>Bills and accounts; receipts

Number of times appearing in last 10 exams: 4
Last appeared in exam: October 2012

The gist of it...
Instructions for obtaining official receipt of payment from remittances to US Customs as well as payment the terms (30 days) that accompany Customs bills.

Excerpt from 19 CFR...

(a) Any bill or account for money due the United States shall be rendered by an authorized Customs officer or employee on an official form.

(b) A receipt for the payment of estimated Customs duties, taxes, fees, and interest, if applicable, shall be provided a payer at the time of payment if he furnishes with his payment an additional copy of the documentation submitted in support of the payment. The appropriate Customs official shall validate the additional copy as paid and return it to the payer. Otherwise, a copy of the document filed by the payer and the payer's cancelled check shall constitute evidence of payment.

(c) A copy of a Customs bill validated as paid will not normally be provided a payer. If a bill is paid by check, the copy of the Customs bill identified as "Payer's Copy" and the payer's cancelled check shall constitute evidence of such payment to Customs. Should a payer desire evidence of receipt, both the "U.S. Customs Service Copy" and the "Payer's Copy" of the bill and, in the case of payments by mail, a stamped, self-addressed envelope, shall be submitted. The "Payer's Copy" of the bill shall then be marked paid by the appropriate Customs official and returned to the payer.

(d) Every payment which is not made in person shall be accompanied by the original bill or by a communication containing sufficient information to identify the account or accounts to which it is to be applied.

(e) Except for bills resulting from dishonored checks or dishonored Automated Clearinghouse (ACH) transactions, all other bills for duties, taxes, fees, interest, or other charges are due and payable within 30 days of the date of issuance of the bill. Bills resulting from dishonored checks or dishonored ACH transactions are due within 15 days of the date of issuance of the bill.

Most Commonly Tested
TITLE 19 CFR

Part 24.5
CUSTOMS FINANCIAL AND ACCOUNTING PROCEDURE>>Filing identification number

Number of times appearing in last 10 exams: 4
Last appeared in exam: April 2013

The gist of it...
     Customs Form 5106 (CBP Form 5106) is used to register an (first time) importer with Customs.

Excerpt from 19 CFR...

(a) Generally. Each person, business firm, Government agency, or other organization shall file Customs Form 5106, Notification of Importer's Number or Application for Importer's Number, or Notice of Change of Name or Address, with the first formal entry which is submitted or the first request for services that will result in the issuance of a bill or a refund check upon adjustment of a cash collection. A Customs Form 5106 shall also be filed for the ultimate consignee for which such entry is being made. Customs Form 5106 may be obtained from any Customs Office.

(b) Preparation of Customs Form 5106. (1) The identification number to be used when filing Customs Form 5106 shall be:

(i) The Internal Revenue Service employer identification number, or

(ii) If no Internal Revenue Service employer identification number has been assigned, the Social Security number.

(2) If neither an Internal Revenue Service employer identification number nor a Social Security number has been assigned, the word "None" shall be written on the line provided for each of these numbers on Customs Form 5106 and the form shall be filed in duplicate.

(c) Assignment of importer identification number. Upon receipt of a Customs Form 5106 without an Internal Revenue Service employer identification number or a Social Security number, an importer identification number shall be assigned and entered on the Customs Form 5106 by the Customs office where the entry or request for services is received. The duplicate copy of the form shall be returned to the filing party. This identification number shall be used in all future Customs transactions when an importer number is required. If an Internal Revenue Service employer identification number, a Social Security number, or both, are obtained after an importer number has been assigned by Customs, a new Customs Form 5106 shall not be filed unless requested by Customs.

... ...

Most Commonly Tested
TITLE 19 CFR

Part 24.23(c)

CUSTOMS FINANCIAL AND ACCOUNTING PROCEDURE>>Fees for processing merchandise>>Exemptions and limitations

Number of times appearing in last 10 exams: 4
Last appeared in exam: October 2013

The gist of it...

      This paragraph lists the transactions that are exempt from the Merchandise Processing Fee (MPF).

Excerpt from 19 CFR...

(c) Exemptions and limitations. (1) The ad valorem fee, surcharge, and specific fees provided for under paragraphs (b)(1) and (b)(2) of this section will not apply to:

(i) Except as provided in paragraph (c)(2) of this section, articles provided for in chapter 98, Harmonized Tariff Schedule of the United States (HTSUS; 19 U.S.C. 1202);

(ii) Products of insular possessions of the U.S. (General Note 3(a)(iv), HTSUS);

(iii) Products of beneficiary countries under the Caribbean Basin Economic Recovery Act (General Note 7, HTSUS);

(iv) Products of least-developed beneficiary developing countries (General Note 4(b)(i), HTSUS); and

(v) Merchandise described in General Note 19, HTSUS, merchandise released under 19 U.S.C. 1321, and merchandise imported by mail.

(2) In the case of any article provided for in subheading 9802.00.60 or 9802.00.80, HTSUS:

(i) The surcharge and specific fees provided for under paragraphs (b)(1)(ii) and (b)(2) of this section will remain applicable; and

(ii) The ad valorem fee provided for under paragraph (b)(1)(i) of this section will be assessed only on that portion of the cost or value of the article upon which duty is assessed under subheadings 9802.00.60 and 9802.00.80.

... ...

Most Commonly Tested
TITLE 19 CFR

Part 24.24
CUSTOMS FINANCIAL AND ACCOUNTING PROCEDURES>>Harbor maintenance fee

Number of times appearing in last 10 exams: 4
Last appeared in exam: October 2011

The gist of it...

Lists the ports for which the harbor maintenance fee (HMF), which is calculated at 0.125 percent (0.00125) of cargo value, is due. Also lists the types of shipments that are exempt from this fee.

Excerpt from 19 CFR...

(a) Fee. Commercial cargo loaded on or unloaded from a commercial vessel is subject to a port use fee of 0.125 percent (.00125) of its value if the loading or unloading occurs at a port within the definition of this section, unless exempt under paragraph (c) of this section or one of the special rules in paragraph (d) of this section is applicable.

(b) Definitions. For the purpose of this section:

(1) Port means any channel or harbor (or component thereof) in the customs territory of the United States which is not an inland waterway and is open to public navigation and at which Federal funds have been used since 1977 for construction, maintenance or operation. It does not include channels or harbors deauthorized by Federal law before 1985. A complete list of the ports subject to the harbor maintenance fee is set forth below:

Port Codes, Names, and Descriptions of Ports Subject to Harbor Maintenance Fee

[Section 1402 of Pub. L. 99-662, as amended]

Port code, port name and state	Port descriptions and notations
Alabama	
1901—Mobile	
Alaska	
3126—Anchorage	*Includes Seldovia Harbor, and Homer. Movements between these points are intraport.*
3106—Dalton Cache	*Includes Haines Harbor.*

… …

Most Commonly Tested
TITLE 19 CFR

Part 102.13
RULES OF ORIGIN>>Rules of Origin>>De Minimis

Number of times appearing in last 10 exams: 4
Last appeared in exam: April 2011

The gist of it...

In general, foreign material with a value of 7% or less of the total value of the good (7% or less by weight for textiles) will be disregarded in determining country of origin with a few exceptions.

Excerpt from 19 CFR...

(a) Except as otherwise provided in paragraphs (b) and (c) of this section, foreign materials that do not undergo the applicable change in tariff classification set out in §102.20 or satisfy the other applicable requirements of that section when incorporated into a good shall be disregarded in determining the country of origin of the good if the value of those materials is no more than 7 percent of the value of the good or 10 percent of the value of a good of Chapter 22, Harmonized System.

(b) Paragraph (a) of this section does not apply to a foreign material incorporated in a good provided for in Chapter 1, 2, 3, 4, 7, 8, 11, 12, 15, 17, or 20 of the Harmonized System.

(c) Foreign components or materials that do not undergo the applicable change in tariff classification set out in §102.21 or satisfy the other applicable requirements of that section when incorporated into a textile or apparel product covered by that section shall be disregarded in determining the country of origin of the good if the total weight of those components or materials is not more than 7 percent of the total weight of the good.

Most Commonly Tested
TITLE 19 CFR

Part 111.2
CUSTOMS BROKERS>>General Provisions>>License and district permit required.

Number of times appearing in last 10 exams: 4
Last appeared in exam: April 2013

The gist of it...

      This section explicitly describes which "customs-related activities" do (and do not) necessitate the possession of a license and permit.

Excerpt from 19 CFR...

(a) License—(1) General. Except as otherwise provided in paragraph (a)(2) of this section, a person must obtain the license provided for in this part in order to transact customs business as a broker.

(2) Transactions for which license is not required—(i) For one's own account. An importer or exporter transacting customs business solely on his own account and in no sense on behalf of another is not required to be licensed, nor are his authorized regular employees or officers who act only for him in the transaction of such business.

(ii) As employee of broker—(A) General. An employee of a broker, acting solely for his employer, is not required to be licensed where:

(1) Authorized to sign documents. The broker has authorized the employee to sign documents pertaining to customs business on his behalf, and has executed a power of attorney for that purpose. The broker is not required to file the power of attorney with the port director, but must provide proof of its existence to Customs upon request; or

(2) Authorized to transact other business. The broker has filed with the port director a statement identifying the employee as authorized to transact customs business on his behalf. However, no statement will be necessary when the broker is transacting customs business under an exception to the district permit rule.

(B) Broker supervision; withdrawal of authority. Where an employee has been given authority under paragraph (a)(2)(ii) of this section, the broker must exercise sufficient supervision of the employee to ensure proper conduct on the part of the employee in the transaction of customs business, and the broker will be held strictly responsible for the acts or omissions of the employee within the scope of his employment and for any other acts or omissions of the employee which, through the exercise of reasonable care and diligence, the broker should have foreseen. The broker must promptly notify the port director if authority granted to an employee under paragraph (a)(2)(ii) of this section is withdrawn. The withdrawal of authority will be effective upon receipt by the port director.

... ...

Most Commonly Tested
TITLE 19 CFR

Part 111.29(b)
CUSTOMS BROKERS>>Duties and Responsibilities of Customs Brokers>>Diligence in correspondence and paying monies>>Notice to client of method of payment

Number of times appearing in last 10 exams: 4
Last appeared in exam: October 2013

The gist of it...

      Customs brokers must provide their importer customers with a statement advising them of their obligation to pay customs charges, and advising them of their option of paying customs charges by check.

Excerpt from 19 CFR...

(b) Notice to client of method of payment—(1) All brokers must provide their clients with the following written notification:

If you are the importer of record, payment to the broker will not relieve you of liability for customs charges (duties, taxes, or other debts owed CBP) in the event the charges are not paid by the broker. Therefore, if you pay by check, customs charges may be paid with a separate check payable to the "U.S. Customs and Border Protection" which will be delivered to CBP by the broker.

(2) The written notification set forth in paragraph (b)(1) of this section must be provided by brokers as follows:

(i) On, or attached to, any power of attorney provided by the broker to a client for execution on or after September 27, 1982; and

(ii) To each active client no later than February 28, 1983, and at least once at any time within each 12-month period after that date. An active client means a client from whom a broker has obtained a power of attorney and for whom the broker has transacted customs business on at least two occasions within the 12-month period preceding notification.

Most Commonly Tested
TITLE 19 CFR

Part 113.62
CUSTOMS BONDS>>Customs Bond Conditions>>Basic importation and entry bond conditions

Number of times appearing in last 10 exams: 4
Last appeared in exam: April 2012

The gist of it...
> This section spells out the various entry bond obligations.

Excerpt from 19 CFR...

A bond for basic importation and entry shall contain the conditions listed in this section and may be either a single entry or a continuous bond.

Basic Importation and Entry Bond Conditions

(a) Agreement to Pay Duties, Taxes, and Charges. (1) If merchandise is imported and released from Customs custody or withdrawn from a Customs bonded warehouse into the commerce of, or for consumption in, the United States, or under §181.53 of this chapter is withdrawn from a duty-deferral program for exportation to Canada or Mexico or for entry into a duty-deferral program in Canada or Mexico, the obligors (principal and surety, jointly and severally) agree to:

(i) Deposit, within the time prescribed by law or regulation, any duties, taxes, and charges imposed, or estimated to be due, at the time of release or withdrawal; and

(ii) Pay, as demanded by Customs, all additional duties, taxes, and charges subsequently found due, legally fixed, and imposed on any entry secured by this bond.

(2) If the principal enters any merchandise into a Customs bonded warehouse, the obligors agree;

(i) To pay any duties, taxes, and charges found to be due on any of that merchandise which remains in the warehouse at the expiration of the warehousing time limit set by law; and

(ii) That the obligation to pay duties, taxes, and charges on the merchandise applies whether it is properly withdrawn by the principal, or by the principal's transferee, or is unlawfully removed by the principal or any other person, without regard to whether the merchandise is manipulated, unless payment was made or secured to be made by some other person.

(3) Under this agreement, the obligation to pay any and all duties, taxes, and charges due on any entry ceases on the date the principal timely files with the port director a bond of the owner in which the owner agrees to pay all duties, taxes, and charges found due on that entry; provided a declaration of the owner has also been properly filed.

... ...

Most Commonly Tested
TITLE 19 CFR

Part 141.113(c)
ENTRY OF MERCHANDISE>>Release of Merchandise>>Recall of merchandise released from CBP custody>>Food, drugs, devices, cosmetics, and tobacco products

Number of times appearing in last 10 exams: 4
Last appeared in exam: October 2013

The gist of it...

Customs conditionally releases shipments subject to FDA. "Conditional" meaning that FDA must also release as explained in this paragraph.

Excerpt from 19 CFR...

(c) Food, drugs, devices, cosmetics, and tobacco products—(1) Conditional release period. For purposes of determining the admissibility of any food, drug, device, cosmetic, or tobacco product imported pursuant to section 801(a) of the Federal Food, Drug, and Cosmetic Act (21 U.S.C. 381(a)), as amended, the release from CBP custody of any such product will be deemed conditional. Unless extended in accordance with paragraph (c)(2) of this section, the conditional release period will terminate upon the earliest occurring of the following events:

(i) The date that FDA issues a notice of refusal of admission;

(ii) The date that FDA issues a notice that the merchandise may proceed; or

(iii) Upon the end of the 30-day period following the date of release.

(2) Extension of conditional release period. The conditional release period provided under this paragraph (c) may be extended. The FDA must issue a written or electronic notice of sampling, detention, or other FDA action to the bond principal (i.e., importer of record) within 30 days of the release of the merchandise in order for the extension of the conditional release period to be valid.

(3) Issuance of a redelivery notice. If FDA refuses admission of a food, drug, device, cosmetic, or tobacco product into the United States, or if any notice of sampling or other request is not complied with, FDA will communicate that fact to the CBP port director who will demand the redelivery of the product to CBP custody. CBP will issue a notice of redelivery within 30 days from the date the product was refused admission by the FDA or from the date FDA determined the noncompliance with a notice of sampling or other request. The demand for redelivery may be made contemporaneously with the notice of refusal issued by the FDA. Notwithstanding the provisions of paragraph (i) of this section, a failure to comply with a demand for redelivery made under this paragraph (c) will result in the assessment of liquidated damages equal to three times the value of the merchandise involved unless the port director has prescribed a bond equal to the domestic value of the merchandise pursuant to §12.3(b) of this Chapter.

Most Commonly Tested
TITLE 19 CFR

Part 152.1(c)
CLASSIFICATION AND APPRAISEMENT OF MERCHANDISE>>General Provisions>>Definitions>>Date of exportation

Number of times appearing in last 10 exams: 4
Last appeared in exam: October 2012

The gist of it...
　　This paragraph defines the term "date of exportation" as the date the merchandise leaves the actual country of export. Note that CBP defines "the country of export" as "the country of which the merchandise was last part of the commerce (i.e. before considered "in-bond") and from which the merchandise was shipped to the U.S. without contingency of diversion".

Excerpt from 19 CFR...

(c) Date of exportation. "Date of exportation," or the "time of exportation" referred to in section 402, Tariff Act of 1930, as amended (19 U.S.C. 1401a), means the actual date the merchandise finally leaves the country of exportation for the United States. If no positive evidence is at hand as to the actual date of exportation, the port director shall ascertain or estimate the date of exportation by all reasonable ways and means in his power, and in so doing may consider dates on bills of lading, invoices, and other information available to him.

Most Commonly Tested
TITLE 19 CFR

Part 152.102(f)
CLASSIFICATION AND APPRAISEMENT OF MERCHANDISE>>Valuation of Merchandise>>Definitions>>Price Actually paid or payable

Number of times appearing in last 10 exams: 4
Last appeared in exam: April 2012

The gist of it...

This paragraph defines the customs phrase "the price actually paid or payable", otherwise known as "the transaction value".

Excerpt from 19 CFR...

(f) Price actually paid or payable. "Price actually paid or payable" means the total payment (whether direct or indirect, and exclusive of any charges, costs, or expenses incurred for transportation, insurance, and related services incident to the international shipment of the merchandise from the country of exportation to the place of importation in the United States) made, or to be made, for imported merchandise by the buyer to, or for the benefit of, the seller.

Most Commonly Tested
TITLE 19 CFR

Part 162.74
INSPECTION, SEARCH, AND SEIZURE>>Special Procedures for Certain Violations>>Prior disclosure

Number of times appearing in last 10 exams: 4
Last appeared in exam: April 2013

The gist of it...

      This section explains in detail, the proper procedure for importers, and subsequently for Customs, in the event of a filing of a prior disclosure by the importer.

Excerpt from 19 CFR...

(a) In general—(1) A prior disclosure is made if the person concerned discloses the circumstances of a violation (as defined in paragraph (b) of this section) of 19 U.S.C. 1592 or 19 U.S.C. 1593a, either orally or in writing to a Customs officer before, or without knowledge of, the commencement of a formal investigation of that violation, and makes a tender of any actual loss of duties, taxes and fees or actual loss of revenue in accordance with paragraph (c) of this section. A Customs officer who receives such a tender in connection with a prior disclosure shall ensure that the tender is deposited with the concerned local Customs entry officer.

(2) A person shall be accorded the full benefits of prior disclosure treatment if that person provides information orally or in writing to Customs with respect to a violation of 19 U.S.C. 1592 or 19 U.S.C. 1593a if the concerned Fines, Penalties, and Forfeitures Officer is satisfied the information was provided before, or without knowledge of, the commencement of a formal investigation, and the information provided includes substantially the information specified in paragraph (b) of this section. In the case of an oral disclosure, the disclosing party shall confirm the oral disclosure by providing a written record of the information conveyed to Customs in the oral disclosure to the concerned Fines, Penalties, and Forfeitures Officer within 10 days of the date of the oral disclosure. The concerned Fines, Penalties and Forfeiture Officer may, upon request of the disclosing party which establishes a showing of good cause, waive the oral disclosure written confirmation requirement. Failure to provide the written confirmation of the oral disclosure or obtain a waiver of the requirement may result in denial of the oral prior disclosure.

(b) Disclosure of the circumstances of a violation. The term "discloses the circumstances of a violation" means the act of providing to Customs a statement orally or in writing that:

(1) Identifies the class or kind of merchandise involved in the violation;

(2) Identifies the importation or drawback claim included in the disclosure by entry number, drawback claim number, or by indicating each concerned Customs port of entry and the approximate dates of entry or dates of drawback claims;

(3) Specifies the material false statements, omissions or acts including an explanation as to how and when they occurred; and

... ...

Most Commonly Tested
TITLE 19 CFR

Part 191.3(b)
DRAWBACK>>General Provisions>>Duties and fees subject or not subject to drawback>>Duties and fees not subject to drawback

Number of times appearing in last 10 exams: 4
Last appeared in exam: April 2014

The gist of it...
     This paragraph states that (in general) fees and duties paid for HMF, MPF, and ADD/CVD will not be refunded with drawback.

Excerpt from 19 CFR...

(b) Duties and fees not subject to drawback include:

(1) Harbor maintenance fee (see §24.24 of this chapter);

(2) Merchandise processing fees (see §24.23 of this chapter), except where unused merchandise drawback pursuant to 19 U.S.C. 1313(j) or drawback for substitution of finished petroleum derivatives pursuant to 19 U.S.C. 1313(p)(2)(A)(iii) or (iv) is claimed; and

(3) Antidumping and countervailing duties on merchandise entered, or withdrawn from warehouse, for consumption on or after August 23, 1988.

---8---

All Sections Appearing on Exams
TITLE 19 CFR

This section of the study guide lists nearly all instances of Title 19 of the United States Code of Federal Regulations (19 CFR) appearing throughout the last 10 exams.

The contents of all titles of the Code of Federal Regulations (CFR) are logically organized in hierarchical order. Instead of a typical reference book's arrangement by parts and then by chapters, the United States CFR's are broken down first by 1) "Title", then 2) "Part", then 3) "Section", then 4) "Paragraph", and then in some cases by 5) "Subparagraph". So, for example, 19 CFR 134.1(b) (the part of the regulations where Customs defines the term "country of origin") is located within Title 19, Part 134, Section 1, Paragraph (b).

Accordingly, the All Sections Appearing on Exams table is arranged in ascending order by "Part", then by "Section", then by "Paragraph" level, and then further sorted by exam date with the most recent exam instances appearing first for each repeating set of section and paragraph occurrences. Within the table, if reference to a specific "Paragraph" has been left blank, then there either may not be a "paragraph" breakdown for that "section", or the answer for that particular exam question may refer to multiple "Paragraphs" within that section. As you can see from the table, we start from "Part" 7, because neither "Part" 0 (Transferred or Delegated Authority) nor "Part" 4 (Vessels in Foreign and Domestic Trades), have appeared in any of the last 10 exams. It is a safe bet to assume that although you can be aware that this part exists, there is no reason to memorize anything contained therein.

The best way to make use of the All Sections Appearing on Exams table is as follows. First, feel free to remove the 19 CFR "Parts" that do not appear on the following "Parts" list from your 19 CFR binder. You can move these extra pages to a different folder or binder that can be label "just in case" if, by chance, they show up in the next exam. By doing so, you reduce the number of pages you must shuffle through to find what you're looking for. This is helpful during both study time and exam time.

Next, go through the remaining part of your newly condensed 19 CFR, and with a highlighter marker, highlight onto your CFR, as many "Sections", and "Paragraphs" as possible that appear in the All Sections Appearing on Exams table. This will allow these frequently tested items to jump out at you when you're scanning through the pages of your reg's when looking up and/or confirming your answers.

$ Money Saving Tip $
Let your employer know that you're interested in taking the exam. Ask if they can help cover some of the expenses. Or, they may do so on the condition that you pass in order to get reimbursed.

Of the 70 Parts that comprise Title 19 CFR, only the following 41 Parts (and even then, some appear only once or twice) have appeared on the last 10 customs broker exams...

Part 7:	CUSTOMS RELATIONS WITH INSULAR POSSESSIONS AND GUANTANAMO BAY
Part 10:	ARTICLES CONDITIONALLY FREE, SUBJECT TO A REDUCED RATE, ETC.
Part 11:	PACKING AND STAMPING; MARKING
Part 12:	SPECIAL CLASSES OF MERCHANDISE
Part 18:	TRANSPORTATION IN BOND AND MERCHANDISE IN TRANSIT
Part 19:	CUSTOMS WAREHOUSES, CONTAINER STATIONS AND CONTROL OF MERCHANDISE THEREIN
Part 24:	CUSTOMS FINANCIAL AND ACCOUNTING PROCEDURE
Part 101:	GENERAL PROVISIONS
Part 102:	RULES OF ORIGIN
Part 103:	AVAILABILITY OF INFORMATION
Part 111:	CUSTOMS BROKERS
Part 113:	CUSTOMS BONDS
Part 114:	CARNETS
Part 122:	AIR COMMERCE REGULATIONS
Part 123:	CBP RELATIONS WITH CANADA AND MEXICO
Part 127:	GENERAL ORDER, UNCLAIMED, AND ABANDONED MERCHANDISE
Part 132:	QUOTAS
Part 133:	TRADEMARKS, TRADE NAMES, AND COPYRIGHTS
Part 134:	COUNTRY OF ORIGIN MARKING
Part 141:	ENTRY OF MERCHANDISE
Part 142:	ENTRY PROCESS
Part 143:	SPECIAL ENTRY PROCEDURES
Part 144:	WAREHOUSE AND REWAREHOUSE ENTRIES AND WITHDRAWALS
Part 145:	MAIL IMPORTATIONS
Part 146:	FOREIGN TRADE ZONES
Part 147:	TRADE FAIRS
Part 148:	PERSONAL DECLARATIONS AND EXEMPTIONS
Part 149:	IMPORTER SECURITY FILING
Part 151:	EXAMINATION, SAMPLING, AND TESTING OF MERCHANDISE
Part 152:	CLASSIFICATION AND APPRAISEMENT OF MERCHANDISE
Part 158:	RELIEF FROM DUTIES ON MERCHANDISE LOST, DAMAGED, ABANDONED, OR EXPORTED
Part 159:	LIQUIDATION OF DUTIES
Part 162:	INSPECTIONS, SEARCH, AND SEIZURE
Part 163:	RECORDKEEPING
Part 171:	FINES, PENALTIES, AND FORFEITURES
Part 172:	CLAIMS FOR LIQUIDATED DAMAGES; PENALTIES SECURED BY BONDS
Part 174:	PROTESTS
Part 181:	NORTH AMERICAN FREE TRADE AGREEMENT (NAFTA)
Part 191:	DRAWBACK
Part 192:	EXPORT CONTROL
Part 351:	ANTIDUMPING AND COUNTERVAILING DUTIES

EXAM DATE	"PART"	"SECTION"	"PARAGRAPH"
Part 7: CUSTOMS RELATIONS WITH INSULAR POSSESSIONS AND GUANTANAMO BAY			
2013 April	7	2	(c)
2012 April	7	2	(c)
Part 10: ARTICLES CONDITIONALLY FREE, SUBJECT TO A REDUCED RATE, ETC.			
2012 October	10	1	(a)
2011 April	10	1	(a)
2009 October	10	8	(a)
2010 April	10	9	(b)
2010 October	10	16	(a)
2013 October	10	16	(b)
2013 October	10	16	(c)
2012 April	10	16	
2010 October	10	31	(f)
2013 October	10	37	
2011 October	10	37	
2011 October	10	39	(f)
2012 October	10	41	(a)
2012 April	10	43	
2010 April	10	66	(a)
2013 April	10	100	
2012 April	10	100	
2012 April	10	133	(a)
2011 October	10	133	
2013 October	10	175	(d)
2014 April	10	176	(a)
2011 October	10	195	
2012 April	10	453	
Part 11: PACKING AND STAMPING; MARKING			
2012 October	11	6	(c)
Part 12: SPECIAL CLASSES OF MERCHANDISE			
2012 October	12	1	(a)
2014 April	12	3	(b)
2012 October	12	26	
2013 October	12	73	(d)
2011 April	12	74	(b)
2010 October	12	112	(a)
2010 April	12	112	(a)
2013 April	12	115	
2011 October	12	118	
2013 April	12	121	(a)
2011 October	12	121	(a)
2010 October	12	121	(a)
2012 April	12	124	
2013 October	12	150	(a)
2010 October	12	150	(a)

EXAM DATE	"PART"	"SECTION"	"PARAGRAPH"
Part 18: TRANSPORTATION IN BOND AND MERCHANDISE IN TRANSIT			
2010 October	18	2	
2011 October	18	5	(a)
2011 April	18	5	(a)
2011 April	18	8	
2011 April	18	10	
2014 April	18	25	(a)
2014 April	18	25	(b)
Part 19: CUSTOMS WAREHOUSES, CONTAINER STATIONS AND CONTROL OF MERCHANDISE THEREIN			
2012 October	19	1	(a)
2010 October	19	1	(a)
2011 April	19	2	(e)
2014 April	19	4	(b)
2011 October	19	11	
2011 October	19	12	(c)
2013 October	19	12	(d)
2011 October	19	12	(d)
2010 October	19	12	(d)
2013 April	19	44	(a)
2012 April	19	44	
Part 24: CUSTOMS FINANCIAL AND ACCOUNTING PROCEDURE			
2009 October	24	1	(a)
2012 October	24	3	(a)
2009 October	24	3	(a)
2011 April	24	3	(b)
2011 October	24	3	(e)
2010 April	24	5	(a)
2013 April	24	5	(e)
2010 October	24	5	(e)
2013 April	24	5	
2009 October	24	23	(a)
2010 April	24	23	(b)
2009 October	24	23	(b)
2014 April	24	23	(c)
2013 October	24	23	(c)
2012 October	24	23	(c)
2010 October	24	23	(c)
2009 October	24	23	(c)
2010 April	24	24	(e)
2009 October	24	24	(e)
2011 October	24	24	
2011 April	24	24	
2012 October	24	36	

EXAM DATE	"PART"	"SECTION"	"PARAGRAPH"
Part 101: GENERAL PROVISIONS			
2014 April	101	1	
2012 October	101	1	
2012 April	101	1	
2012 April	101	1	
2011 October	101	1	
2011 April	101	1	
Part 102: RULES OF ORIGIN			
2010 April	102	1	(f)
2009 October	102	1	(k)
2011 April	102	13	(b)
2010 April	102	13	(c)
2009 October	102	13	
2009 October	102	13	
2009 October	102	15	
2011 October	102	17	(a)
2013 April	102	20	(g)
2011 October	102	20	
2010 October	102	21	(b)
2012 October	102	21	
2011 October	102	21	
2010 April	102	24	
2011 October	102	25	
2010 October	102	Appendix	
Part 103: AVAILABILITY OF INFORMATION			
2013 October	103	31	(d)
Part 111: CUSTOMS BROKERS			
2014 April	111	1	
2011 October	111	1	
2011 October	111	1	
2011 October	111	1	
2011 April	111	1	
2011 April	111	1	
2010 April	111	1	
2012 October	111	2	(a)
2013 April	111	2	(b)
2013 April	111	2	(b)
2013 April	111	2	
2014 April	111	11	(a)
2012 October	111	11	(a)
2012 October	111	11	(c)
2010 April	111	11	(c)
2010 October	111	11	
2011 October	111	15	
2009 October	111	19	(b)
2011 October	111	19	(c)
2009 October	111	19	(c)
2009 October	111	19	(f)

EXAM DATE	"PART"	"SECTION"	"PARAGRAPH"
2011 October	111	19	
2011 April	111	19	
2011 April	111	19	
2013 October	111	21	(a)
2011 October	111	23	(a)
2010 April	111	23	(a)
2013 October	111	23	(b)
2013 October	111	23	(b)
2009 October	111	23	(b)
2011 April	111	23	
2009 October	111	24	
2014 April	111	28	(b)
2014 April	111	28	(b)
2012 October	111	28	(b)
2011 October	111	28	(b)
2014 April	111	28	(c)
2010 April	111	28	(d)
2011 October	111	28	
2013 October	111	29	(a)
2013 October	111	29	(a)
2013 April	111	29	(a)
2011 October	111	29	(a)
2011 April	111	29	(a)
2013 October	111	29	(b)
2011 October	111	29	(b)
2011 October	111	29	(b)
2010 October	111	29	(b)
2013 October	111	30	(a)
2014 April	111	30	(d)
2014 April	111	30	(d)
2013 October	111	30	(d)
2013 April	111	30	(d)
2013 April	111	30	(d)
2009 October	111	30	
2013 April	111	31	(c)
2012 April	111	31	(c)
2011 October	111	32	
2013 April	111	36	(c)
2011 April	111	36	
2013 April	111	37	
2011 October	111	37	
2013 April	111	39	(b)
2014 April	111	42	(a)
2011 October	111	45	(a)
2010 October	111	45	(a)
2010 April	111	45	(a)
2013 April	111	45	(b)
2011 April	111	45	
2012 April	111	53	(a)

EXAM DATE	"PART"	"SECTION"	"PARAGRAPH"
2013 October	111	53	(e)
2013 April	111	53	(e)
2010 October	111	53	
2010 October	111	53	
2010 April	111	74	
2010 April	111	74	
2011 April	111	75	
2010 April	111	78	
2014 April	111	79	
2013 April	111	81	
2013 October	111	91	(b)
2010 October	111	91	(b)
2010 October	111	92	(a)
2011 April	111	92	
2014 April	111	96	(c)
2011 October	111	96	(c)
2013 October	111	96	(d)
Part 113: CUSTOMS BONDS			
2014 April	113	1	
2011 October	113	4	(b)
2012 October	113	13	(a)
2011 April	113	13	(b)
2009 October	113	13	
2014 April	113	23	(b)
2011 October	113	24	
2010 October	113	37	(g)
2014 April	113	40	(a)
2010 April	113	62	(d)
2011 October	113	62	(m)
2011 October	113	62	(m)
2012 April	113	62	
2011 October	113	63	(d)
2014 April	113	66	
Part 114: CARNETS			
2012 April	114	23	(a)
2011 October	114	23	(a)
2010 October	114	23	(a)
2009 October	114	25	
Part 122: AIR COMMERCE REGULATIONS			
2011 April	122	119	(b)
2012 October	122	119	
Part 123: CBP RELATIONS WITH CANADA AND MEXICO			
2009 October	123	92	(a)
Part 127: GENERAL ORDER, UNCLAIMED, AND ABANDONED MERCHANDISE			
2009 October	127	1	(c)
2011 October	127	1	
2012 April	127	2	
2012 April	127	12	(a)
2011 October	127	28	(a)

EXAM DATE	"PART"	"SECTION"	"PARAGRAPH"
Part 132: QUOTAS			
2011 April	132	1	
2014 April	132	3	
2010 April	132	5	(c)
2013 April	132	5	
2012 April	132	5	
2010 April	132	12	(a)
Part 133: TRADEMARKS, TRADE NAMES, AND COPYRIGHTS			
2013 April	133	1	
2014 April	133	21	
2013 April	133	21	
2013 October	133	23	(a)
2011 April	133	23	(b)
2011 April	133	23	(d)
2013 October	133	25	(a)
2011 April	133	25	
2009 October	133	27	
2013 October	133	34	(b)
Part 134: COUNTRY OF ORIGIN MARKING			
2013 April	134	1	(b)
2012 April	134	1	(b)
2014 April	134	2	
2014 April	134	2	
2011 April	134	4	
2009 October	134	32	(d)
2012 October	134	32	(i)
2012 October	134	33	
2011 April	134	33	
2010 October	134	33	
2010 April	134	41	(a)
2012 April	134	41	(b)
2012 October	134	43	(a)
2010 October	134	46	
2013 October	134	51	(a)
Part 141: ENTRY OF MERCHANDISE			
2012 October	141	3	
2012 April	141	5	
2012 October	141	13	
2011 October	141	31	(d)
2012 October	141	31	
2012 April	141	32	
2010 April	141	32	
2014 April	141	34	
2012 October	141	34	
2012 October	141	36	
2010 April	141	36	
2010 April	141	36	
2013 October	141	37	

EXAM DATE	"PART"	"SECTION"	"PARAGRAPH"
2014 April	141	39	(a)
2011 October	141	43	(a)
2010 April	141	43	(c)
2011 October	141	46	
2010 April	141	46	
2014 April	141	61	(b)
2010 October	141	61	(d)
2012 October	141	68	(c)
2010 October	141	68	(c)
2010 April	141	68	(c)
2011 April	141	68	(d)
2014 April	141	69	(b)
2012 October	141	69	(b)
2010 October	141	69	
2013 October	141	86	(a)
2012 April	141	86	
2012 April	141	89	(a)
2011 October	141	89	(a)
2011 April	141	89	(a)
2014 April	141	89	
2012 April	141	89	
2012 April	141	89	
2010 October	141	89	
2010 October	141	89	
2013 April	141	92	(a)
2011 October	141	113	(a)
2011 April	141	113	(a)
2013 April	141	113	(b)
2013 October	141	113	(c)
2012 October	141	113	(c)
2011 April	141	113	(c)
2010 April	141	113	(c)
2012 October	141	113	(i)
Part 142: ENTRY PROCESS			
2009 October	142	3	(a)
2011 October	142	4	(a)
2012 October	142	6	
2012 April	142	6	
2009 October	142	11	(a)
2011 October	142	12	(b)
2011 October	142	12	(b)
2009 October	142	15	
2009 October	142	17	
2009 October	142	21	(b)
2009 October	142	21	
2009 October	142	22	
2011 October	142	23	
2011 October	142	24	(a)
2009 October	142	25	(a)

EXAM DATE	"PART"	"SECTION"	"PARAGRAPH"
Part 143: SPECIAL ENTRY PROCEDURES			
2011 April	143	23	(d)
2009 October	143	23	(j)
2011 April	143	26	(a)
2010 October	143	26	(b)
2012 April	143	43	(b)
2011 April	143	44	(e)
Part 144: WAREHOUSE AND REWAREHOUSE ENTRIES AND WITHDRAWALS			
2011 October	144	1	(a)
2010 April	144	1	(a)
2012 October	144	5	
2010 October	144	5	
2010 April	144	11	(d)
2012 April	144	15	(c)
2009 October	144	34	(a)
2010 April	144	37	(b)
2010 April	144	37	(b)
2010 April	144	37	(c)
2010 April	144	37	(e)
2010 April	144	37	(g)
Part 145: MAIL IMPORTATIONS			
2010 April	145	11	(a)
2012 October	145	35	
Part 146: FOREIGN TRADE ZONES			
2013 October	146	22	(a)
2010 October	146	22	(a)
2014 April	146	25	(a)
2010 April	146	25	(a)
2014 April	146	35	(b)
2011 October	146	35	(e)
2010 April	146	41	(e)
2010 April	146	42	(b)
2011 October	146	44	(d)
2014 April	146	53	(b)
2012 April	146	67	(c)
2010 October	146	67	(c)
2012 April	146	71	(c)
2011 April	146	71	(c)
Part 147: TRADE FAIRS			
2011 October	147	42	(a)

EXAM DATE	"PART"	"SECTION"	"PARAGRAPH"
Part 148: PERSONAL DECLARATIONS AND EXEMPTIONS			
2011 October	148	6	
2010 October	148	114	
Part 149: IMPORTER SECURITY FILING			
2010 October	149	2	(b)
2010 April	149	2	
2012 April	149	3	(a)
2011 April	149	3	(a)
2011 October	149	5	(a)
Part 151: EXAMINATION, SAMPLING, AND TESTING OF MERCHANDISE			
2013 October	151	16	(c)
Part 152: CLASSIFICATION AND APPRAISEMENT OF MERCHANDISE			
2012 October	152	1	(c)
2012 October	152	1	(c)
2012 April	152	1	(c)
2010 April	152	1	(c)
2011 April	152	2	
2013 April	152	13	
2014 April	152	101	(d)
2011 April	152	101	(d)
2010 April	152	101	(d)
2014 April	152	102	(a)
2014 April	152	102	(d)
2012 April	152	102	(f)
2010 October	152	102	(f)
2009 October	152	102	(f)
2009 October	152	102	(f)
2010 April	152	102	(g)
2014 April	152	102	(i)
2009 October	152	102	
2014 April	152	103	(a)
2013 October	152	103	(a)
2013 October	152	103	(a)
2013 October	152	103	(a)
2013 April	152	103	(a)
2012 October	152	103	(a)
2012 April	152	103	(a)
2011 October	152	103	(a)
2011 October	152	103	(a)
2010 October	152	103	(a)
2009 October	152	103	(a)
2009 October	152	103	(a)
2014 April	152	103	(b)
2013 October	152	103	(b)
2012 October	152	103	(b)
2011 October	152	103	(b)
2010 October	152	103	(b)
2010 October	152	103	(b)

EXAM DATE	"PART"	"SECTION"	"PARAGRAPH"
2009 October	152	103	(b)
2012 October	152	103	(c)
2009 October	152	103	(c)
2014 April	152	103	(d)
2013 October	152	103	(d)
2013 October	152	103	(d)
2012 April	152	103	(d)
2012 April	152	103	(d)
2013 October	152	103	(e)
2012 October	152	103	(f)
2013 October	152	103	(j)
2012 October	152	103	(j)
2012 October	152	103	(j)
2012 October	152	103	(j)
2012 October	152	103	(j)
2010 October	152	103	(j)
2010 April	152	103	(j)
2009 October	152	103	(j)
2013 October	152	103	(k)
2012 October	152	103	(k)
2012 October	152	103	(k)
2012 April	152	103	
2014 April	152	105	(d)
2014 April	152	105	(d)
2013 October	152	106	(a)
2013 October	152	106	(b)
2011 April	152	106	
2009 October	152	106	
2014 April	152	107	(b)
Part 158: RELIEF FROM DUTIES ON MERCHANDISE LOST, DAMAGED, ABANDONED, OR EXPORTED			
2009 October	158	2	
2011 April	158	21	(a)
2011 April	158	23	
2011 October	158	41	
2012 October	158	43	(a)
Part 159: LIQUIDATION OF DUTIES			
2011 October	159	1	(c)
2013 October	159	1	
2010 April	159	2	(a)
2011 April	159	2	
2011 October	159	6	(a)
2014 April	159	9	(c)
2010 April	159	11	(a)
2010 April	159	11	(a)
2013 April	159	12	(a)
2011 October	159	12	(a)
2013 April	159	12	(e)
2011 October	159	22	(c)
2009 October	159	32	(d)

EXAM DATE	"PART"	"SECTION"	"PARAGRAPH"
2013 October	159	32	
2012 October	159	32	
2012 October	159	32	
2010 April	159	32	
2011 April	159	34	
2011 October	159	35	
2012 April	159	41	
2011 April	159	52	
Part 162: INSPECTIONS, SEARCH, AND SEIZURE			
2009 October	162	23	(a)
2011 April	162	72	(a)
2010 April	162	73	(a)
2013 October	162	73	(b)
2011 October	162	74	(a)
2010 October	162	74	(b)
2013 April	162	74	
2011 October	162	74	
2010 April	162	80	
Part 163: RECORDKEEPING			
2012 October	163	2	(a)
2012 October	163	2	(a)
2010 October	163	2	(a)
2012 October	163	2	(c)
2012 April	163	2	(c)
2011 October	163	4	(a)
2010 October	163	4	(a)
2013 October	163	5	(b)
2011 April	163	6	(a)
2013 October	163	6	(b)
2009 October	163	6	(b)
2009 October	163	6	(b)
Part 171: FINES, PENALTIES, AND FORFEITURES			
2009 October	171	2	(b)
2013 April	171	23	
2009 October	171	Appendix A	
2013 October	171	Appendix B	(e)
2013 October	171	Appendix B	(f)
2010 October	171	Appendix B	(f)
2012 April	171	Appendix B	
2010 October	171	Appendix B	
2012 April	171	Appendix C	
2010 October	171	Appendix C	
Part 172: CLAIMS FOR LIQUIDATED DAMAGES; PENALTIES SECURED BY BONDS			
2012 April	172	1	
2011 October	172	1	
2011 October	172	3	
2012 April	172	11	
2013 October	172	41	
2011 October	172	41	

EXAM DATE	"PART"	"SECTION"	"PARAGRAPH"
Part 174: PROTESTS			
2013 October	174	12	(b)
2009 October	174	21	(b)
2012 April	174	21	
2014 April	174	22	(d)
2012 October	174	31	
Part 181: NORTH AMERICAN FREE TRADE AGREEMENT (NAFTA)			
2014 April	181	21	(b)
2013 April	181	21	
2010 April	181	22	(a)
2012 October	181	22	(b)
2010 April	181	22	(b)
2009 October	181	22	(c)
2012 October	181	22	(d)
2010 October	181	22	
2012 October	181	31	
2010 October	181	31	
2009 October	181	44	(a)
2012 October	181	45	(b)
2010 April	181	53	(a)
2010 April	181	53	(a)
2012 April	181	64	(a)
2012 April	181	64	(b)
Part 191: DRAWBACK			
2014 April	191	2	(g)
2014 April	191	2	(i)
2011 October	191	3	(a)
2014 April	191	3	(b)
2014 April	191	3	(b)
2012 October	191	3	(b)
2011 October	191	3	(b)
2011 April	191	10	(a)
2010 April	191	11	(a)
2013 October	191	15	
2011 April	191	26	(a)
2014 April	191	28	
2012 October	191	33	(a)
2011 April	191	33	(a)
2011 October	191	35	(a)
2012 October	191	42	(c)
2012 October	191	51	(a)
2014 April	191	51	(e)
2012 October	191	51	(e)
2011 April	191	52	(c)
2012 October	191	53	(b)

EXAM DATE	"PART"	"SECTION"	"PARAGRAPH"
Part 192: EXPORT CONTROL			
2010 October	192	2	(d)
2012 April	192	4	
2012 April	192	14	(b)
Part 351: ANTIDUMPING AND COUNTERVAILING DUTIES			
2013 April	351	206	(a)

Exam with Commentary
Apr. 2014 Customs Broker License Examination

This section of the study guide analyzes an actual customs broker exam. It presents the actual question and its multiple choices. For HTSUS classification questions (e.g. Question 1), the HTSUS Article Descriptions have also been notated directly to the right of each multiple choice for your convenience and ease of reference purposes. As necessary, and in proportion to the complexity of each particular exam question, an analysis of the question and path to the correct answer has been provided. Direct excerpts from the HTSUS, 19 CFR, etc. are also included as supporting points of reference for each answer. This exam (without commentary) and its answer key, as well as other previous customs exams can be downloaded directly from Customs' website at...

http://www.cbp.gov/document/publications/past-customs-broker-license-examinations-answer-keys

Exam Refs: **Harmonized Tariff Schedule of the United States**
Title 19, Code of Federal Regulations
Customs and Trade Automated Interface Requirements (CATAIR)
Instructions for Preparation of CBP Form 7501
Right to Make Entry Directive, 3530-002A

Exam Breakdown by Subject:

I Power of Attorney	**Questions 1 - 2**
II Practical Exercises	**Questions 3 - 11**
III Entry	**Questions 12 - 20**
IV Foreign Trade Zone/Warehouse	**Questions 21 - 26**
V Bonds	**Questions 27 - 31**
V1 Classification	**Questions 32 - 45**
VII Valuation	**Questions 46 - 54**
VII Free Trade Agreements	**Questions 55 – 64**
IX Drawback	**Questions 65 - 68**
X Intellectual Property Rights	**Questions 69**
XI Marking	**Questions 70 - 71**
XII Broker Compliance	**Questions 72 - 80**

Section I: Powers of Attorney
1. A Customs Power of Attorney may be issued by a partnership for a period not to exceed _____ years.

A. 1
B. 2
C. 5
D. 10
E. 20

As per 19 CFR 141.34:

§141.34   Duration of power of attorney.

Powers of attorney issued by a partnership shall be limited to a period not to exceed 2 years from the date of execution. All other powers of attorney may be granted for an unlimited period.

"B" is the correct answer.

2. Don Murphy is the Import Manager of ABC Imports. He hires XYZ Brokers to clear shipments for ABC Imports. ABC Imports is a limited partnership under state law. Which of the following is required as part of, or must accompany, the power of attorney from ABC Imports?

A. The signature of Don Murphy
B. The signature of the President of ABC Imports and a certification supporting the President's authority to sign the power of attorney.
C. The signature of all members of the limited partnership.
D. The names of all the general partners who have authority to bind ABC Imports and a copy of the partnership agreement.
E. The names of all members of the partnership and the signature of two of the partners.

As per 19 CFR 141.39(a):

§141.39   Partnerships.

(a)(1) General. A power of attorney granted by a partnership shall state the names of all members of the partnership. One member of the partnership may execute a power of attorney in the name of the partnership for the transaction of all its Customs business.

(2) Limited partnership. **A power of attorney granted by a limited partnership need only state the names of the general partners who have authority to bind the firm unless the partnership agreement provides otherwise. A copy of the partnership agreement must accompany the power of attorney.** *For this purpose, a partnership or limited partnership means any business association recognized as such under the laws of the state where the association is organized.*

"D" is the correct answer.

Section II: Practical Exercises

Practical Exercise A:

Using the invoice provided below, answer questions 3 through 5.

COMMERCIAL INVOICE Mario's Foods		
4. **Shipper/Exporter** Mario's Foods Atlixco 100B Mexico City Mexico	5. **No. and Date of Invoice** US001836 Monday, January 13, 2014	
	6. **No. and Date of L/C**	
7. **For Account and Risk of Messers** Jones Cafe 301 Texan Plaza Dallas, TX 78205	8. **L/C Issuing Bank**	
9. **Notify Party** 10. R.Schaub, 231-423-1234	11. **Remarks** P/O No.: TPS001 Not subject to AD/CVD cases	
12. **Port of Lading** Mexico City, Mexico	13. **Final Destination** Dallas	
14. **Carrier**	15. **Departure on or about** January 20, 2014	Marks and Numbers of Pkgs. Fernando's Pickles 25/1. 16 Ounce Jar.

16. **Description of Goods**	17. **Quantity**	18. **Unit Price**	19. **Amount**
Country of Origin: Mexico Pickled cucumbers $7,000 One pound jar	10000 pieces	0.70 USD	
TOTAL $7,000			
Master Bill: 001-63324833 House Bill: COSC56676406 Estimated Entry Date 01/20/2014			

3. If Dallas, TX is the port of entry, what is the port code?

A. 2101
B. 5311
C. 5501
D. 5507
E. 6420

 As per HTSUS Annex C:

55. DALLAS-FORT WORTH, TEXAS
    01. Dallas-Fort Worth, TX
    02. Amarillo, TX
    03. Lubbock, TX
    04. Oklahoma City, OK
    05. Tulsa, OK
    06. Austin, TX
    07. San Antonio, TX
    82. Midland International Airport,
        Midland, TX
    83. Fort Worth Alliance Airport, TX
    84. Addison Airport, Addison, TX
    88. Dallas Love Field User Fee
        Airport, Dallas, TX

"C" is the correct answer. Note also that although not even a multiple choice option, port code 5588 (for Dallas Love Field, Dallas, TX) should not qualify as a suitable answer as this (seemingly obscure) destination airport is not specifically mentioned on the commercial invoice, or otherwise indicated.

4. Block 31 of the CBP Form 7501 should indicate _____ for the pickles.

A. 16 ounces
B. 10,000 pounds
C. 10,000 pieces
D. 10,000 kilograms
E. 4,536 kilograms

 As per the HTSUS Chapter 20:

Heading/ Subheading	Stat. Suf-fix	Article Description	Unit of Quantity
2001		Vegetables, fruit, nuts and other edible parts of plants, prepared or preserved by vinegar or acetic acid:	
2001.10.00	00	Cucumbers including gherkins.	kg. . . . . . .

The correct HTSUS classification for pickled cucumbers is 2001.10.0000. The reporting unit if quantity (column) of which is in "kg" (kilograms). So, the number input into block 31 of CBP Form 7501 for this specific entry should accordingly be in "kg". The commercial invoice provided quantifies the merchandise as 10,000 each of "one pound jar". This equals a total of 10,000 pounds. Convert the 10,000 pounds into kilograms by dividing the 10,000 by 2.20462 to equal 4536 (rounded to the nearest whole number) kg. "E" is the correct answer.

5. The Manufacturer's Identification Code is.

A. MXELGOR2568MEX
B. MXGORDES2BAGTA
C. MXMARFOO100MEX
D. NAFTAMARFOOMX
E. TAELGOR2568MAT

 As per CBP Form 7501 Instructions:

RULES FOR CONSTRUCTING THE MANUFACTURER IDENTIFICATION CODE
These instructions provide for the construction of an identifying code for a manufacturer or shipper from its name and address. The code can be up to 15 characters in length, with no inserted spaces.

To begin, for the first 2 characters, use the ISO code for the actual country of origin of the goods. The exception to this rule is Canada. "CA" is NOT a valid country for the manufacturer code; instead, show as one of the appropriate province code.

Next, use the first three characters from the first two "words" of the name. If there is only one "word" in the name, then use only the first three characters from the first name. For example, Amalgamated Plastics Corp. would be "AMAPLA;" Bergstrom would be "BER."

Next, find the largest number on the street address line and use up to the first four numbers. For example, "11455 Main Street Suite 9999" would yield "1145." A suite number or a post office box should be used if it contains the largest number. For example, "232 Main Street Suite 1234" would yield "1234." If the numbers in the street address are spelled out, such as "One Thousand Century Plaza," there will be no numbers in this section of the MID. However, if the address is "One Thousand Century Plaza Suite 345," this would yield "345."

Finally, use the first three alpha characters from the city name. "Tokyo" would be "TOK," "St. Michel" would be "STM," "18-Mile High" would be "MIL," and "The Hague" would be "HAG." Notice that numerals in the city line are to be ignored.

"C" is the correct answer. Note, however, that a typo was made on this question when creating the exam. The actual multiple choice for "C" was originally "MXMARFOO301MEX", which was incorrect. Although credit was probably given to all answers on the actual exam, "MXMARFOO100MEX" is indeed the correct answer.

Practical Exercise B:

Using the following abbreviated CBP Form 7501 "Entry Summary," answer questions 6 through 8.

DEPARTMENT OF HOMELAND SECURITY U.S. Customs and Border Protection			1. Filer Code / Entry No. ABC-1234567-8		2. Entry Type 01 ABI/A		3. Summary Date 01/17/14
ENTRY SUMMARY			4. Surety No. 891	5 Bond Type 8	6. Port Code 1101		7. Entry Date 01/04/14
8. Importing Carrier MAERSK SENANG		9. Mode of Transport 11	10. Country of Origin SG				11. Import Date 01/02/14
12. B/L or AWB No. MAEU751824346		13. Manufacturer ID SGHSEXT1234NOR	14. Exporting Country MY				15. Export Date 12/03/13
16. I.T. No. V0670830522	17. I.T. Date 01/02/14	18 Missing Docs	19. Foreign Port of Lading 55700			20. U.S. Port of Unlading 1001	
21. Location of Goods/GO No. H572 BNSF LOGISTICS PARK PHL		22. Consignee No. SAME	23. Importer No. 04-0422353-00			24. Reference No.	
26. Ultimate Consignee Name and Address City State Zip			26. Importer of Record Number and Address HS Exteriors 1234 Main Street Norristown, PA 19401				

6. Which date is used for calculating the applicable rate of duty?

A. Export
B. Import
C. Entry
D. Entry Summary
E. Immediate Transportation

 As per 19 CFR 141.69(b):

(b) Merchandise entered for immediate transportation. Merchandise which is not subject to a quantitative or tariff-rate quota and which is covered by an entry for immediate transportation made at the port of original importation, if entered for consumption at the port designated by the consignee or his agent in such transportation entry without having been taken into custody by the port director for general order under

section 490, Tariff Act of 1930, as amended (19 U.S.C. 1490), **shall be subject to the rates in effect when the immediate transportation entry was accepted at the port of original importation.**

As per the Entry Summary provided, there is proof of an I.T. (Immediate Transportation) number and I.T. date. Thus "E" is the correct answer. If this shipment had not been on an I.T. then the rate of duty applicable would have been the rate in effect at the Entry Date (as per 19 CFR 141.69 & 141.68).

7. Which of the following is the port of processing?

A. Lubbock, Texas
B. New York, New York
C. Seattle, Washington
D. Philadelphia, Pennsylvania
E. Miami, Florida

 As per HTSUS Annex C:

   11. PHILADELPHIA, PENNSYLVANIA
     01. Philadelphia, PA
     02. Chester, PA
     03. Wilmington, DE
     04. Pittsburgh, PA
     05. Paulsboro, NJ
     06. Wilkes-Barre/Scranton, PA
     07. Camden, NJ
     08. Philadelphia International Airport, PA
     09. Harrisburg, PA
     13. Gloucester City, NJ
     19. Allentown, PA (Lehigh Valley
        International Airport), PA
     81. Allentown-Bethlehem, PA (Easton
        Airport)
     82. Atlantic City Regional Airport, NJ
     83. Trenton/Mercer County Airport, NJ
     95. UPS, Philadelphia, PA

The question's CBP Form 7501 lists two different U.S. port codes. Block 6 indicates Port Code 1101. Block 20 indicates U.S. Port of Unlading port code 1001. Although in some instances the U.S. Port of Unlading will be the same as the Port of Entry, the primary "Port Code" (Block 6) is considered the port of entry, and also known as the port of processing. "D" is the correct answer.

 8. What is the entry type?

A. Warehouse Withdrawal for Consumption
B. Consumption Foreign Trade Zone
C. Consumption Free and Dutiable
D. Transportation and Exportation
E. Consumption Anti-dumping/Countervailing Duty

As per CBP Form 7501 Instructions:

BLOCK 2) ENTRY TYPE

Record the appropriate entry type code by selecting the two-digit code for the type of entry summary being filed. The first digit of the code identifies the general category of the entry (i.e., consumption = 0, informal = 1, warehouse = 2). The second digit further defines the specific processing type within the entry category. The following codes shall be used:

Consumption Entries	
Free and Dutiable	01
Quota/Visa	02
Antidumping/Countervailing Duty (AD/CVD)	03
Appraisement	04
Vessel Repair	05
Foreign Trade Zone Consumption	06
Quota/Visa and AD/CVD combinations	07
Duty Deferral	08
Informal Entries	
Free and Dutiable	11
Quota Other than textiles	12
Warehouse Entries	
Warehouse	21
Re-Warehouse	22
Temporary Importation Bond	23

The Entry Summary (CBP Form 7501) provided for this set of questions lists Entry Type (Block 2) as "01". This is the code for Consumption Entry, Free and Dutiable Entries. "C" is the correct answer.

Practical Exercise C:

Using the abbreviated Entry Summary below, answer questions 9 through 11.

27. Line No.	28. Description of Merchandise			32. A. Entered Value B. CHGS C. Relationship	33. A. HTSUS Rate B. ADA/CVD Rate C. IRC Rate D. Visa No.	34. Duty and I.R. Tax Dollars Cents
	29. A. HTSUS No. B. ADA/CVD Case No	30. A. Gross Weight B. Manifest Qty.	31. Net Quantity in HTSUS Units			
001 D	M 55217035541 LADIES / MEN'S POLO SHIRTS 384 CTNS Invoice Number – 24011 04/2013 APPL AGOA, FROM NON US FABRICS 9819.11.09 WOMENS COTN BLOUS/SHIRS, NIT/C 6106.10.0010 905 225 DOZ CAT 339 (810 KG)			384 CTNS NOT-RELATED 0 9536 C 1339	FREE FREE V3ET022805 DOE 08/18/13 0.010717 / KG	0.00 0.00 8.68
Other Fee Summary for Block 39	35. Total Entered Value					

9. If the country of export of this shipment was Ghana, then the International Standard Organizational country code identified as Block 14 of CBP Form 7501 would be:

A. GH
B. LY
C. US
D. DE
E. D

 As per HTSUS Annex B:

Gabon..	GA
Gambia..	GM
Gaza Strip (administered by Israel).	GZ
Georgia..	GE
Germany..	DE
Ghana..	GH

"GH" is the correct ISO country code for Ghana. "A" is the correct answer.

10. The "Total Entered Value" at Block 35 is:

A. $0
B. $1,339
C. $9,536
D. $10,875
E. $63,490

 As per CBP Form 7501 Instructions:

COLUMN 32)

A. ENTERED VALUE

Record the U.S. dollar value as defined in 19 U.S.C. § 1401a for all merchandise.

Record the value for each line item on the same line as the HTS number.

Report the value in whole dollars rounded off to the nearest whole dollar (if the total entered value for a line item is less than 50 cents report as "0"). Dollar signs are omitted.

Report the total entered value for all line items in block 35.

B. CHARGES (CHGS)

Record the aggregate cost in U.S. dollars of freight, insurance and all other charges, costs and expenses incurred while bringing the merchandise from alongside the carrier at the port of exportation in the country of exportation and placing it alongside the carrier at the first U.S. port of entry. *Do not include U.S. import duties. In the case of overland shipments originating in Canada or Mexico, such costs shall include freight, insurance, and all other charges, costs and expenses incurred in bringing the merchandise from the point of origin (where the merchandise begins its journey to the United States) in Canada or Mexico to the first U.S. port of entry.*

This value shall be shown in whole numbers for each HTS number. It is to be placed beneath the entered value and identified with the letter 'C' (e.g., C550). *Dollar signs are omitted.*

As per the CBP Form 7501 Instructions, the US Dollar value for each item on the entry is to be recorded in Column 32. For the Entry Summary in this scenario, we can assume that there is only 1 line item (indicated by the lone "001" in Column 27) as there is no reference made to any additional merchandise, any additional Entry Summary lines, or any additional Entry Summary pages. Due to the nature of the singular merchandise being entered here (the circumstances of which are not relevant to the solution of this question), two different HTS numbers are referenced. Entered values for the merchandise should be on the same line(s) as HTS number(s), though this is not reflected in the exam question's "abbreviated" Entry Summary for reasons unknown. However, we can assume that the value "C 1339" is the recorded cost of transportation charges. The aggregate of the remaining values (that actually should have been shown as immediately following their HTS numbers) is 0 + 9536 = 9536. "C" is the correct answer.

11. What free trade agreement is claimed on this entry summary?

A. Generalized System of Preferences
B. African Growth and Opportunity Act
C. U.S.-Colombia Free Trade Agreement
D. North American Free Trade Agreement
E. There is no free trade agreement claim on this entry summary.

 As per HTSUS General Note 3(c):

(c) Products Eligible for Special Tariff Treatment.

    (i)   Programs under which special tariff treatment may be provided, and the corresponding symbols for such programs as they are indicated in the "Special" subcolumn, are as follows:

Generalized System of Preferences.................................... A, A* or A+
United States-Australia Free Trade Agreement......................... AU
Automotive Products Trade Act....................................... B
United States-Bahrain Free Trade Agreement Implementation Act.......... BH
Agreement on Trade in Civil Aircraft................................. C
North American Free Trade Agreement:
    Goods of Canada, under the terms of
      general note 12 to this schedule............................. CA
    Goods of Mexico, under the terms of
      general note 12 to this schedule............................. MX
United States-Chile Free Trade Agreement............................. CL
African Growth and Opportunity Act.................................. D

And as per CBP Form 7501 Instructions:

Where a reporting number is preceded by an alpha character designating a special program (i.e., NAFTA = "CA" or "MX"; GSP = "A"), that indicator is to be placed in column 27, directly below the line number. The special program indicator (SPI) should be right justified on the same line and immediately preceding the HTS number to which it applies. If more than one HTS number is required for a line item, place the SPI on the same line as the HTS number upon which the rate of duty is based. If more than one SPI is used, the primary indicator that establishes the rate of duty is shown first, followed by a period and the secondary SPI immediately following.

The letter "D", which is the Special Program Indicator (SPI) for the African Growth and Opportunity Act (AGOA) Free Trade Agreement (FTA) has been included in Column 27 of the Entry Summary, and thus multiple choice "B" is the correct answer.

Section III: Entry
12. Please construct the Manufacturer Identification Code (MID) for the following company:

D.A.A.S.J. Manufacturing and Designing Corporation
82467 North Pixie Lane
Suite 14
Green Gables, Prince Edward Island, Canada C0A 1M0

A. CADAASJMAN8246GRE
B. CADMADC14 PEI
C. XPCAMDC14PEI
D. XPDAAMAN8246GRE
E. XPDAMAD8214GGPEI

 As per CBP Form 7501 Instructions:

RULES FOR CONSTRUCTING THE MANUFACTURER IDENTIFICATION CODE

These instructions provide for the construction of an identifying code for a manufacturer or shipper from its name and address. The code can be up to 15 characters in length, with no inserted spaces.

To begin, for the first 2 characters, use the ISO code for the actual country of origin of the goods. The exception to this rule is Canada. "CA" is NOT a valid country for the manufacturer code; instead, show as one of the appropriate province codes listed below:

ALBERTA	*XA*
BRITISH COLUMBIA	*XC*
MANITOBA	*XM*
NEW BRUNSWICK	*XB*
NEWFOUNDLAND (LABRADOR)	*XW*
NORTHWEST TERRITORIES	*XT*
NOVA SCOTIA	*XN*
NUNAVUT	*XV*
ONTARIO	*XO*
PRINCE EDWARD ISLAND	*XP*
QUEBEC	*XQ*
SASKATCHEWAN	*XS*
YUKON TERRITORY	*XY*

Next, use the first three characters from the first two "words" of the name. If there is only one "word" in the name, then use only the first three characters from the first name. For example, Amalgamated Plastics Corp. would be "AMAPLA;" Bergstrom would be "BER."

If there are two or more initials together, treat them as a single word. For example, A.B.C. Company or A B C Company would yield "ABCCOM." O.A.S.I.S. Corp. would yield "OASCOR." Dr. S.A. Smith yields "DRSA." Shavings B L Inc. yields "SHABL."

Next, find the largest number on the street address line and use up to the first four numbers. For example, "11455 Main Street Suite 9999" would yield "1145." A suite number or a post office box should be used if it contains the largest number. For example, "232 Main Street Suite 1234" would yield "1234." If the numbers in the street address are spelled out, such as "One Thousand Century Plaza," there will be no numbers in this section of the MID. However, if the address is "One Thousand Century Plaza Suite 345," this would yield "345."

Finally, use the first three alpha characters from the city name. "Tokyo" would be "TOK," "St. Michel" would be "STM," "18-Mile High" would be "MIL," and "The Hague" would be "HAG." Notice that numerals in the city line are to be ignored.

"D" is the correct answer.

13. Quota Class merchandise is any imported merchandise subject to limitations under an absolute or tariff rate quota. Entry summaries for consumption or withdrawal for consumption shall be presented during official office hours. Official office hours for purposes of administering quotas shall be:

A. 8:00 am to 4:30 pm PST
B. 8:30 am to 4:40 pm EST
C. 8:30 am to 4:30 pm in all time zones
D. 8:00 am to 4:30 pm in all time zones
E. 8:30 am to 5:00 pm in all time zones

 As per 19 CFR 132.3:

§132.3   Observation of official hours.

*An entry summary for consumption or a withdrawal for consumption for quota-class merchandise shall be presented only during official office hours, except as provided in §§132.12 and 141.62(b) of this chapter. **For purposes of administering quotas, "official office hours" shall mean 8:30 a.m. to 4:30 p.m. in all time zones.***

"C" is the correct answer.

14. How much Antidumping Duties/Countervailing Duties (AD/CVD) are entitled to drawback, for entries made after August 23, 1988?

A. Up to 99 percent of AD/CVD may be refunded if approved by CBP
B. Only the initial cash deposit amount for AD/CVD duties may be refunded under drawback
C. The entire amount of AD/CVD paid may be refunded
D. The first $1,000 of AD/CVD paid may be refunded
E. AD/CVD will not be refunded because they are not subject to drawback

 As per 19 CFR 191.3(b):

*(b) **Duties and fees not subject to drawback include**:*

(1) Harbor maintenance fee (see §24.24 of this chapter);

(2) Merchandise processing fees (see §24.23 of this chapter), except where unused merchandise drawback pursuant to 19 U.S.C. 1313(j) or drawback for substitution of finished petroleum derivatives pursuant to 19 U.S.C. 1313(p)(2)(A)(iii) or (iv) is claimed; and

*(3) **Antidumping and countervailing duties** on merchandise entered, or withdrawn from warehouse, for consumption on or after August 23, 1988.*

"E" is the correct answer.

15. Turtle Clothing Line is a new company getting started in China. They would like to solicit orders in the United States. They are planning to import samples. The merchandise will be filed under classification 9811.00.60. Which of the following does not qualify for 9811.00.60?

A. Merchandise unsuitable for sale.
B. Items marked, torn, or perforated.
C. Merchandise valued not over $10 each.
D. Merchandise valued not over $1 each.
E. None of the above.

 As per HTSUS:

9811.00.60	1/	Any sample (except samples covered by heading 9811.00.20 or 9811.00.40), valued not over $1 each, or marked, torn, perforated or otherwise treated so that it is unsuitable for sale or for use otherwise than as a sample, to be used in the United States only for soliciting orders for products of foreign countries. . . . . .Free

The article description for 9811.00.60 includes items "valued not over $1 each", but does not mention "valued not over $10 each" as a qualifying condition. "C" is the correct answer.

16. When admission into the United States for a shipment is prohibited, the importer has the option to file for a direct exportation (without transportation to another port) instead of an entry for consumption. Which of the following documents must be provided?

A. A copy of the commercial invoice.
B. Proof of payment to foreign shipper and a bond on CBP Form 301 containing the bond conditions set forth in 19 CFR 113.63.
C. Four copies of CBP Form 7512, and a bond on CBP Form 301 containing the bond conditions set forth in 19 CFR 113.63.
D. A copy of the airway bill or bill of lading.
E. CBP Form 7512 and a carrier's certificate.

 As per 19 CFR 18.25(a) & (b):

§18.25   Direct exportation.

*(a) Except as otherwise provided for in subpart F of part 145 of this chapter, relating to exportations by mail, when no entry has been made or completed for merchandise in Customs custody, or when the merchandise is covered by an unliquidated consumption entry, or when merchandise which has been entered in good faith is found to be prohibited under any law of the United States, and such merchandise is to be exported directly without transportation to another port, **four copies of Customs Form 7512 shall be filed**. If a TIR carnet covers the merchandise which is to be exported directly without transportation, the carnet shall be discharged or canceled, as appropriate (see part 114 of this chapter), and four copies of Form 7512 shall be filed. The port director may require an extra copy or copies of Form 7512 to be furnished for use in connection with delivery of the merchandise to the carrier named in the entry. If an A.T.A. carnet covers the merchandise which is to be exported directly without transportation, the carnet shall be discharged by the certification of the appropriate transportation and reexportation vouchers by Customs officers as necessary.*

*(b) **A bond on Customs Form 301, containing the bond conditions set forth in §113.63 of this chapter, shall be required.** (See also §158.45 of this chapter.)*

"C" is the correct answer.

17. Which of the following dates would be the date of liquidation of an entry?

A. The date of the courtesy notice of liquidation provided to the importer.
B. 314 days from the date of entry.
C. The date the duties are paid the CBP.
D. The bulletin notice date posted in the customs house.
E. 90 days from the date the bulletin notice is posted.

 As per 19 CFR 159.9(c):

*(c) Date of liquidation—(1) Generally. **The bulletin notice of liquidation will be dated with the date it is posted or lodged in the customhouse** for the information of importers. This posting or lodging will be deemed the legal evidence of liquidation. For electronic entry summaries, the date of liquidation will be the date of posting of the bulletin notice of liquidation. CBP will endeavor to provide the filer with electronic notification of this date as an informal, courtesy notice of liquidation.*

"D" is the correct answer.

18. If accelerated disposition is requested on a protest and it is not allowed or denied within 30 days from request for accelerated disposition what would the status of the protest be?

A. The protest is deemed approved.
B. The protest is forwarded to a secondary port for further review.
C. The protest is deemed denied.
D. The protest stays open until a decision is reached or 2 years from the filing date is reached when it will be deemed approved.
E. The protest is withdrawn allowing protestant to resubmit its claim within 180 days of the protest withdrawal.

 As per 19 CFR 174.22(d):

(d) Failure to allow or deny protest within 30-day period. If the port director fails to allow or deny a protest which is the subject of a request for accelerated disposition within 30 days from the date of mailing of such request, the protest shall be deemed to have been denied at the close of the 30th day following such date of mailing.

"C" is the correct answer.

19. Which of the following is not required to complete the paper CBP Form 7501?

A. The signature of the importer
B. The identification number for merchandise subject to an antidumping or countervailing duty order
C. The importer's identification number
D. The marks and numbers previously provided for packages released or withdrawn
E. The value of each invoice

 As per 19 CFR 141.61(b):

(b) Marks and numbers previously provided. **An importer may omit from entry summary (CBP Form 7501) the marks and numbers previously provided for packages released or withdrawn.**

At first glance, it may make sense that "A" could be a correct answer as the importer's customs broker (not the importer of record) is the party that actually signs the CBP Form 7501 (on the importer's behalf). However, as per 19 CFR 101.1:

Importer. "Importer" means the person primarily liable for the payment of any duties on the merchandise, or an authorized agent acting on his behalf. ...

"D" is the correct answer.

20. Any parties participating in an import transaction with a financial interest in the transaction may make entry on his own behalf, or may designate a licensed customs broker to make entry on his behalf, and may be shown as the importer of record on CBP Form 7501, except:

A. The buying agent to the transaction
B. The selling agent to the transaction
C. A person or firm who is importing on consignment
D. A person who imports under loan or lease
E. The nominal consignee to the transaction

 As per Directive 3530-002A (Right to Make Entry):

*5.3.1 The terms "owner" and "purchaser" include any party with a financial interest in a transaction, including, but not limited to, the actual owner of the goods, the actual purchaser of the goods, a buying or selling agent, a person or firm who imports on consignment, a person or firm who imports under loan or lease, a person or firm who imports for exhibition at a trade fair, a person or firm who imports goods for repair or alteration or further fabrication, etc. Any such owner or purchaser may make entry on his own behalf or may designate a licensed Customs broker to make entry on his behalf and may be shown as the importer of record on the CF 7501. **The terms "owner" or "purchaser" would not include a "nominal consignee" who effectively possesses no other right, title, or interest in the goods except as he possessed under a bill of lading, air waybill, or other shipping document.***

5.3.2 Examples of nominal consignees not authorized to file Customs entries are express consignment operators (ECO), freight consolidators who handle consolidated shipments as described in 5.10 below, and Customs brokers who are not permitted to transact business in Customs ports where a shipment is being entered.

"E" is the correct answer.

Section IV: Foreign Trade Zone and Warehouse
21. Antidumping/Countervailing merchandise is placed in a bonded warehouse facility and re-warehoused at a second warehouse. What is the appropriate entry type to be included on the U.S. CBP Form 7501?

A. Entry type 07
B. Entry type 21
C. Entry type 22
D. Entry type 32
E. Entry type 34

 As per CBP Form 7501 Instructions:

Consumption Entries
      Free and Dutiable   *01*
      Quota/Visa   *02*
      Antidumping/Countervailing Duty (AD/CVD)   *03*
      Appraisement   *04*
      Vessel Repair   *05*
      Foreign Trade Zone Consumption   *06*
      Quota/Visa and AD/CVD combinations   *07*
      Duty Deferral   *08*
Informal Entries
      Free and Dutiable   *11*
      Quota Other than textiles   *12*
Warehouse Entries
      Warehouse   *21*
      Re-Warehouse   *22*
      Temporary Importation Bond   *23*
      Trade Fair   *24*
      Permanent Exhibition   *25*
      Foreign Trade Zone Admission   *26*
Warehouse Withdrawal
      For Consumption   *31*
      Quota/Visa   *32*
      AD/CVD   *34*
      Quota/Visa and AD/CVD combinations   *38*

... ...

"C" is the correct answer.

22. What entry type is used to file for non-quota merchandise to be withdrawn for consumption from a bonded warehouse?

A. Entry type 21
B. Entry type 22
C. Entry type 23
D. Entry type 31
E. Entry type 32

 The key words to in the verbiage of the question are "withdrawn", "consumption", and "(bonded) warehouse". "D" is the correct answer.

23. What form is required for a temporary deposit of merchandise in a Foreign Trade Zone, provided that it is signed, numbered, and marked as "Temporary Deposit in a Zone"?

A. CBP Form 214
B. CBP Form 3461
C. CBP Form 3499
D. CBP Form 6043
E. CBP Form 7512

 As per 19 CFR 146.35(b):

(b) Application. An application for temporary deposit will be made to the port director on a properly signed and uniquely numbered Customs Form 214, annotated clearly "Temporary Deposit in a Zone".

"A" is the correct answer.

24. How long must a proprietor of a bonded warehouse retain all records pertaining to bonded merchandise after the date of the final withdrawal under the entry?

A. One year
B. Two years
C. Three years
D. Four years
E. Five years

As per 19 CFR 19.4(b)(4)(B):

(B) Retain all records required in this part and defined in §163.1(a) of this chapter, pertaining to bonded merchandise for 5 years after the date of the final withdrawal under the entry.

"E" is the correct answer.

25. Except in a case of theft or suspected theft, the Foreign Trade Zone (FTZ) operator need not file a report with the port director, or note in the annual reconciliation report, any _____.

A. shortage of six percent (6%) of the quantity of merchandise in a lot that would have been subject to duties and taxes in the amount of $1,000.
B. merchandise not properly admitted to the zone.
C. shortage of one percent (1%) of the quantity of merchandise covered by a unique identifier that would have been subject to duties and taxes in the amount of $1,000.
D. shortage of one percent (1%) or more of the quantity of merchandise in a lot that would have been subject to duties and taxes of $100 or more upon entry into the Customs territory.
E. shortage or overage concerning domestic status merchandise for which no permit is required.

 As per 19 CFR 146.53(b):

(b) Certain domestic merchandise. Except in a case of theft or suspected theft, the operator need not file a report with the port director, or note in the annual reconciliation report, any shortage or overage concerning domestic status merchandise for which no permit is required.

"E" is the correct answer.

26. For a Foreign Trade Zone, the operator shall prepare a reconciliation report within _____ days after the end of the zone/subzone year unless the port director authorizes an extension for reasonable cause.

A. 30
B. 60
C. 90
D. 120
E. 180

 As per 19 CFR 146.25(a):

§146.25   Annual reconciliation.

*(a) Report. **The operator shall prepare a reconciliation report within 90 days after the end of the zone/subzone year** unless the port director authorizes an extension for reasonable cause. The operator shall retain that annual reconciliation report for a spot check or audit by Customs, and need not furnish it to Customs unless requested. There is no form specified for the preparation of the report.*

"C" is the correct answer.

Section V: Bonds
27. Modifications to a bond made prior to its signing by the parties to the bond require:

A.   Initials of the parties placed adjacent to the modification
B.   Nothing because the bond has not yet been signed by the parties
C.   A statement of approval by the principal attached to the bond
D.   Initials of the agent of the surety company placed adjacent to the modification
E.   A statement by an agent of the surety company or by the personal sureties to that effect placed on the bond

 As per 19 CFR 113.23(b):

(b) Prior to signing. When erasures, alterations, modifications, or interlineations are made on the bond prior to its signing by the parties to the bond, a statement by an agent of the surety company or by the personal sureties to that effect shall be placed upon the bond.

"E" is the correct answer.

28. An importer wants to clear its instruments of international traffic. However, it does not have a bond on file with CBP and only needs the customs bond for this one time shipment. To import the instruments of international traffic, it would need a _____.

A.   Single Entry Basic Importation Bond
B.   Single Entry Instruments of International Traffic Bond
C.   Single Entry international Carrier Bond
D.   Continuous International Carrier Bond
E.   Continuous Instruments of International Traffic Bond

 As per 19 CFR 113.66:

§113.66   Control of containers and instruments of international traffic bond conditions.

A bond for control of containers and instruments of international traffic *shall contain the conditions listed in this section and* **shall be a continuous bond***.*

"E" is the correct answer.

29. When a bond or other security is not specifically required by law, CBP possesses the regulatory authority to require security or execution of a bond pursuant to which regulation?

A.   19 CFR 113.1
B.   19 CFR 113.2
C.   19 CFR 113.11
D.   19 CFR 113.12
E.   19 CFR 113.13

 As per 19 CFR 113.1:

§113.1   Authority to require security or execution of bond.

Where a bond or other security is not specifically required by law, the Commissioner of Customs, pursuant to Treasury Department Order No. 165 Revised, as amended (T.D. 53654, 19 FR 7241, November 6, 1954), may by regulation or specific instruction require, or authorize the port director to require, such bonds or other security considered necessary for the protection of the revenue or to assure compliance with any pertinent law, regulation, or instruction.

"A" is the correct answer.

30. Which of the following obligations will CBP not accept in lieu of sureties on a bond required or authorized by any law, regulation, or instruction?

A.   United States money
B.   United States certificates of indebtedness
C.   Treasury notes
D.   Treasury bills
E.   Savings bonds

 As per 19 CFR 113.40(a):

§113.40   Acceptance of cash deposits or obligations of the United States in lieu of sureties on bonds.

*(a) General provision. In lieu of sureties on any bond required or authorized by any law, regulation, or instruction which the Secretary of the Treasury or the Commissioner of Customs is authorized to enforce, **the port director is authorized to accept United States money, United States bonds (except for savings bonds), United States certificates of indebtedness, Treasury notes, or Treasury bills in an amount equal to the amount of the bond.***

"E" is the correct answer.

Note: A United States bond is a form of a "United States certificate of indebtedness".

31. Merchandise subject to the Federal Food, Drug, and Cosmetic Act requires a single entry bond. The amount of the entry bond is equal to the domestic value of the merchandise at the time of release as if the merchandise were admissible and otherwise in compliance; or:

A.   three times the value of the merchandise.
B.   the total entered value plus all duties, taxes and fees.
C.   the total entered value.
D.   equal to 110% of the total estimated duties determined at time of entry.
E.   three times the total entered value of the merchandise plus duties, taxes, and fees.

 As per 19 CFR 12.3(b):

(b) Bond amount. The bond referred to in paragraph (a) (FDA) of this section must be in a specific amount prescribed by the port director based on the circumstances of the particular case that is either:

(1) Equal to the domestic value (see §162.43(a) of this chapter) of the merchandise at the time of release as if the merchandise were admissible and otherwise in compliance; or

(2) ***Equal to three times the value of the merchandise*** *as provided in §113.62(m)(1) of this chapter.*

"A" is the correct answer.

Section VI: Classification
32. What is the classification of a men's woven solid color dress shirt composed of 45 percent cotton, 40 percent polyester and 15 percent spandex?

A. 6205.20.2026   Men's or boys' shirts>>Of cotton>>Other>>Dress shirts>>Other>>Men's

B. 6205.30.2010   Men's or boys shirts>>Of man-made fibers>>Other>>Other>>Dress>>With two or more colors in the warp and/or the filling>>Men's

C. 6205.30.2030   Men's or boys shirts>>Of man-made fibers>>Other>>Other>>Dress>>Other>>Men's

D. 6205.90.4010   Men's or boys' shirts>>Of other textile materials>>Other>>Subject to cotton restraints

E. 6205.90.4030   Men's or boys' shirts>>Of other textile materials>>Other>>Subject to man-made fiber restraints

 As per HTSUS Section XI (Chapters 50 thru 63) Note 2:

2. (A) Goods classifiable in chapters 50 to 55 or in heading 5809 or 5902 and of a mixture of two or more textile materials are to be classified as if consisting wholly of that one textile material which predominates by weight over each other single textile material.

     When no one textile material predominates by weight, the goods are to be classified as if consisting wholly of that one textile material which is covered by the heading which occurs last in numerical order among those which equally merit consideration.

  (B) For the purposes of the above rule:

    (a) Gimped horsehair yarn (heading 5110) and metalized yarn (heading 5605) are to be treated as a single textile material the weight of which is to be taken as the aggregate of the weights of its components; for the classification of woven fabrics, metal thread is to be regarded as a textile material;

    (b) The choice of appropriate heading shall be effected by determining first the chapter and then the applicable heading within that chapter, disregarding any materials not classified in that chapter;

    (c) When both chapters 54 and 55 are involved with any other chapter, chapters 54 and 55 are to be treated as a single chapter;

    (d) Where a chapter or a heading refers to goods of different textile materials, such materials are to be treated as a single textile material.

AND as per HTSUS Section XI (Chapters 50 thru 63) Subheading Note 2:

2. (A) Products of chapters 56 to 63 containing two or more textile materials are to be regarded as consisting wholly of that textile material which would be selected under note 2 to this section for the classification of a product of chapters 50 to 55 or of heading 5809 consisting of the same textile materials.

  (B) For the application of this rule:

    (a) Where appropriate, only the part which determines the classification under general interpretative rule 3 shall be taken into account;

    (b) In the case of textile products consisting of a ground fabric and a pile or looped surface no account shall be taken of the ground fabric;

    (c) In the case of embroidery of heading 5810 and goods thereof, only the ground fabric shall be taken into account. However, embroidery without visible ground, and goods thereof, shall be classified with reference to the embroidering threads alone.

The main trick here is to combine the "man-made" fiber percentages, essentially treating them as a single textile material. Both the polyester (40%) and spandex (15%) are man-made fibers. Together, they comprise 55% of the whole dress shirt, which exceeds that of the cotton (45%). Accordingly, the classification 6205.30.2030 best describes this "sold color" (i.e. NOT with two or more colors) dress shirt. "C" is the correct answer.

Heading/ Subheading	Stat. Suf- fix	Article Description	Unit of Quantity	Rates of Duty		
				1		2
				General	Special	
6205 (con.) 6205.30 6205.30.10	00	Men's or boys' shirts (con.): Of man-made fibers: Certified hand-loomed and folklore products (640)..............................	doz...... kg	12.2%	Free (BH,CA, CL,CO,E,IL,JO, KR,MA,MX,OM, P,PA,PE,SG) 8% (AU)	76%
6205.30.15		Other: Containing 36 percent or more by weight of wool or fine animal hair......................		49.6¢/kg + 19.7%	Free (BH,CA, CL,CO,IL,JO,KR, MA,MX,OM,P, PA,PE,SG) 8% (AU)	52.9¢/kg + 45%
	10	Men's (440).........................	doz. kg			
	20	Boys' (440).	doz. kg			
6205.30.20		Other...........................		29.1¢/kg + 25.9%	Free (BH,CA, CL,CO,IL,JO,KR, MA,MX,OM,P, PA,PE,SG) 8% (AU)	30.9¢/kg + 76%
		Dress: With two or more colors in the warp and/or the filling:				
	10	Men's (640).	doz. kg			
	20	Boys' (640)...................	doz. kg			
		Other:				
	30	Men's (640).	doz. kg			
	40	Boys' (640)...................	doz. kg			
		Other: With two or more colors in the warp and/or the filling:				
	50	Men's (640).	doz. kg			
		Boys':				
	55	Imported as parts of play- suits (237).................	doz. kg			
	60	Other (640)................	doz. kg			
		Other:				
	70	Men's (640).	doz. kg			
		Boys':				
	75	Imported as parts of play- suits (237).................	doz. kg			
	80	Other (640)................	doz. kg			

33. What is the correct tariff classification of a perfume containing alcohol?

A. 3302.10.1000   Mixtures of odoriferous substances and mixtures (including alcoholic solutions) with a basis of one or more of these substances, of a kind used as raw materials in industry; …>>Of a kind used in the food or drink industries>>Not containing alcohol.

B. 3303.00.1000   Perfumes and toilet waters>>Not containing alcohol>>Floral or flower waters

C. 3303.00.2000   Perfumes and toilet waters>>Not containing alcohol>>Other

D. 3303.00.3000   Perfumes and toilet waters>>Containing alcohol

E. 3307.10.2000   Pre-shave, shaving or after-shave preparations, personal deodorants, bath preparations, depilatories and other perfumery, cosmetic or toilet preparations, not elsewhere specified or included; …>>Pre-shave, shaving or after-shave preparations>>Containing alcohol

 As per HTSUS Chapter 33 Notes, 2, 3, & 4:

2. The expression "odoriferous substances" in heading 3302 refers only to the substances of heading 3301, to odoriferous constituents isolated from those substances or to synthetic aromatics.

3. Headings 3303 to 3307 apply, inter alia, to products, whether or not mixed (other than aqueous distillates and aqueous solutions of essential oils), suitable for use as goods of these headings and put up in packings of a kind sold by retail for such use.

4. The expression "perfumery, cosmetic or toilet preparations" in heading 3307 applies, inter alia, to the following products: scented sachets; odoriferous preparations which operate by burning; perfumed papers and papers impregnated or coated with cosmetics; contact lens or artificial eye solutions; wadding, felt and nonwovens, impregnated, coated or covered with perfume or cosmetics; animal toilet preparations.

Multiple choices "A", "B", and "C" may all be disregarded as they describe articles "not containing alcohol". "E" may also be disregarded as the item description for "D" more specifically describes the item than does "E". "D" is the correct answer.

Note: The actual exam uses HTSUS 3307.10.0000 for multiple choice "E". This HTS number, however, does not appear in the recent editions of the HTSUS, so the author of this book took the liberty of replacing this entry with HTS number 3307.10.2000 for the sake of this exercise.

Heading/ Subheading	Stat. Suf- fix	Article Description	Unit of Quantity	Rates of Duty 1 General	Rates of Duty 1 Special	Rates of Duty 2
3303.00		Perfumes and toilet waters:				
		Not containing alcohol:				
3303.00.10	00	Floral or flower waters.........................	liters.....	Free		20%
3303.00.20	00	Other..	kg......	Free		75%
3303.00.30	00	Containing alcohol.............................	kg......	Free		88¢/kg + 75%
3304		Beauty or make-up preparations and preparations for the care of the skin (other than medicaments), including sunscreen or sun tan preparations; manicure or pedicure preparations:				
3304.10.00	00	Lip make-up preparations.........................	X.......	Free		75%
3304.20.00	00	Eye make-up preparations........................	X.......	Free		75%
3304.30.00	00	Manicure or pedicure preparations..................	X.......	Free		75%
		Other:				
3304.91.00		Powders, whether or not compressed.............		Free		75%
	10	Rouges....................................	X			
	50	Other......................................	X			
		Other:				
3304.99.10	00	Petroleum jelly put up for retail sale...........	X.......	Free		75%
3304.99.50	00	Other......................................	X.......	Free		75%
3305		Preparations for use on the hair:				
3305.10.00	00	Shampoos.....................................	X.......	Free		75%
3305.20.00	00	Preparations for permanent waving or straightening.................................	X.......	Free		75%
3305.30.00	00	Hair lacquers..................................	kg......	Free		88¢/kg + 75%
3305.90.00	00	Other..	kg......	Free		88¢/kg + 75%
3306		Preparations for oral or dental hygiene, including denture fixative pastes and powders; yarn used to clean between the teeth (dental floss), in individual retail packages:				
3306.10.00	00	Dentifrices....................................	X.......	Free		75%
3306.20.00	00	Yarn used to clean between the teeth (dental floss).....	kg......	Free		88¢/kg + 75%
3306.90.00	00	Other..	kg......	Free		88¢/kg + 75%

34. What is the proper classification of high fashion snakeskin men's anoraks from Canada?

A. 4203.10.2000   Articles of apparel and clothing accessories, of leather or of composition leather>>Articles of apparel>>Of retile leather

B. 4203.10.4010   Articles of apparel and clothing accessories, of leather or of composition leather>>Articles of apparel>>Other>>Coats and jackets>>Anoraks

C. 4203.10..4030   Articles of apparel and clothing accessories, of leather or of composition leather>>Articles of apparel>>Other>>Coats and jackets>>Other>>Men's and boys'

D. 4203.10.4060   Articles of apparel and clothing accessories, of leather or of composition leather>>Articles of apparel>>Other>>Coats and jackets>>Other>>Women's, girls' and infants'

E. 4203.10.4085   Articles of apparel and clothing accessories, of leather or of composition leather>>Articles of apparel>>Other>>Other>>Men's and boys'

"B" thru "E" may be eliminated as possible answers as the article description for each of these four HTS numbers are "Other (than of reptile leather)", which from the get-go precludes them from further consideration. And, as per GRI 6, only subheadings at the same level are comparable. "A" is the most suitable answer.

Heading/ Subheading	Stat. Suffix	Article Description	Unit of Quantity	Rates of Duty 1 General	Rates of Duty 1 Special	Rates of Duty 2
4203		Articles of apparel and clothing accessories, of leather or of composition leather:				
4203.10		Articles of apparel:				
4203.10.20	00	Of reptile leather.	No..	4.7%	Free (A,AU,BH,CA, CL,CO,E,IL,JO, KR,MA,MX,OM,P, PA,PE,SG)	35%
4203.10.40		Other.	. . . .	6%	Free (AU,BH,CA, CL,CO,D,IL, JO,MA,MX,OM,P, PA,PE,R,SG) 2.4% (KR) 4.8% (E)	35%
		Coats and jackets:				
	10	Anoraks.	No.			
		Other:				
	30	Men's and boys'.	No.			
	60	Women's, girls' and infants'.	No.			
		Other:				
	85	Men's and boys'.	No.			
	95	Women's, girls' and infants'.	No.			
		Gloves, mittens and mitts:				
4203.21		Specially designed for use in sports: Baseball and softball gloves and mitts (including batting gloves):				
4203.21.20	00	Batting gloves.	No..	3%	Free (A,AU,BH,CA, CL,CO,E,IL,JO, KR,MA,MX,OM,P, PA,PE,SG)	30%
4203.21.40	00	Other.	No..	Free		30%
		Ski or snowmobile gloves, mittens and mitts:				
4203.21.55	00	Cross-country ski gloves, mittens and mitts.	prs.	3.5%	Free (A,AU,BH,CA, CL,CO,E,IL,JO, KR,MA,MX,OM,P, PA,PE,SG)	45%
4203.21.60	00	Other.	prs.	5.5%	Free (A,AU,BH,CA, CL,CO,E,IL,JO, KR,MA,MX,OM,P, PA,PE,SG)	45%
4203.21.70	00	Ice hockey gloves.	prs.	Free		30%
4203.21.80		Other.	. . . .	4.9%	Free (A,AU,BH,CA, CL,CO,E,IL,JO, KR,MA,MX,OM,P, PA,PE,SG)	30%
	30	Golf gloves.	doz.			
	60	Other.	X			

35. What is the correct classification of raw cane sugar from Columbia with an entered polarization of 94.5 degrees? The raw cane sugar is described in Additional U.S. Note 5 to Chapter 17 and is entered pursuant to its provisions.

A. 1701.12.1000   Cane or beet sugar and chemically pure sucrose, in solid form>>Raw sugar not containing added flavoring or coloring matter>>Beet sugar>>Described in additional U.S. note 5 to this chapter and entered pursuant to its provisions.

B. 1701.13.1000   Cane or beet sugar and chemically pure sucrose, in solid form>>Raw sugar not containing added flavoring or coloring matter>>Cane sugar specified in subheading note 2 to this chapter>>Described in additional U.S. note 5 to this chapter and entered pursuant to its provisions.

C. 1701.14.1000   Cane or beet sugar and chemically pure sucrose, in solid form>>Raw sugar not containing added flavoring or coloring matter>>Other cane sugar>>Described in additional U.S. note 5 to this chapter and entered pursuant to its provisions.

D. 1701.99.1010   Cane or beet sugar and chemically pure sucrose, in solid form>>Other>>Other>> Described in additional U.S. note 5 to this chapter and entered pursuant to its provisions>>Specialty sugars.

E. 1701.99.1025   Cane or beet sugar and chemically pure sucrose, in solid form>>Other>>Other>> Described in additional U.S. note 5 to this chapter and entered pursuant to its provisions>>Other>>Sugar not for further processing

 As per HTSUS Chapter 17 Subheading Notes:

Subheading Notes

1. For the purposes of subheadings 1701.12, 1701.13 and 1701.14, "raw sugar" means sugar whose content of sucrose by weight, in the dry state, corresponds to a polarimeter reading of less than 99.5 degrees.

2. Subheading 1701.13 covers only cane sugar obtained without centrifugation, whose content of sucrose by weight, in the dry state, corresponds to a polarimeter reading of 69° or more but less than 93°. The product contains only natural anhedral microcrystals, of irregular shape, not visible to the naked eye, which are surrounded by residues of molasses and other constituents of sugar cane.

As per Subheading Note 1, the cane sugar in question, which has an entered polarization of 94.5 degrees, does, in fact, conform to customs' definition of "raw sugar". At this point, "B" appears to be a suitable classification. However, as per Subheading Note 2, this polarization of 94.5 degrees precludes the cane sugar in question from being classified as "B" (1701.13). Subsequently, "C", which has an article description of "Other (than specified in Subheading Note 2) cane sugar, is the most suitable classification. The correct answer is "C".

Note: The references in this question to "U.S. Note 5 to Chapter 17" and "General Note 15 of the tariff schedule" are merely quota-related items, the details of which are of no consequence to this question.

Heading/ Subheading	Stat. Suf- fix	Article Description	Unit of Quantity	Rates of Duty		
				1		2
				General	Special	
1701 (con.)		Cane or beet sugar and chemically pure sucrose, in solid form:(con.) Raw sugar not containing added flavoring or coloring matter:(con.)				
1701.13 (con.)		Cane sugar specified in subheading note 2 to this chapter: (con.)				
1701.13.50	00	Other 1/..............................	kg.......	33.87¢/kg	Free (JO,MX,SG) 23.7¢/kg (KR) See 9822.05.20 (P+) See 9822.06.10 (PE) See 9822.08.01 (CO) See 9822.09.17- 9822.09.20 (PA) See 9911.17.05- 9911.17.10 (CL) See 9912.17.05- 9912.17.10 (MA) See 9914.17.05, 9914.17.10 (BH) See 9916.17.05- 9916.17.10 (OM)	39.85¢/kg
1701.14 1701.14.05	00	Other cane sugar: Described in general note 15 of the tariff schedule and entered pursuant to its provisions............................	kg.......	1.4606¢/kg less 0.020668¢/kg for each degree under 100 degrees (and fractions of a degree in proportion) but not less than 0.943854¢/kg	Free (A*,AU,BH, CA,CL,CO,E*,IL, JO,KR,MA,MX, OM,P,PA,PE,SG)	4.3817¢/kg less 0.0622005¢ /kg for each degree under 100 degrees (and fractions of a degree in proportion) but not less than 2.831562¢ /kg
1701.14.10	00	Described in additional U.S. note 5 to this chapter and entered pursuant to its provisions...	kg.......	1.4606¢/kg less 0.020668¢/kg for each degree under 100 degrees (and fractions of a degree in proportion) but not less than 0.943854¢/kg	Free (A*,BH,CA, CL,CO,E*,IL,JO, MA,MX,OM,P,PA, PE,SG) See 9822.05.15 (P+) 0.5¢/kg less 0.01¢/kg for each degree under 100 degrees (and fractions of a degree in pro- portion) but not less than 0.3¢/kg (KR)	4.3817¢/kg less 0.0622005¢ /kg for each degree under 100 degrees (and fractions of a degree in proportion) but not less than 2.831562¢ /kg

36. A fabricated one-piece stainless steel sink unit is composed of a molded stainless steel sink welded to stainless steel countertops fabricated of steel sheet. The stainless steel sink provides the principal function to this article. What is the classification of the fabricated one-piece stainless steel sink?

A. 6910.10.0030   Ceramic sinks, wash basins, washbasin pedestals, baths, bidets, water closet bowls, flush tanks, urinals and similar sanitary fixtures.

B. 7324.10.0010   Sanitary ware and parts thereof, of iron or steel>>Sinks and wash basins, of stainless steel>>Stainless steel sinks with one or more drawn bowls (basins).

C. 7324.90.0000   Sanitary ware and parts thereof, of iron or steel>>Other, including parts.

D. 7326.90.8588   Other articles of iron or steel>>Other>>Other>>Other>>Other>>Other.

E. 9403.20.0020   Other furniture and parts thereof>>Other metal furniture>>Other>>Counters, lockers, racks, display cases, shelves, partitions and similar fixtures.

The key here is that the question states that "the stainless steel sink (not the countertop) provides the principal function to this article". Accordingly, multiple choice "E" may be disregarded as this classification is for counters. "A" may be disregarded as this is for ceramic articles. Stainless steel sinks are specifically provided for in HTS 7324.10.0000, and apparently no Section of Chapter Notes advise otherwise. The correct answer is "B".

Note: The actual exam uses HTSUS 7324.10.0000 for multiple choice "B". This HTS number, however, does not appear in the recent HTSUS, so the author of this book took the liberty of replacing this entry with HTS number 7324.10.0010 for the sake of this exercise. Additionally, the actual exam uses HTSUS 7326.90.8587 for multiple choice "D". This HTS number, however, does not appear in the recent editions of the HTSUS, so the author of this book took the liberty of replacing this entry with HTS number 7326.90.8588 for the sake of this exercise.

Heading/ Subheading	Stat. Suffix	Article Description	Unit of Quantity	Rates of Duty		
				1		2
				General	Special	
7324		Sanitary ware and parts thereof, of iron or steel:				
7324.10.00		Sinks and wash basins, of stainless steel...........		3.4%	Free (A,AU,BH,C, CA,CL,CO,E,IL, JO,KR,MA,MX, OM,P,PA,PE,SG)	40%
	10	Stainless steel sinks with one or more drawn bowls (basins)........................	No.			
	50	Other....................................	No.			
		Baths:				
7324.21		Of cast iron, whether or not enamelled:				
7324.21.10	00	Coated or plated with precious metal.........	No.......	Free		20%
7324.21.50	00	Other..................................	No.......	Free		40%
7324.29.00	00	Other...................................	No.......	Free		40%
7324.90.00	00	Other, including parts........................	X.......	Free		40%
7325		Other cast articles of iron or steel:				
7325.10.00		Of nonmalleable cast iron...................		Free		10%
	10	Manhole covers, rings and frames.............	kg			
	20	Catch basins, grates and frames.............	kg			
	25	Cleanout covers and frames.................	kg			
	30	Valve and service boxes....................	kg			
	35	Meter boxes.............................	kg			
	80	Other...................................	kg			
		Other:				
7325.91.00	00	Grinding balls and similar articles for mills........	kg......	2.9%	Free (A,AU,BH,CA, CL,CO,E,IL,JO, KR,MA,MX,OM,P, PA,PE,SG)	45%
7325.99		Other:				
7325.99.10	00	Of cast iron.............................	kg......	Free		20%
7325.99.50	00	Other...................................	kg......	2.9%	Free (A,AU,B,BH, CA,CL,CO,E,IL, JO,KR,MA,MX, OM,P,PA,PE,SG)	45%

37. What is the classification of plastic swimming goggles with rubber straps?

A. 3926.90.9980   Other articles of plastics ...>>Other>>Other>>Other

B. 4015.19.1050   Articles of apparel and clothing accessories (including gloves, mittens and mitts), for all purposes, of vulcanized rubber other than hard rubber>>Gloves, mittens and mitts>>Other>>Other>>Other

C. 9004.90.0000   Spectacles, goggles and the like, corrective, protective or other>>Other

D. 9506.29.0080   Articles and equipment for general physical exercise, gymnastics, athletics, other sports (including table-tennis) or outdoor games, not specified or included elsewhere in this chapter; swimming pools and wading pools; parts and accessories thereof>>Water skis, surf boards, sailboards and other watersport equipment; parts and accessories thereof>>Other>>Other

E. 9506.99.6080   Articles and equipment for general physical exercise, gymnastics, athletics, other sports (including table-tennis) or outdoor games, not specified or included elsewhere in this chapter; swimming pools and wading pools; parts and accessories thereof>>Other>>Other>>Other>>Other

 As per HTSUS Chapter 39 Note 2(u):

2. This chapter does not cover:

...

(u) Articles of chapter 90 (for example, optical elements, spectacle frames, drawing instruments);

AND as per HTSUS Chapter 40 Note 2(e):

2. This chapter does not cover:

...

(e) Articles of chapter 90, 92, 94 or 96; or

AND as per HTSUS Chapter 95 Note 1(q):

1. This chapter does not cover:

...

(q) Spectacles, goggles or the like, for sports or outdoor games (heading 9004);

As per GRI 1, items are to be classified based on the Headings of the HTSUS Classifications, and the HTSUS Section Notes and Chapter Notes. It may seem unreasonable to expect the examinee to comb through all the Section Notes and Chapter Notes of the various chapters referenced in each question, and through the process of elimination, arrive at the correct classification. However, the heading 9004 does specifically provide for "...goggles...protective or other". This means that the solution to this question could have been derived based on utilizing either the Classification Heading OR the Chapter Notes. "C" is the correct answer.

Heading/ Subheading	Stat. Suf- fix	Article Description	Unit of Quantity	Rates of Duty		
				1		2
				General	Special	
9003		Frames and mountings for spectacles, goggles or the like, and parts thereof: Frames and mountings:				
9003.11.00	00	Of plastics............................	Doz.....	2.5%	Free (A,AU,BH,CA, CL,CO,E,IL,JO, KR,MA,MX,OM,P, PA,PE,SG)	50%
9003.19.00	00	Of other materials....................	Doz.....	Free		50%
9003.90.00	00	Parts................................	X.......	2.5%	Free (A,AU,BH, CA,CL,CO,E,IL, JO,KR,MA,MX, OM,P,PA,PE,SG)	50%
9004		Spectacles, goggles and the like, corrective, protective or other:				
9004.10.00	00	Sunglasses.............................	Doz.....	2%	Free (A,AU,BH,CA, CL,CO,E,IL,JO, KR,MA,MX,OM,P, PA,PE,SG)	40%
9004.90.00	00	Other..................................	Doz.....	2.5%	Free (A,AU,BH,CA, CL,CO,E,IL,JO, KR,MA,MX,OM,P, PA,PE,SG)	40%
9005		Binoculars, monoculars, other optical telescopes, and mountings therefor; other astronomical instruments and mountings therefor, but not including instruments for radio-astronomy; parts and accessories thereof:				
9005.10.00		Binoculars.............................		Free		60%
	20	Prism binoculars for use with infrared light.........	No.			
	40	Other prism binoculars......................	No.			
	80	Other................................	No.			
9005.80		Other instruments:				
9005.80.40		Optical telescopes......................		8% 1/	Free (A,AU,BH,CA, CL,CO,E,IL,JO, KR,MA,MX,OM,P, PA,PE,SG)	45%
	20	For use with infrared light.................	No.			
	40	Other................................	No.			
9005.80.60	00	Other................................	No......	6%	Free (A,AU,BH,CA, CL,CO,E,IL,JO, KR,MA,MX,OM,P, PA,PE,SG)	45%
9005.90		Parts and accessories (including mountings):				
9005.90.40	00	Incorporating goods of heading 9001 or 9002.	X........	The rate applicable to the article of which it is a part or accessory	Free (A,AU,BH,CA, CL,CO,E,IL,JO, KR,MA,MX,OM,P, PA,PE,SG)	The rate applicable to the article of which it is a part or accessory
9005.90.80	00	Other................................	X........	The rate applicable to the article of which it is a part or accessory 1/	Free (A,AU,BH,CA, CL,CO,E,IL,JO, KR,MA,MX,OM,P, PA,PE,SG)	The rate applicable to the article of which it is a part or accessory

38. Frozen veal bones with adhering meat are being imported. The bones are from the neck, vertebrae, atich, blade, brisket, knuckle tip and rib. The meat has been removed from the bones by hand. They are not further processed. After importation, they will be cooked in water to make veal broth and then discarded. What is the classification for the frozen veal bones?

A. 0201.20.5000   Meat of bovine animals, fresh or chilled>>Other cuts with bone in>>Described in additional U.S. note 3 to this chapter and entered pursuant to its provisions>>Other

B. 0202.20.3000   Meat of bovine animals, frozen>>Other cuts with bone in>>Described in additional U.S. note 3 to this chapter and entered pursuant to its provisions>>Processed>>Other

C. 0202.20.5000   Meat of bovine animals, frozen>>Other cuts with bone in>>Described in additional U.S. note 3 to this chapter and entered pursuant to its provisions>>Other

D. 0208.90.9100   Other meat and edible meat offal, fresh, chilled or frozen>>Other>>Other

E. 0506.90.0020   Bones and horn cores, unworked, defatted, simply prepared (but not cut to shape), treated with acid or degelatinized, powder and waste of these products>>Other>>Bones, crude, steamed or ground

 As per HTSUS Chapter 5 Note 1(a):

1. This chapter does not cover:

(a) Edible products (other than guts, bladders and stomachs of animals, whole and pieces thereof, and animal blood, liquid or dried);

Accordingly, multiple choice "E" may be eliminated as a possible answer, as the item is undoubtedly being processed into an edible product.

AND, as per HTSUS Chapter 2 Additional U.S. Note 1(a):

1. For the purposes of this chapter—

(a) The term "processed" covers meats which have been ground or comminuted, diced or cut into sizes for stew meat or similar uses, rolled and skewered, or specially processed into fancy cuts, special shapes, or otherwise made ready for particular uses by the retail consumer.

Accordingly, the classification article description for "C", is preferred to either "A" or "B" for this frozen and unprocessed commodity. "C" also more specifically describes the item than does "D". The correct answer is "C".

Note: References to "Described in additional U.S. note 3 to this chapter" refers to Chapter 2 quota quantity limits, and has no relevance to the question.

Heading/ Subheading	Stat. Suf- fix	Article Description	Unit of Quantity	Rates of Duty		
				1		2
				General	Special	
0202 (con.) 0202.20 (con.)		Meat of bovine animals, frozen (con.): Other cuts with bone in (con.):				
		Described in additional U.S. note 3 to this chapter and entered pursuant to its provisions: Processed:				
0202.20.10	00	High-quality beef cuts...................	kg.......	4%	Free (A+,AU,BH, CA,CL,CO,D,E*, IL,JO,MA,MX, OM,P,PA,PE,SG) 1.6% (KR)	20%
0202.20.30	00	Other................................	kg.......	10%	Free (A+,AU,BH, CA,CL,CO,D,E*, IL,JO,MA,MX, OM,P,PA,PE,SG) 4% (KR)	20%
0202.20.50	00	Other.	kg.......	4.4¢/kg	Free (A+,AU,BH, CA,CL,CO,D,E*, IL,JO,MA,MX, OM,P,PA,PE,SG) 1.7¢/kg (KR)	13.2¢/kg
0202.20.80	00	Other 1/............................	kg.......	26.4%	Free (CA,JO,MX, SG) 10.5% (P) 15.8% (PE) 21.1% (KR) See 9911.02.05- 9911.02.10 (CL) See 9912.02.05- 9912.02.10 (MA) See 9913.02.05- 9913.02.30 (AU) See 9914.02.05- 9914.02.10 (BH) See 9915.02.05- 9915.02.10 (P+) See 9916.02.05- 9916.02.10 (OM) See 9918.02.01- 9918.02.03 (CO) See 9919.02.01- 9919.02.02 (PA)	31.1%

39. A woven silk tie is composed of 80 percent silk and 20 percent polyester outer shell and 100 percent polyester lining. The tie, inclusive of the linings and interlining, is greater than 50 percent by weight of polyester. What is the classification of the woven silk tie?

A. 6215.10.0025   Ties, bow ties and cravats>>Of silk or silk waste>>Containing 50 percent or more by weight (including any linings and interlinings) of textile materials other than silk or silk waste

B. 6215.10.0040   Ties, bow ties and cravats>>Of silk or silk waste>>Containing less than 50 percent by weight (including any linings and interlinings) of textile materials other than silk or silk waste>>With outer shell containing 70 percent or more by weight of silk or silk waste

C. 6215.10.0090   Ties, bow ties and cravats>>Of silk or silk waste>>Containing less than 50 percent by weight (including any linings and interlinings) of textile materials other than silk or silk waste>>Other

D. 6215.20.0000   Ties, bow ties and cravats>>Of man-made fibers

E. 6217.10.1090   Other made up clothing accessories; parts of garments or of clothing accessories, other than those of heading 6212>>Accessories>>Containing 70 percent or more by weight of silk or silk waste>>Other

At a glance, it may appear that "D" is the most likely candidate as the correct answer, as the item is greater than 50% by weight of polyester. However, a closer look should be taken at "A", "B", and "C". "A" thru "C" are all under the Subheading of "Of silk or silk waste". Although the question's description of the item states that the tie is "(inclusive of linings and interlinings) greater than 50 percent by weight of polyester" (which would in most cases qualify a textile article as man-made), "A", "B", and "C" all have provisions written within their article descriptions that allow an item to be classified as "A", "B", or "C", even if silk comprises a minority of the total by weight. Accordingly, "A" accurately describes the item and is thus the correct answer.

Heading/ Subheading	Stat. Suffix	Article Description	Unit of Quantity	Rates of Duty		
				1		2
				General	Special	
6215		Ties, bow ties and cravats:				
6215.10.00		Of silk or silk waste..............................		7.2%	Free (BH,CA, CL,CO,E*,IL, JO,KR, MA,MX,OM,P, PA,PE,SG) 3% (AU)	65%
	25	Containing 50 percent or more by weight (including any linings and interlinings) of textile materials other than silk or silk waste (659)....................	doz. kg			
		Containing less than 50 percent by weight (including any linings and interlinings) of textile materials other than silk or silk waste:				
	40	With outer shell containing 70 percent or more by weight of silk or silk waste (758)...........	doz. kg			
	90	Other (858).	doz. kg			
6215.20.00	00	Of man-made fibers (659)........................	doz. kg	24.8¢/kg + 12.7%	Free (BH,CA, CL,CO,IL,JO,KR, MA,MX,OM, P,PA,PE,SG) 3% (AU)	26.5¢/kg + 65%
6215.90.00		Of other textile materials........................		5%	Free (BH,CA, CL,CO,E*,IL,JO, KR,MA,MX, P,PA,PE,SG) 2% (OM) 3% (AU)	52%
	10	Of wool or fine animal hair (459)................	doz. kg			
	15	Of cotton (359).	doz. kg			
	20	Other (858).	doz. kg			

40. What is the classification of a men's knit two button polo shirt composed of 100% cotton with 8 stitches per linear centimeter in each direction?

A. 6105.10   Men's or boys shirts, knitted or crocheted>>Of cotton

B. 6105.20   Men's or boys shirts, knitted or crocheted>>Of man-made fibers

C. 6105.90   Men's or boys shirts, knitted or crocheted>>Of other textile materials

D. 6110.20   Sweaters, pullovers, sweatshirts, waistcoats (vests) and similar articles, knitted or crocheted>>Of cotton

E. 6110.90   Sweaters, pullovers, sweatshirts, waistcoats (vests) and similar articles, knitted or crocheted>>Of other textile materials

 As per HTSUS Chapter 61 Note 4:

*4. **Headings 6105 and 6106 do not cover** garments with pockets below the waist, with a ribbed waistband or other means of tightening at the bottom of the garment, **or garments having an average of less than 10 stitches per linear centimeter in each direction** counted on an area measuring at least 10 centimeters by 10 centimeters. Heading 6105 does not cover sleeveless garments.*

First off, note that the question is not asking for the full 10 digit classification of the described item. Rather, for the sake of brevity, it is asking just for the correct HTSUS number up to the first 6 digits (this is not a typo). Without consulting the Chapter Notes, "A" appears to be the correct classification. However, this is another example of a trick question. Per the above-mentioned Chapter 61 Note 4, the men's polo shirt in question, which has 8 stitches per linear centimeter, cannot be classified in Heading 6105 because of stitch count restrictions, thus excluding "A", "B", and "C" from the realm of possible answers. And, "D" is a more appropriate answer than is "E" being that the shirt is 100% cotton. The correct answer is "D".

Heading/ Subheading	Stat. Suf- fix	Article Description	Unit of Quantity	Rates of Duty		
				1		2
				General	Special	
6110 (con.)		Sweaters, pullovers, sweatshirts, waistcoats (vests) and similar articles, knitted or crocheted (con.): Of wool or fine animal hair (con.):				
6110.19.00		Other............................	....	16%	Free (BH,CA, CL,CO,IL,JO,KR, MA,MX,OM,P, PA,PE,SG) 8% (AU)	54.5%
		Sweaters:				
	15	Men's (445).........................	doz. kg			
	25	Boys' (445).........................	doz. kg			
	30	Women's (446).......................	doz. kg			
	40	Girls' (446)........................	doz. kg			
		Vests. other than sweater vests:				
	50	Men's or boys' (459).................	doz. kg			
	60	Women's or girls' (459)..............	doz. kg			
		Other:				
	70	Men's or boys' (438).................	doz. kg			
	80	Women's or girls' (438)..............	doz. kg			
6110.20		Of cotton:				
6110.20.10		Containing 36 percent or more by weight of flax fibers................................	....	5%	Free (BH,CA, CL,CO,IL,JO,KR, MA,MX,OM,P, PA,PE,SG) 4.5% (AU)	45%
		Sweaters:				
	10	Men's or boys' (345)..................	doz. kg			
	20	Women's or girls' (345)...............	doz. kg			
		Vests other than sweater vests:				
	22	Men's or boys' (359)..................	doz. kg			
	24	Women's or girls' (359)...............	doz. kg			
		Other: Men's or boys':				
	26	Knit to shape articles described in statistical note 6 to this chapter (338)....	doz. kg			
	29	Other (338).....................	doz. kg			
		Women's or girls':				
	31	Knit to shape articles described in statistical note 6 to this chapter (339)....	doz. kg			
	33	Other (339).....................	doz. kg			

41. Artic Ships Inc. intends to import a woman's knit cardigan with decorative beads and embroidery into the United States from Hong Kong. The cardigan consists of 73% polyester, 25% rayon, and 2% spandex. The outer surface of the garment measures more than 9 stitches per 2 centimeters in the direction in which the stitches were formed. The garment also features a rounded front neckline, straight hemmed bottom, and extends below the waist. What is the classification of this garment?

A. 6110.20.2079   Sweaters, pullovers, sweatshirts, waistcoats (vests) and similar articles, knitted or crocheted>>Of cotton>>Other>>Other>>Other>>Other

B. 6110.30.1020   Sweaters, pullovers, sweatshirts, waistcoats (vests) and similar articles, knitted or crocheted>>Of man-made fibers>>Containing 25 percent or more by weight of leather>>Sweaters>>Women's or girls'

C. 6110.30.3020   Sweaters, pullovers, sweatshirts, waistcoats (vests) and similar articles, knitted or crocheted>>Of man-made fibers>>Other>>Other>>Other>>Other>>Sweaters>>Women's

D. 6110.30.3059   Sweaters, pullovers, sweatshirts, waistcoats (vests) and similar articles, knitted or crocheted>>Of man-made fibers>>Other>>Other>>Other>>Other>>Other>>Women's or girls'>>Other

E. 6110.90.9022   Sweaters, pullovers, sweatshirts, waistcoats (vests) and similar articles, knitted or crocheted>>Of other textile materials>>Other>>Sweaters for men or boys>>Other>>Other>>Assembled in Hong Kong from knit-to-shape component parts knitted elsewhere

 As per HTSUS Chapter 61 Statistical Note 3:

*3. For purposes of this chapter, statistical provisions for **sweaters include garments, whether or not known as pullovers, vests or cardigans, the outer surfaces of which are constructed essentially with 9 or fewer stitches per 2 centimeters measured in the direction the stitches were formed**, and garments, known as sweaters, where, due to their construction, the stitches on the outer surface cannot be counted in the direction the stitches were formed.*

Based on the question's item description and the five classifications' article descriptions, both "C" and "D" stand out as likely answers. The key question behind the question is "does the item, which is described in the narrative of the question as a 'cardigan', meet the Customs' definition of a 'sweater' or not?" As per the above-mentioned Statistical Note, regardless of whether a person considers a cardigan to be a sweater or not, if the outer surface is constructed with more than 9 stitches per 2 cm, then the article cannot be classified as a "sweater". Accordingly, the answer cannot be "C". The correct answer is "D".

Heading/ Subheading	Stat. Suffix	Article Description	Unit of Quantity	Rates of Duty		
				1		2
				General	Special	
6110 (con.)		Sweaters, pullovers, sweatshirts, waistcoats (vests) and similar articles, knitted or crocheted (con.):				
6110.30 (con.)		Of man-made fibers (con.):				
		Other (con.):				
		Other (con.):				
6110.30.30		Other..		32%	Free (BH,CA, CL,CO,IL,JO,KR, MA,MX,OM,P, PA,PE,SG) 8% (AU)	90%
	05	Boys' and girls' garments imported as parts of playsuits (237).	doz. kg			
		Other:				
		Sweaters:				
	10	Men's (645).	doz. kg			
	15	Boys' (645).	doz. kg			
	20	Women's (646).	doz. kg			
	25	Girls' (646).	doz. kg			
		Vests, other than sweater vests:				
	30	Men's or boys' (659).	doz. kg			
	35	Women's or girls' (659).	doz. kg			
		Sweatshirts:				
	40	Men's or boys' (638).	doz. kg			
	45	Women's or girls' (639).	doz. kg			
		Other:				
		Men's or boys':				
	51	Knit to shape articles described in statistical note 6 to this chapter (638). .	doz. kg			
	53	Other (638).	doz. kg			
		Women's or girls':				
	57	Knit to shape articles described in statistical note 6 to this chapter (639).	doz. kg			
	59	Other (639).	doz. kg			

128

42. What is the classification of Italian glazed ceramic tiles each covering 2855 tiles per square meter?

A. 6802.10.0000   Worked monumental or building stone (except slate) and articles thereof, other than goods of heading 6801; mosaic cubes and the like, of natural stone (including slate), whether or not on a backing; artificially colored granules, chippings and powder, of natural stone (including slate)>>Tiles, cubes and similar articles, whether or not rectangular (including square), the largest surface area of which is capable of being enclosed in a square the side of which is less than 7 cm; artificially colored granules, chippings and powder

B. 6810.19.5000   Articles of cement, of concrete or of artificial stone, whether or not reinforced>>Tiles, flagstones, bricks and similar articles>>Other>>Other

C. 6905.10.0000   Roofing tiles, chimney pots, cowls, chimney liners, architectural ornaments and other ceramic constructional goods>>Roofing tiles

D. 6907.10.0000   Unglazed ceramic flags and paving, hearth or wall tiles; unglazed ceramic mosaic cubes and the like, whether or not on a backing>>Tiles, cubes and similar articles, whether or not rectangular, the largest surface area of which is capable of being enclosed in a square the side of which is less than 7 cm

E. 6908.10.1000   Glazed ceramic flags and paving, hearth or wall tiles; glazed ceramic mosaic cubes and the like, whether or not on a backing>>Tiles, cubes and similar articles, whether or not rectangular, the largest surface area of which is capable of being enclosed in a square the side of which is less than 7 cm>>Having not over 3229 tiles per square meter, most of which have faces bounded entirely by straight lines

Here we have one of the more straight-forward exam questions and solutions. The classification for "E" correctly describes the item, no Section Notes or Chapter Notes state otherwise, and thus "E" is the correct answer.

Heading/ Subheading	Stat. Suffix	Article Description	Unit of Quantity	Rates of Duty 1 General	Rates of Duty 1 Special	Rates of Duty 2
6908		Glazed ceramic flags and paving, hearth or wall tiles; glazed ceramic mosaic cubes and the like, whether or not on a backing:				
6908.10		Tiles, cubes and similar articles, whether or not rectangular, the largest surface area of which is capable of being enclosed in a square the side of which is less than 7 cm:				
6908.10.10	00	Having not over 3229 tiles per square meter, most of which have faces bounded entirely by straight lines........................	m²	10%	Free (AU,CA,CL, CO,D,E,IL,JO, MA,MX,P,PA, PE,SG) 1.1% (BH) 4% (OM) 8.3% (KR)	55%
		Other:				
6908.10.20	00	The largest surface area of which is less than 38.7 cm²........................	m²	10%	Free (A*,AU,BH, CA,CL,CO,E,IL, JO,MA,MX,OM, P,PA,PE,SG) 8.3% (KR)	55%
6908.10.50	00	Other........................	m²	8.5%	Free (AU,CA,CL, CO,D,E,IL,JO, MA,MX,P,PA, PE,SG) 0.9% (BH) 3.4% (OM) 7% (KR)	55%
6908.90.00		Other........................		8.5%	Free (AU,CA,CL, CO,D,E,IL,JO, MA,MX,P,PA, PE,SG) 0.9% (BH) 3.4% (OM) 7% (KR)	55%
	11	Tiles, the largest surface area of which is capable of being enclosed in a square the side of which is 30 cm or less........................	m²			
	51	Other........................	m²			

43. Your client is importing "Super flowGro," a product described as a natural fertilizer manufactured in the Dominican Republic, exclusively from plant matter. This fertilizer is intended to be used to grow flowers. "Super flowGro" is imported in tablet form, in twelve kilogram, retail-ready packages. What is the tariff classification for this product?

A. 3101.00.0000   Animal or vegetable fertilizers, whether or not mixed together or chemically treated; fertilizers produced by the mixing or chemical treatment of animal or vegetable products

B. 3105.10.0000   Mineral or chemical fertilizers containing two or three of the fertilizing elements nitrogen, phosphorous and potassium; other fertilizers; goods of this chapter in tablets or similar forms on in packages of a gross weight not exceeding 10 kg: >>Products of this chapter in tablets or similar forms or in packages of a gross weight not exceeding 10 kg

C. 3105.20.0000   Mineral or chemical fertilizers containing two or three of the fertilizing elements nitrogen, phosphorous and potassium; other fertilizers; goods of this chapter in tablets or similar forms on in packages of a gross weight not exceeding 10 kg: >>Mineral or chemical fertilizers containing the three fertilizing elements nitrogen, phosphorous and potassium

D. 3105.90.0050   Mineral or chemical fertilizers containing two or three of the fertilizing elements nitrogen, phosphorous and potassium; other fertilizers; goods of this chapter in tablets or similar forms or in packages of a gross weight not exceeding 10 kg: >>Other>>Other

E. 3824.90.9290   Prepared binders for foundry molds or cores; chemical products and preparations of the chemical or allied industries…>>Other>>Other>>Other>>Other>>Other>>Other

On the surface it appears that "A" is the obvious answer, as this classification's article description references "vegetable fertilizer". However, the item in question is manufactured exclusively "from plant matter", which is not necessarily the equivalent of "vegetable" fertilizer. Therefore, "B", which includes "; other fertilizers" in its heading, as well as a qualifying description of products "in tablets … OR" in its subheading is the most appropriate answer to the question.

Heading/ Subheading	Stat. Suf- fix	Article Description	Unit of Quantity	Rates of Duty		
				1		**2**
				General	Special	
3105		Mineral or chemical fertilizers containing two or three of the fertilizing elements nitrogen, phosphorus and potassium; other fertilizers: goods of this chapter in tablets or similar forms or in packages of a gross weight not exceeding 10 kg:				
3105.10.00	00	Products of this chapter in tablets or similar forms or in packages of a gross weight not exceeding 10 kg	kg	Free		Free
3105.20.00	00	Mineral or chemical fertilizers containing the three fertilizing elements nitrogen, phosphorus and potassium	t	Free		Free
3105.30.00	00	Diammonium hydrogenorthophosphate (Diammonium phosphate)	t	Free		Free
3105.40.00		Ammonium dihydrogenorthophosphate (Mono-ammonium phosphate) and mixtures thereof with diammonium hydrogenorthophosphate (Diammonium phosphate)		Free		Free
	10	Ammonium dihydrogenorthophosphate (Monoammonium phosphate)	t			
	50	Other . . . . Other mineral or chemical fertilizers containing the two fertilizing elements nitrogen and phosphorus:	t			
3105.51.00	00	Containing nitrates and phosphates	t	Free 1/		Free
3105.59.00	00	Other	t	Free		Free
3105.60.00	00	Mineral or chemical fertilizers containing the two fertilizing elements phosphorus and potassium	t	Free		Free
3105.90.00		Other		Free		Free
	10	Potassium nitrate-sodium nitrate mixtures	t			
	50	Other	t			

44. What is the classification of a handbag with an outer surface of 1cm-wide, interwoven palm leaf strips?

A. 4202.22.6000   Trunks, suitcases, ... ; ... handbags, ... and similar containers, of leather or of composition leather, of sheeting of plastics, of textile materials, of vulcanized fiber or of paperboard, or wholly or mainly covered with such materials or with paper

B. 4601.29.6000   Plaits and similar products of plaiting materials, whether or not assembled in strips; plaiting materials, plaits and similar products of plaiting materials, bound together in parallel strands or woven, in sheet form, whether or not being finished articles (for example, mats, matting, screens)>>Mats, matting and screens of vegetable materials>>Other>>Woven or partly assembled>>Other

C. 4602.12.2500   Basketwork, wickerwork and other articles, made directly to shape from plaiting materials or made up from articles of heading 4601; articles of loofah>>Of vegetable materials>>Of rattan>>Luggage, handbags and flatgoods, whether or not lined>>Other

D. 4602.19.1600   Basketwork, wickerwork and other articles, made directly to shape from plaiting materials or made up from articles of heading 4601; articles of loofah>>Of vegetable materials>>Other>>Other baskets and bags, whether or not lined>>Of palm leaf>>Other

E. 4602.19.2500   Basketwork, wickerwork and other articles, made directly to shape from plaiting materials or made up from articles of heading 4601; articles of loofah>>Of vegetable materials>>Other>>Luggage, handbags and flatgoods, whether or not lined>>Of palm leaf>>Other

 As per HTSUS Chapter 42 Note 3(A)(b):

*(A) In addition to the provisions of note 2, above, **heading 4202 does not cover**: (a) Bags made of sheeting of plastics, whether or not printed, with handles, not designed for prolonged use (heading 3923); (b) **Articles of plaiting materials (heading 4602)**.*

As per HTSUS Chapter 46 Note 1:

*1. In this chapter the expression **"plaiting materials" means materials in a state or form suitable for plaiting, interlacing or similar processes; it includes** straw, osier or willow, bamboos, rattans, rushes, reeds, strips of wood, **strips of other vegetable material (for example, strips of bark, narrow leaves** and raffia or other strips obtained from broad leaves), unspun natural textile fibers, monofilament and strip and the like of plastics and strips of paper, but not strips of leather or composition leather or of felt or nonwovens, human hair, horsehair, textile rovings or yarns, or monofilament and strip and the like of chapter 54.*

As per Chapter 42 Note 3(A)(b), multiple choice "A" may be excluded, as Chapter 42 does not include articles of plaiting materials. "B" may be eliminated as the item in question is neither matting nor screen. "C" may be excluded as the item in question is not "of rattan". "E" (which includes "handbags") provides a more specific description of the item in question than does "D" (which includes generically "other baskets and bags"), and so "E" is thus the correct answer.

Note: The common definition for "Rattan" is "a species of palm, the stems of which are often used in wickerwork".

Heading/ Subheading	Stat. Suf-fix	Article Description	Unit of Quantity	Rates of Duty 1 General	Rates of Duty 1 Special	2
4602 (con.)		Basketwork, wickerwork and other articles, made directly to shape from plaiting materials or made up from articles of heading 4601; articles of loofah (con.):				
4602.19 (con.)		Of vegetable materials (con.): Other (con.):				
		Luggage, handbags and flatgoods, whether or not lined:				
4602.19.22	00	Of willow...............................	No......	5.8%	Free (AU,BH,CA, CL,CO,D,IL, JO,KR,MA,MX, OM,P,PA,PE,R, SG) 4.6% (E)	50%
		Of palm leaf:				
4602.19.23	00	Articles of a kind normally carried in the pocket or in the handbag............	No......	9%	Free (A,AU,BH,CA, CL,CO,E,IL,JO, KR,MA,MX,OM,P, PA,PE,SG)	50%
4602.19.25	00	Other............................	No......	18%	Free (AU,BH,CA, CL,CO,D,IL, JO,MA,MX,OM,P, PA,PE,R,SG) 12.6% (KR) 15.5% (E)	50%
4602.19.29		Other...........................	....	5.3%	Free (AU,BH,CA, CL,CO,D,IL, JO,KR,MA,MX, OM,P,PA,PE,R, SG) 4.2% (E)	50%
	20	Handbags.......................	No.			
	40	Other...........................	No.			
		Other: Of willow or wood:				
4602.19.35	00	Wickerwork...................	No......	Free		45%
4602.19.45	00	Other.........................	No......	6.6%	Free (A,AU,BH,CA, CL,CO,E,IL,JO, KR,MA,MX,OM, P,PA,PE,SG)	45%
		Other:				
4602.19.60	00	Wickerwork...................	X.......	Free		25%
4602.19.80	00	Other.........................	X.......	2.3%	Free (A,AU,BH,CA, CL,CO,E,IL,JO, KR,MA,MX,OM, P,PA,PE,SG)	25%
4602.90.00	00	Other..............................	X.......	3.5%	Free (A,AU,BH,CA, CL,CO,E,IL,JO, KR,MA,MX,OM,P, PA,PE,SG)	80%

45. A men's lightweight upper body garment is cut and sewn from 45% cotton, 35% polyester, 20% linen, pique knitted fabric. The fabric measures 12 stitches per linear centimeter counted in the horizontal direction and 14 stitches per linear centimeter counted in the vertical direction. The garment is designed for wear over the skin or underwear and has a rib knit spread collar. It has a partial front opening at the neck with a three button placket, short sleeves with rib knit cuffs, and a ribbed knit waistband. What is the classification of this garment?

A. 6105.10.0010   Men's or boys' shirts, knitted or crocheted>>Of cotton>>Men's

B. 6106.10.0010   Women's or girls' blouses and shirts, knitted or crocheted>>Of cotton>>Women's

C. 6109.10.0004   T-shirts, singlets, tank tops and similar garments, knitted or crocheted>>Of cotton>>Men's or boys'>>T-shirts, all white, short hemmed sleeves, hemmed bottom, crew or round neckline, or V-neck with a mitered seam at the center of the V, without pockets, trim or embroidery

D. 6110.20.2067   Sweaters, pullovers, sweatshirts, waistcoats (vests) and similar articles, knitted or crocheted>>Of cotton>>Other>>Other>>Other>>Men's or boys'>>Knit to shape articles described in statistical note 6 to this chapter

E. 6110.20.2069   Sweaters, pullovers, sweatshirts, waistcoats (vests) and similar articles, knitted or crocheted>>Of cotton>>Other>>Other>>Other>>Men's or boys'>>Other

 As per HTSUS Chapter 61 Note 4 & Note 5:

*4. **Headings 6105 and 6106 do not cover garments with** pockets below the waist, with a **ribbed waistband** or other means of tightening at the bottom of the garment, or garments having an average of less than 10 stitches per linear centimeter in each direction counted on an area measuring at least 10 centimeters by 10 centimeters. Heading 6105 does not cover sleeveless garments.*

*5. **Heading 6109 does not cover garments with** a drawstring, **ribbed waistband** or other means of tightening at the bottom of the garment.*

As per HTSUS Chapter 61 Statistical Note 6:

*6. For the purposes of statistical reporting **under heading 6110, the term "knit to shape" means garments knit to shape on flat-knitting machines, having a stitch count exceeding 9 stitches per 2 centimeters, but less than or equal to 18 stitches per 2 centimeters, measured on the outer surfaces of the fabric, in the direction on which the stitches are formed.** ...*

As per Chapter 61 Note 4 and Note 5, multiple choices "A", "B", and "C" may all be eliminated. Now, whether the answer is "D" or "E" depends on if the item in question is considered "knit to shape" (as defined by Customs) or not. That's easy enough, because, measured in either direction (horizontal or vertical), the item in question has 24 (12 x 2) and 28 (14 x 2) stitches per 2 cm, which exceeds Customs' limit for an item to qualify as "knit to shape" of 18 stitches per 2 cm. "E" is the correct answer.

Note: "Pique Knitted" is a method of knitting characterized by a fine-textured surface, and sometimes called mesh. "Placket" is an opening at the upper part of a garment.

Heading/ Subheading	Stat. Suf- fix	Article Description	Unit of Quantity	Rates of Duty		
				1		2
				General	Special	
6110		Sweaters, pullovers, sweatshirts, waistcoats (vests) and similar articles, knitted or crocheted (con.):				
6110.20 (con.)		Of cotton (con.):				
6110.20.20		Other....................................		16.5%	Free (BH,CA, CL,CO,IL,JO, MA,MX,OM,P, PA,PE,SG) 8% (AU) 11.5% (KR)	50%
	05	Boys' or girls' garments imported as parts of playsuits (237)........................	doz. kg			
		Other:				
		Sweaters:				
	10	Men's (345).....................	doz. kg			
	15	Boys' (345).....................	doz. kg			
	20	Women's (345).................	doz. kg			
	25	Girls' (345).....................	doz. kg			
		Vests, other than sweater vests:				
	30	Men's or boys' (359)...............	doz. kg			
	35	Women's or girls' (359).............	doz. kg			
		Sweatshirts:				
	40	Men's or boys' (338)...............	doz. kg			
	45	Women's or girls' (339).............	doz. kg			
		Other:				
		Men's or boys':				
	67	Knit to shape articles described in statistical note 6 to this chapter (338)........................	doz. kg			
	69	Other (338)...................	doz. kg			
		Women's or girls':				
	77	Knit to shape articles described in statistical note 6 to this chapter (339)........................	doz. kg			
	79	Other (339)...................	doz. kg			

Section VII: Valuation
46. Which of the following is not an assist, and should not be included in entered value?

A. Artwork created by a company in England
B. Molds supplied free of charge by the importer to a Vietnamese manufacturer
C. Design work created by the US importer domestically and supplied free of charge to the manufacturer
D. Component parts supplied free of charge by the US importer
E. Engineering performed by a Chinese engineering firm

 As per 19 CFR 152.102(a)(1)(iv):

(a) Assist. (1) "Assist" means any of the following if supplied directly or indirectly, and free of charge or at reduced cost, by the buyer of imported merchandise for use in connection with the production or the sale for export to the United States of the merchandise:

(i) Materials, components, parts, and similar items incorporated in the imported merchandise.

(ii) Tools, dies, molds, and similar items used in the production of the imported merchandise.

(iii) Merchandise consumed in the production of the imported merchandise.

*(iv) Engineering, development, artwork, **design work**, and plans and sketches that are **undertaken elsewhere than in the United States** and are necessary for the production of the imported merchandise.*

Services such as engineering, design work, etc. may not qualify as an assist nor increase the value of the shipment if the service was of U.S. origin. "C" is the correct answer.

47. The Transaction Value of imported merchandise is the price actually paid or payable for the merchandise when sold for exportation to the United States. The Transaction Value can include which of the following additions.

A. Packing, Selling Commissions, Assists, Royalties, Proceeds, and Discounts.
B. Selling Commissions, Royalties, and Copy Rights and Trade Mark fees.
C. Packing, Selling Commissions, Assist, Royalties, and Proceeds.
D. Only Selling Commissions, International Freight, and Insurance.
E. Antidumping and Countervailing Duty.

 As per 19 CFR 152.103(b)(1):

(b) Additions to price actually paid or payable. (1) The transaction value of imported merchandise is the price actually paid or payable for the merchandise when sold for exportation to the United States, plus amounts equal to:

(i) The packing costs incurred by the buyer with respect to the imported merchandise;

(ii) Any selling commission incurred by the buyer with respect to the imported merchandise;

(iii) The value, apportioned as appropriate, of any assist;

(iv) Any royalty or license fee related to the imported merchandise that the buyer is required to pay, directly or indirectly, as a condition of the sale of the imported merchandise for exportation to the United States; and

(v) The proceeds of any subsequent resale, disposal, or use of the imported merchandise that accrue, directly or indirectly, to the seller.

An acronym to "assist" the customs broker in remembering the five types of additions to the price actually paid or payable is "CRAPP". C-ommissions (selling), R-oyalties, A-ssists, P-acking, P-roceeds (of subsequent disposition). The correct answer is "C".

48. After liquidation, the importer has _____ days to request a written explanation of how the value of the imported merchandise was determined?

A. 20
B. 30
C. 90
D. 180
E. 360

 As per 19 CFR 152.101(d):

(d) Explanation to importer. **Upon receipt of a written request from the importer within 90 days after liquidation, the port director shall provide a reasonable and concise written explanation of how the value of the imported merchandise was determined.** *The explanation will apply only to the imported merchandise being appraised and will not serve as authority with respect to the valuation of importations of any other merchandise at the same or a different port of entry. This procedure is for informational purposes only, and will not affect or replace the protest or administrative ruling procedures contained in parts 174 and 177, respectively, of this chapter, or any other Customs procedures. ...*

"C" is the correct answer.

49. According to 19 CFR 141.89, "additional information for certain classes of merchandise," what is the requirement for classifiable items of iron or steel classifiable in Chapter 72 or headings 7301 to 7307?

A. A statement of the weight of articles of copper, and a statement of percentage of copper content and all other elements, by weight, to articles classifiable according to copper content.

B. Statement specifying the kind of machine for which the parts are intended, or if this is not known to the shipper, the kinds of machines for which the parts are suitable.

C. Statement of the percentages by weight of carbon and any metallic elements contained in the articles, in the form of a mill analysis or mill test certificate.

D. Furnish the use and Chemical Abstracts Service number of chemical compounds.

E. A statement of the method of preparation of the oxide, together with the patent number, if any.

 As per 19 CFR 141.89:

Iron or steel classifiable in Chapter 72 or headings 7301 to 7307, HTSUS (T.D. 53092, 55977)—Statement of the percentages by weight or carbon and any metallic elements contained in the articles, in the form of a mill analysis or mill test certificate.

"C" is the correct answer.

50. When considering test values in a related party transaction, which of the following choices does the appraising officer have?

        1. Previously established Customs values
        2. Goods produced in the same country as the merchandise under appraisement
        3. Goods exported from the same country as the merchandise under appraisement.
        4. Goods exported at or about the same time as the merchandise under appraisement

A.   (1), (2), and (3)
B.   (2), (3), and (4)
C.   (1), (3), and (4)
D.   (1), (2), and (4)
E.   (1) and (2)

 As per 19 CFR 152.107(b):

*(b) Identical merchandise or similar merchandise. **The requirement that identical merchandise, or similar merchandise, should be exported at or about the same time of exportation as the merchandise being appraised may be interpreted flexibly.** Identical merchandise, or similar merchandise, produced in any country other than the country of exportation or production of the merchandise being appraised may be the basis for customs valuation. **Customs values of identical merchandise, or similar merchandise, already determined on the basis of deductive value or computed value may be used.***

AND as per 19 CFR 152.102(d) and 152.102(i):

*(d) **Identical merchandise. "Identical merchandise" means merchandise identical in all respects to, and produced in the same country and by the same person as, the merchandise being appraised.** If identical merchandise cannot be found (or for purposes of related buyer and seller transactions (see §152.103 (j)(2)(i)(A)) regardless of whether identical merchandise can be found), merchandise identical in all respects to, and produced in the same country as, but not produced by the same person as, the merchandise being appraised, may be treated as "identical merchandise". ...*

*(i) Similar **merchandise. "Similar merchandise" means merchandise produced in the same country and by the same person as the merchandise being appraised**, like the merchandise being appraised in characteristics and component material, and commercially interchangeable with the merchandise being appraised. If similar merchandise cannot be found (or for purposes of related buyer and seller transactions (see §152.103 (j)(2)(i)(A)) regardless of whether similar merchandise can be found), merchandise produced in the same country as, but not produced by the same person as, the merchandise being appraised, like the merchandise being appraised in characteristics and component material, and commercially interchangeable with the merchandise being appraised, may be treated as "similar merchandise". ...*

Per above regulations, "D" is the correct answer.

51. An importer is entering $50,000 worth of gold jewelry which had previously been imported from Thailand and then exported for repairs under warranty. The broker classifies the repaired jewelry in subheading 9802.00.4040 of the HTSUS with a secondary classification of subheading 7113.19.5085 of the HTSUS.

Which one of the following statements is TRUE regarding the duty due?

A.   The importer owes 5.5% duty on the value of the repairs.

B.   The importer owes 5.5% duty on the total value of the jewelry, $50,000.

C.   The importer owes no duty since the importer was not charged for the repairs under warranty.

D.   The importer owes duty on the total value of the jewelry minus the value of the repairs.

E.   The importer owes no duty because the goods qualify for duty free treatment under the GSP trade agreement.

 As per HTSUS Chapter 98 Classification 9802.00.4040:

Heading/ Subheading	Stat. Suf- fix	Article Description	Unit of Quantity	Rates of Duty	
				1	
				General	Special
9802.00.40		Articles returned to the United States after having been exported to be advanced in value or improved in condition by any process of manufacture or other means: Articles exported for repairs or alterations: Repairs or alterations made pursuant to a warranty.		A duty upon the value of the repairs or alterations (see U.S. note 3 of this subchapter)	Free (AU,B,BH,C, CA,CL,CO,IL,JO, KR,MA,MX,OM, P,PA,PE,SG)
	20 1/	Internal combustion engines.	1/		
	40	Other.	1/		

AND as per HTSUS Chapter 98 Subchapter II U.S. Note 3:

3. Articles repaired, altered, processed or otherwise changed in condition abroad.--The following provisions apply only to subheadings 9802.00.40 through 9802.00.60, inclusive:
*(a) The value of repairs, alterations, processing or other change in condition outside the United States shall be: (i) The cost to the importer of such change; or (ii) **If no charge is made, the value of such change,** as set out in the invoice and entry papers; except that, if the appraiser concludes that the amount so set out does not represent a reasonable cost or value, then the value of the change shall be determined in accordance with section 402 of the Tariff Act of 1930, as amended.*

AND as per HTSUS Chapter 73 Classification 7113.19.5085:

Heading/ Subheading	Stat. Suf- fix	Article Description	Unit of Quantity	Rates of Duty General	Rates of Duty Special
7113.19.50		Other......................................	....	5.5%	Free (A*,AU,BH, CA,CL,CO,E,IL, JO,KR,MA,MX, OM,P,PA,PE,SG)
	15	Containing jadeite or rubies...........	X		
		Other:			
		Of ISO standard platinum:			
	22	Necklaces and neck chains.....	pcs 1/		
	24	Rings....................	pcs 1/		
	28	Earrings..................	pcs 1/		
	40	Other....................	pcs 1/		
	85	Other.......................	X		

First, we'll take a look at what the HTSUS rate of duty is for the primary HTSUS classification 9802.00.4040. Although Thailand is in fact a Generalized System of Preferences (GSP) beneficiary country, the "Special" (Reduced) Rate of Duty Column does not apply as the letter "A", the Special Program Indicator (SPI) Symbol for GSP, is absent from this column for this classification. Subsequently, we take a look at the "General" Rate of Duty Column, which states that the duty rate is "A duty upon the value of the repairs or alterations". Note that even though the repairs were under warranty and free of charge, the value of the charge shall be assessed per above-mentioned Ch. 98 Note.

For the secondary HTS 7113.19.5085, let's start by looking at the "Special" Rates of Duty Column for this classification. This column contains an "A*", which is indicative of GSP. However, what is the asterisk (*) that appears after the "A"? As per HTSUS General Note (GN) 4, "the symbol "A*" indicates that for certain HTS headings and subheadings, certain beneficiary developing countries, specifically enumerated in subdivision (d) of this note, are not eligible for such preferential treatment". This subdivision (d) of GN 4 lists the subject classification and Thailand as one of the ineligible countries as per below...

7113.19.50   India;
                Thailand;
                Turkey

Thus after this long and laborious process we come to the conclusion that the importer here owes 5.5%, the general rate of duty, on whatever the value of the repairs may be. Multiple choice "A" is the correct answer.

Note: The actual exam uses HTSUS 7113.19.5000 as the secondary classification. This HTS number, however, does not appear in the recent editions of the HTSUS, so the author of this book took the liberty of replacing this entry with HTS number 7113.19.5085 for the sake of this exercise.

52. Which of the following is the transaction value of a shipment of lithium-ion batteries with the following details?

       1. Invoice value of $100,000
       2. Terms of sales CIF duty paid, merchandise processing fee (MPF) included
       3. Air freight of $3,000 and insurance of $100 included in the invoice value of $100,000
       4. The actual duty rate is 3.4%
       5. The actual MPF rate is 0.3464%

A. $93,270
B. $93,401
C. $93,605
D. $96,254
E. $96,900

 As per 19 CFR 152.103(a):

(a) Price actually paid or payable—(1) General. In determining transaction value, the price actually paid or payable will be considered without regard to its method of derivation. It may be the result of discounts, increases, or negotiations, or may be arrived at by the application of a formula, such as the price in effect on the date of export in the London Commodity Market. The word "payable" refers to a situation in which the price has been agreed upon, but actual payment has not been made at the time of importation. Payment may be made by letters of credit or negotiable instruments and may be made directly or indirectly.

... ...

Example 4. Company X in the United States pays $2,000 to Y Toy Factory abroad for a shipment of toys. The $2,000 consists of $1,850 for the toys and $150 for ocean freight and insurance. Y Toy Factory would have charged Company X $2,200 for the toys; however, because Y owed Company X $350, Y charged only $1,850 for the toys. What is the transaction value?

The transaction value of the imported merchandise is $2,200, that is, the sum of the $1,850 plus the $350 indirect payment. Because the transaction value excludes C.I.F. charges, the $150 ocean freight and insurance charge is excluded.

First off, let's deduct the Insurance and Freight from the invoice value since the terms are "CIF".

$100,000 (invoice value)
-   $3,000 (freight)
-     $100 (insurance)

= $96,900

Now, to back out the duty and MPF for this DDP (Delivered Duty Paid) shipment divide this amount by the duty factor of 1.037464 (1 + duty rate of 0.034 + MPF 0.003464)

$96,900 ÷ 1.037464 = $93,400.83

Finally, round this figure up to $93,401 for the "entered value". "B" is the correct answer.

Note: The author is unaware where the procedure of "the backing out of duties" is officially referenced in the exam reference material (HTSUS, 19 CFR, etc.). It may not be. However, they regularly include this type of question on the exam, nonetheless.

53. A U.S. importer contracts the services of a foreign company that works with aluminum to manufacture 300 aluminum windows at $40.00 per window. The manufacturer contacts the U.S. importer and asks him for some special tools to cut the aluminum profiles. The importer agrees to send $500.00 worth of tools to the manufacturer through an air carrier. The carrier charges the U.S. importer $300.00. The importer tells the manufacturer to repay him the $300.00 dollars for the carrier charges. A month later the U.S. importer receives the 300, cut and assembled, windows accompanied by an invoice for $12,000.00 dollars.

What is the transaction value?

A. $11,200
B. $11,800
C. $12,000
D. $12,200
E. $12,800

 As per 19 CFR 152.103(d)(2):

*(2) If the assist consists of tools, dies, molds, or similar items used in the production of the imported merchandise, acquired by the buyer from an unrelated seller, the value of the assist is the cost of its acquisition. If the assist were produced by the buyer or a person related to the buyer, its value would be cost of its production. If the assist has been used previously by the buyer, regardless of whether it had been acquired or produced by him, the original cost of acquisition or production would be adjusted downward to reflect its use before its value could be determined. If the assist were leased by the buyer from an unrelated seller, the value of the assist would be the cost of the lease. **In either case, the value of the assist would include transportation costs to the place of production.** Repairs or modifications to an assist may increase its value.*

Regardless of the value on the commercial invoice or invoice from the foreign manufacturer, the transaction value should include the value of any assist, including the transportation costs associated with providing the assist.

$12,000.00 (value of goods)
+   500.00 (value of tools/assist)
+   300.00 (assist transport cost)
= $12,800.00

"E" is the correct answer.

54. A shipment of 860 dozen scissors, manufactured in China, is invoiced at $74.77 per dozen CIF San Juan. The invoice shows an estimate of marine insurance at $0.03 per unit and an estimate of ocean freight at $6200. The bill of lading shows the actual ocean freight to be $4,750. The insurance bill provided shows a rate of $0.005 per unit. What is the transaction value for the shipment?

A. $57,792
B. $59,501
C. $62,852
D. $64,302
E. $115,584

 As per 19 CFR 152.105(d)(2):

(d) Deductions from price. The price determined under paragraph (c) of this section will be reduced by an amount equal to:

... ...

*(2) **The actual costs and associated costs of transportation and insurance** incurred with respect to international shipments of the merchandise concerned from the country of exportation to the United States;*

Regardless of the estimates for freight and insurance on the commercial invoice or invoice from the foreign manufacturer, the freight and insurance costs actually incurred (if known) should be the amounts to be deducted from the invoice value to most accurately figure the transaction value of the shipment.

$64,302.20 (value of goods 860 doz. X $74.77/doz.)
-   4,750.00 (actual freight cost)
-        51.60 (actual ins. cost of 10,320 units x $0.005/unit)
= $59,500.60

Round this total to $59,501 for the total entered/transaction value for the shipment. "B" is the correct answer.

Section VIII: Trade Agreements
55. Which country below is designated as a beneficiary country for purposes of the Andean Trade Preferences Act (ATPA)?

A. Brazil
B. Venezuela
C. Panama
D. Ecuador
E. Chile

 As per HTSUS General Note 11(a):

11. Products of Countries Designated as Beneficiary Countries for Purposes of the Andean Trade Preference Act (ATPA).

   (a) The following countries or successor political entities are designated beneficiary countries for purposes of the ATPA, pursuant to section 203 of the Act (19 U.S.C. 3202):

      Ecuador

In 2013, Ecuador was the only ATPA beneficiary country. "D" is the correct answer.

Note: The ATPA expired as of July 31, 2013.

56. Which of the following countries is considered a "Least Developed Beneficiary Country" for purposes of the General System of Preferences (GSP)?

A. Mozambique
B. Algeria
C. China
D. Saint Lucia
E. Italy

 As per HTSUS General Note 4(b):

(b)   (i)   The following beneficiary countries are designated as least-developed beneficiary developing countries pursuant to section 502(a)(2) of the Trade Act of 1974, as amended:

Afghanistan	Congo (Kinshasa)	Mali	The Solomon Islands
Angola	Djibouti	Mauritania	Somalia
Benin	Ethiopia	Mozambique	South Sudan
Bhutan	Gambia, The	Nepal	Tanzania
Burkina Faso	Guinea	Niger	Timor-Leste
Burundi	Guinea-Bissau	Rwanda	Togo
Cambodia	Haiti	Samoa	Tuvalu
Central African	Kiribati	Sao Tomé and	Uganda
Republic	Lesotho	Principe	Vanuatu
Chad	Liberia	Senegal	Republic of
Comoros	Madagascar	Sierra Leone	Yemen
	Malawi		Zambia

Along with about 40 other member countries, Mozambique is designated as a least-developed GSP beneficiary country. Multiple choice "A" is the correct answer.

57. Canadian Hockey Equipment issues a NAFTA Certificate of Origin for its shipment of hockey sticks to its U.S. customer, Hockey Sticks, Inc. Canadian Hockey Equipment discovers that the sticks do not qualify for NAFTA and provides a written statement to Hockey Sticks, Inc. advising them of the mistake. In order to rectify the situation with CBP, Hockey Sticks, Inc. must do which of the following:

A. Advise CBP that Canadian Hockey Equipment owes them the duty due
B. Notify CBP and pay the duties within 10 calendar days of having reason to believe the goods do not quailify
C. Continue to file claims for NAFTA for the hockey sticks
D. Advise Canadian Hockey Equipment that they must notify CBP of the error and pay the duties due
E. Notify CBP and pay the duties due within 30 calendar days of making discovery of the error

 As per 19 CFR 181.21(b):

*(b) Corrected declaration. If, after making the declaration required under paragraph (a) of this section or under §181.32(b)(2) of this part, **the U.S. importer has reason to believe that a Certificate of Origin on which a declaration was based contains information that is not correct, the importer shall within 30 calendar days after the date of discovery of the error make a corrected declaration and pay any duties that may be due.** A corrected declaration shall be effected by submission of a letter or other written statement to the CBP office where the original declaration was filed.*

"E" is the correct answer.

58. Korean Boat Restorations LLP is investigating the viability of restoring used inboard motorboats (HTSUS 8903.92.00) of unknown origin in S. Korea for export to the United States. The restoration will include the disassembly, cleaning, replacing inoperable parts and reassembly. Can the motorboat enter the United States duty free under the Korea FTA?

A.   Yes, the Korea FTA has a "recovered goods" provision and these boats meet the definition of a "recovered good".

B.   No, since the boats were not manufactured in S. Korea, they cannot meet the terms of Korea FTA.

C.   No, although the Korea FTA has a "remanufactured goods" provision, goods of chapter 89 are ineligible.

D.   Yes, the Korea FTA has a "remanufactured goods" provision and these boats meet the definition of a "remanufactured good".

E.   No, although the goods can enter the U.S. under the Korea FTA, they will not be duty free because the duties are still phasing out.

 As per HTSUS General Note 33(c)(i) & (ii):

(c)   (i)   For purposes of subdivision (b)(i) of this note, the expression "<u>wholly obtained or produced entirely in the territory of Korea or of the United States, or both</u>" means any of the following–

... ...

    (K)   recovered goods derived in the territory of Korea or of the United States, or both, from used goods; or

    (L)   goods, at any stage of production, produced in the territory of Korea or of the United States, or both, exclusively from–

        (i)   goods referred to in any of subdivisions (A) through (J) above, or

        (ii)   the derivatives of goods referred to in clause (L)(i).

    (ii)   (A)   For the purposes of subdivision (i)(K), the term "<u>recovered goods</u>" means materials in the form of individual parts that are the result of:

        (1)   the disassembly of used goods into individual parts; and

        (2)   the cleaning, inspecting, testing or other processing that is necessary for improvement to sound working condition of such individual parts.

    (B)   The term "<u>remanufactured good</u>" for purposes of this note means a good that is classified under chapter 84, 85, 87 or 90 or heading 9402, and that--

Per GN 33(c)(ii)(A), there is a provision that qualifies the restoration process in question as eligible "recovered goods". However, read further, and as per GN 33(c)(ii)(B), goods of Chapter 89, which covers the motorboats in question, do not qualify as eligible "remanufactured goods". "C" is the correct answer.

59. Automatic teller machines (ATMs) in HTS 8472.90.10 are manufactured in Malaysia, imported into Singapore and subsequently imported into the United States with the country of origin "Malaysia" and country of export "Singapore". Which of the following statements is true regarding the Singapore Free Trade Agreement (SGFTA)?

A.   ATMs are ineligible for SGFTA preference because the special program indicator (SG) is not listed in the "Special" column for HTS 8472.90.10.

B.   Although ATMs are eligible for SGFTA preference, there is no reason to claim it since they are unconditionally free.

C.   Only goods of a Party can benefit from the SGFTA, not goods of a 3rd-country.

D.   ATMs originate under the SGFTA irrespective of where they are manufactured.

E.   ATMs are provided for in the World Trade Organization (WTO) Information Technology Agreement (ITA) and thus enter the US free of duty and MPF irrespective of where they are manufactured.

 As per HTSUS General Note 25(m):

(m)   <u>Goods that shall be considered originating goods</u>. For the purposes of subdivision (b)(ii) of this note, goods that, in their condition as imported, are classifiable in the tariff provisions enumerated in the first column and are described opposite such provisions, when such goods are imported into the customs territory of the United States from the territory of Singapore, shall be considered originating goods for the purposes of this note:

... ...

(28)   8472.90.10   Automatic teller machines

Although, not at all considered common knowledge, it appears ATMs, as well as many other items are eligible for SFTA if merely exported to the U.S. from Singapore, regardless of actual country of origin. "D" is the correct answer.

Note: The exam describes this free trade agreement as the "Singapore Free Trade Agreement" and abbreviates it as "SGFTA". However, the free trade agreement is officially called the "United States-Singapore Free Trade Agreement" and abbreviated as "SFTA". The Special Program Indicator (SPI) symbol for this FTA is "SG".

60. Under the Australia FTA, which of the following are not indirect materials?

A. Catalysts and solvents
B. Discards unsuitable for sale
C. Lubricants, greases, compounding materials used to operate equipment and buildings
D. Dies and molds
E. Safety clothing and equipment for employees

 As per HTSUS General Note 28(k):

(k)   Indirect materials.

An indirect material shall be considered to be an originating material for purposes of this note without regard to where it is produced, and its value shall be the cost registered in the accounting records of the producer of the good. The term "indirect material" means a good used in the production, testing or inspection of a good but not physically incorporated into the good, or a good used in the maintenance of buildings or the operation of equipment associated with the production of a good, including–

(i)   fuel and energy;

(ii)   tools, dies and molds;

(iii)   spare parts and materials used in the maintenance of equipment or buildings;

(iv)   lubricants, greases, compounding materials and other materials used in production or used to operate equipment and buildings;

(v)   gloves, glasses, footwear, clothing, safety equipment and supplies;

(vi)   equipment, devices and supplies used for testing or inspecting the goods;

(vii)   catalysts and solvents; and

(viii)   any other goods that are not incorporated into the good but the use of which in the production of the good can reasonably be demonstrated to be a part of that production.

Although it is true that "discards unsuitable for sale" are not physically incorporated into the good, the fact that they (discards) are not used in the production, testing or inspection of a good, means that they are not defined as "indirect materials". "B" is the correct answer.

61. Ski board boots in HTS 6403.12.30 are manufactured in Canada of both NAFTA and 3rd-country materials in such a manner as to comply with the applicable General Note 12(t) requirement and subsequently imported into the U.S. The importation meets the NAFTA's direct shipment and all other requirements. Which of the following is true regarding whether NAFTA preference may be claimed to obtain the MPF exemption?

A.   Although virtually all Canadian goods benefit from NAFTA preference, since HTS 6403.12.30 does not show "CA" in the "Special" column of the HTSUS, it is an exception and is not NAFTA eligible.

B.   The "CA" in the "Special" column of the HTSUS is not necessary to claim NAFTA preference on Canadian-manufactured goods in HTS 6403.12.30 because all Canadian-manufactured goods enter the U.S. free of duty and MPF.

C.   Footwear importations into the U.S. are particularly restrictive and the fact that HTS 6403.12.30 does not list "CA" in the "Special" column indicates that it is ineligible for NAFTA preference.

D.   HTS 6403.12.30 is unconditionally free, so there is no benefit to claiming NAFTA preference.

E.   Notwithstanding that HTS 6403.12.30 does not show "CA" in the "Special" column of the HTSUS, since the good meets all of the requirements, NAFTA preferences may be claimed to obtain the MPF exemption.

Heading/ Subheading	Stat. Suf- fix	Article Description	Unit of Quantity	Rates of Duty	
				1	
				General	Special
6403		Footwear with outer soles of rubber, plastics, leather or composition leather and uppers of leather: Sports footwear:			
6403.12		Ski-boots, cross-country ski footwear and snowboard boots:			
6403.12.30	00	Welt footwear.	prs.	Free	

 As per 19 CFR 24.23(c)(3):

(3) The ad valorem, surcharge, and specific fees provided for under paragraphs (b)(1) and (b)(2) of this section will not apply to goods originating in Canada or Mexico within the meaning of General Note 12, HTSUS...

Translated, the above-mentioned statement says that the MPF will not be assessed for NAFTA qualifying shipments. As per the item's description for this question, the goods do, in fact, qualify for NAFTA in terms of both origination and routing. However, no Special Program Indicator (SPI), namely "CA" for NAFTA, is listed in the "Special" rates of duty column. In general, this is the case for classifications that are already unconditionally free (i.e. "Free" in "General" column of the HTSUS). This is also the case for 6403.12.30000 as shown in the above excerpt from the HTUSU. Even so, in order to be exempt from MPF, "CA" may be claimed for qualifying shipments. "E" is the correct answer.

Note: The question's reference to "General Note 12(t)" refers to NAFTA's Change in Tariff Classification Rules. These rules describe how an exported product made from non-NAFTA originating input materials (e.g. parts from China, etc.) may still qualify for NAFTA. These non-NAFTA originating inputs must have different HTSUS headings or subheadings relative to the exported product, and the transforming "tariff shift" must be specifically listed in the General Note. The NAFTA Change in Tariff Classification Rules for Chapter 64 are:

Chapter 64.

1.   A change to headings 6401 through 6405 from any heading outside that group, except from subheading 6406.10, provided there is a regional value content of not less than 55 percent under the net cost method.

2.   A change to subheading 6406.10 from any other subheading, except from headings 6401 through 6405, provided there is a regional value content of not less than 55 percent under the net cost method.

3.   A change to subheadings 6406.20 through 6406.99 from any other chapter.

62. Importer XYZ wants to know if the shipment of flashlights that he is importing from Pakistan can qualify for preferential tariff treatment. He supplies the cost breakdown as:

$4.68 aluminum - Pakistan
$0.36 copper wire – India
$0.48 screw – Korea
$1.20 light bulb - China
$1.59 plastic – Korea
$0.87 lens – Peru
$2.40 labor - Pakistan

Which trade agreement could this shipment be qualified for?

A.   United States-Korea Free Trade Agreement Implementation Act
B.   North American Free Trade Agreement Implementation Act
C.   United States-Peru Trade Promotion Agreement
D.   Generalized System of Preferences
E.   United States-China Free Trade Agreement

 As per 19 CFR 10.176(a):

§10.176   Country of origin criteria (for GSP).

(a) Merchandise produced in a beneficiary developing country or any two or more countries which are members of the same association of countries—(1) General. Except as otherwise provided in this section, any article which either is wholly the growth, product, or manufacture of, or is a new or different article of commerce that has been grown, produced, or manufactured in, a beneficiary developing country may qualify for duty-free entry under the Generalized System of Preferences (GSP). No article will be considered to have been grown, produced, or manufactured in a beneficiary developing country by virtue of having merely undergone simple (as opposed to complex or meaningful) combining or packaging operations or mere dilution with water or mere dilution with another substance that does not materially alter the characteristics of the article. **Duty-free entry under the GSP may be accorded to an article only if the sum of the cost or value of the materials produced in the beneficiary developing country or any two or more countries that are members of the same association of countries and are treated as one country** *under section 507(2) of the Trade Act of 1974, as amended (19 U.S.C. 2467(2)),* **plus the direct costs of processing operations performed in the beneficiary developing country or member countries, is not less than 35 percent of the appraised value of the article at the time it is entered.**

As per the preceding note, if the sum of the Pakistani costs, and costs from any of its fellow GSP co-members (see General Note 4(a)), comprise at least 35% of the total value of the finished good, then GSP may be claimed. So, we add up the Pakistani and Indian (both members of SAARC Association) inputs and get $7.44. This is approximately 64% of the total $11.58 of all listed inputs, which is well over the 35% minimum threshold. So, based on the information at hand, these flashlights from Pakistan do qualify for GSP and a reduced rate of duty. "D" is the correct answer.

Note: The classification for flashlights is 8513.10.2000 as per the below excerpt from the HTSUS. The SPI symbol "A" for GSP is listed in the "Special" duly rate column for this classification.

8513.10.20	00	Flashlights...	No......	12.5%	Free (A,AU,BH,CA, CL,CO,E,IL,JO, MA,MX,OM,P,PA, PE,SG)

63. After extensive market research, a Korean manufacturer of a canned peach and apricot fruit medley (HTS 2008.97) made of domestically grown Korean fruit is considered adding 9% Malaysian pears to the recipe and exporting the medley to the United States where consumers love pears. Will the fruit medley be eligible for Korea FTA preferences and if so, what duty rate will it pay?

A.   Eligible at 0.0%
B.   Eligible at 10.6%
C.   Ineligible at 5.6%
D.   Ineligible at 14.9%
E.   Ineligible at 20.0%

 As per HTSUS Chapter 20:

Heading/ Subheading	Stat. Suf- fix	Article Description	Unit of Quantity	Rates of Duty	
				1	
				General	Special
... ...					
2008.97.90		Other....................................	...........14.9%		Free (A+,BH,CA, CO,E,IL,J,JO, MX,P,PA,PE,SG) 7.4% (OM) 10.6% (KR) See 9911.96.96- 9911.97.25 (CL) See 9912.95.66- 9912.95.86 (MA) See 9913.95.86- 9913.96.06 (AU)

AND as per HTSUS General Note 33(o) (Product-specific rules):

Chapter 20.

*Chapter rule 1: Fruit, nut and vegetable preparations of headings 2001 through 2008 that have been prepared or preserved by freezing, by packing (including canning) in water, brine or natural juices or by roasting, either dry or in oil (including processing incidental to freezing, packing or roasting) shall be treated as originating only if the fresh good were wholly obtained or produced entirely in the territory of Korea or of the United States, or both. Furthermore, **fruit preparations of heading 2008 that contain peaches, pears or apricots, either alone or mixed with other fruits, shall be treated as originating only if the peaches, pears, or apricots were wholly obtained or produced entirely in the territory of Korea or of the United States, or both**.*

As per the immediately preceding note above, certain Korea FTA eligible items classified in HTSUS heading 2008 must be wholly from Korea, the United States, or both. This includes the canned fruit medley in question, which would not eligible for Korea FTA because of the presence of the Malaysian pears. Accordingly, the product will not receive a reduced duty rate of 10.6% per the "Special" rate of duty column. Instead, the 14.9% "General" rate of duty is what will be resorted to for duty assessment. "D" is the correct answer.

<u>Note:</u> With the limited information provided to the examinee, the classification for the canned peach and apricot fruit medley can be ascertained up to 8 digits as 2008.97.90. The SPI symbol for the Korea FTA is notated in the "Special" duly rate column as a "KR".

64. Assuming that substantial transformation, 35 percent value added, imported directly and all other requirements of the Generalized System of Preferences (GSP) are met, which of the following goods would not qualify for preferential tariff treatment under the GSP?

A.   0404.10.05 produced in and imported from Thailand
B.   4015.19.10 produced in and imported from Albania
C.   6912.00.45 produced in and imported from Haiti
D.   7604.10.30 produced in and imported from Venezuela
E.   8419.50.10 produced in and imported from Brazil

 As per HTSUS Chapter 20:

Heading/ Subheading	Stat. Suf- fix	Article Description	Unit of Quantity	Rates of Duty	
				1	
				General	Special
... ...					
0404.10.05	00	Whey protein concentrates..................	kg...... kg cmsc	8.5%	Free (A,BH,CA,CL, CO,E, IL,JO, MA,MX,OM,P,PA, PE,SG) 3.4% (KR) 3.7% (AU)
... ...					
4015.19.10		Seamless.	....	3%	Free (A,AU,BH, CA,CL,CO,E,IL, JO,KR,MA, MX,OM,P, PA,PE,SG)
... ...					
6912.00.45	00	Cups valued over $5.25 per dozen; saucers valued over $3 per dozen; soups, oatmeals and cereals valued over $6 per dozen; plates not over 22.9 cm in maximum diameter and valued over $6 per dozen; plates over 22.9 but not over 27.9 cm in maximum diameter and valued over $8.50 per dozen; platters or chop dishes valued over $35 per dozen; sugars valued over $21 per dozen; creamers valued over $15 per dozen; and beverage servers valued over $42 per dozen......................	doz.pcs..	4.5%	Free (A+,AU,CA, CL,CO,D,E,IL, JO,KR,MA,MX,P, PA,PE,SG) 0.4% (BH) 1.8% (OM)
... ...					
7604.10.30		Having a round cross section.................	....	2.6%	Free (A*,AU,BH, CA,CL,CO,E,IL, JO,KR,MA,MX, OM,P,PA,PE,SG)
... ...					
8419.50.10	00	Brazed aluminum plate-fin heat exchangers........	No.......	4.2%	Free (A,AU,BH,C, CA,CL,CO,E,IL, JO,KR,MA,MX, OM,P,PA,PE,SG)

To begin with, all of the countries named in the question are listed as GSP beneficiary countries as per General Note 4(a). The associated GSP SPI symbols are "A", "A+", and "A*".

"Haiti" is the only country of the bunch designated as a "least-developed beneficiary country" for purposes of GSP. The associated GSP SPI symbol for this is "A+"

What does the "A*" symbol mean in terms of an item classified as 7604.10.30 and imported from Venezuela in relation to its GSP eligibility?

As per HTSUS General Note 4(d):

*(d) Articles provided for in a provision for which a rate of duty of "Free" appears in the "Special" sub column of rate of duty column 1 followed by the **symbol "A*" in parentheses, if imported from a beneficiary developing country set out opposite the provisions enumerated below, are not eligible for the duty-free treatment provided in subdivision (c) of this note:***

7604.10.30   Venezuela

As per the General Note above, classification 7604.10.30 does not qualify for GSP preferential tariff treatment if imported from Venezuela. "D" is the correct answer.

Section IX: Drawback

65. In general, a complete drawback claim, with all required documents, shall be filed within _____ after the date of exportation or destruction of the merchandise or articles that are subject of the claim.

A. 3 years
B. 5 years
C. 6 years
D. 10 years
E. an unlimited number of years

 As per 19 CFR 191.51(e):

(e) Time of filing—(1) General. **A completed drawback claim, with all required documents, shall be filed within 3 years after the date of exportation or destruction of the merchandise or articles** *which are the subject of the claim. Except for landing certificates (see §191.76 of this part), or unless this time is extended as provided in paragraph (e)(2) of this section, claims not completed within the 3-year period shall be considered abandoned. Except as provided in paragraph (e)(2) of this section, no extension will be granted unless it is established that Customs was responsible for the untimely filing.*

"A" is the correct answer.

66. The definition of a "Destruction" of merchandise that is part of a claim for drawback duty means:

A. The complete destruction of over 50% of the value of the merchandise.
B. The complete destruction of over 90% of the value of the merchandise.
C. The complete recycling of the merchandise.
D. The recycling of less than 50% of the merchandise and the destruction of the remaining.
E. The complete destruction of the merchandise to the extent that it has no commercial value.

 As per 19 CFR 191.2(g):

(g) Destruction. Destruction means the complete destruction of articles or merchandise to the extent that they have no commercial value.

"E" is the correct answer.

67. The _____ shall be entitled to claim drawback unless this party, by means of certification, assigns the right to claim drawback to an intermediate party in the following scenario:

1. Company Alpha imports CBP duty assessed graphite from a seller, MNO, in Australia and issues a certificate of delivery to Company Beta.
2. Company Beta uses all of the imported graphite to manufacture pencils and issues a certificate of manufacture and delivery to Company Delta.
3. Company Delta is the exporter of record for all of the pencils to a buyer XYZ in China.

A. importer
B. manufacturer
C. exporter
D. seller MNO in Australia
E. buyer XYZ in China

 As per 19 CFR 191.28:

§191.28   Person entitled to claim drawback.

The exporter (or destroyer) shall be entitled to claim drawback, *unless the exporter (or destroyer), by means of a certification, assigns the right to claim drawback to the manufacturer, producer, importer, or intermediate party. Such certification shall also affirm that the exporter (or destroyer) has not and will not itself claim drawback or assign the right to claim drawback on the particular exportation or destruction to any other party. The certification provided for under this section may be a blanket certification for a stated period. Drawback is paid to the claimant, who may be the manufacturer, producer, intermediate party, importer, or exporter (destroyer).*

"C" is the correct answer.

68. What are all of the types of monies imposed on imported merchandise that may be requested on a drawback claim submitted on, or after, October 1, 2010?

A. Customs Duties and Harbor Maintenance Fees
B. Customs Duties and Merchandise Processing Fees
C. Customs Duties, Fees, and Internal Revenue Tax
D. Customs Duties, Anti-Dumping Duties, Fees, and Internal Revenue Tax
E. Customs Duties, Anti-Dumping Duties, Countervailing Duties, Fees, and Internal Revenue Tax

 As per 19 CFR 191.2(i):

*(i) Drawback. Drawback **means the refund or remission, in whole or in part, of a customs duty, fee or internal revenue tax** which was imposed on imported merchandise under Federal law because of its importation, and the refund of internal revenue taxes paid on domestic alcohol as prescribed in 19 U.S.C. 1313(d) (see also §191.3 of this subpart).*

AND as per 19 CFR 191.3(b):

*(b) **Duties and fees not subject to drawback include**:*

*(1) **Harbor maintenance fee** (see §24.24 of this chapter);*

*(2) **Merchandise processing fees** (see §24.23 of this chapter), except where unused merchandise drawback pursuant to 19 U.S.C. 1313(j) or drawback for substitution of finished petroleum derivatives pursuant to 19 U.S.C. 1313(p)(2)(A)(iii) or (iv) is claimed; and*

*(3) **Antidumping and countervailing duties** on merchandise entered, or withdrawn from warehouse, for consumption on or after August 23, 1988.*

"C" is the correct answer.

Section X: Intellectual Property Rights
69. Articles suspected of bearing counterfeit marks are detained. If the importer of the article does not provide timely information or the information provided is insufficient for CBP to determine that the merchandise does not bear a counterfeit mark, CBP may provide the owner of the mark with all of the following EXCEPT:

A.   Serial numbers and/or lot codes appearing on the merchandise
B.   Serial numbers and/or lot codes appearing on the merchandise's retail packaging
C.   Any entry documents accompanying the shipment
D.   A sample of the merchandise and/or its retail packaging in its condition as presented for examination, subject to bond and return requirements
E.   Images of the merchandise and/or its retail packaging in its condition as presented for examination

 As per 19 CFR 133.21:

(1) Notice to importer of detention and possible disclosure. Within five days (excluding weekends and holidays) from the date of a decision to detain, CBP will notify the importer in writing of the detention. The notice will inform the importer that a disclosure of information concerning the detained merchandise may be made to the owner of the mark to assist CBP in determining whether any marks are counterfeit, unless the importer presents information within seven days of the notification (excluding weekends and holidays) establishing to CBP's satisfaction that the detained merchandise does not bear a counterfeit mark. ***CBP may disclose information appearing on the merchandise and/or its retail packaging, images (including photographs) of the merchandise and/or its retail packaging in its condition as presented for examination, or a sample of the merchandise and/or its retail packaging in its condition as presented for examination. The release (disclosure) of a sample is subject to the bond and return requirements of paragraph (c) of this section.*** *Where the importer does not timely provide information or the information provided is insufficient for CBP to determine that the merchandise does not bear a counterfeit mark, CBP may proceed with the disclosure to the owner of the mark, and will so notify the importer. Disclosure under this section* ***may include any serial numbers, dates of manufacture, lot codes, batch numbers, universal product codes, or other identifying marks appearing on the merchandise or its retail packaging,*** *in alphanumeric or other formats.*

"C" is the correct answer.

Section XI: Marking

70. Articles not properly marked under the Country of Origin regulations shall, unless excluded, be subject to additional duties of what percentage of the final appraised value of the imported goods, unless those articles are exported or destroyed under Customs supervision prior to liquidation of the entry?

A. 1
B. 5
C. 10
D. 20
E. 25

 As per 19 CFR 134.2:

§134.2 Additional duties.

Articles not marked as required by this part shall be subject to additional duties of 10 percent of the final appraised value unless exported or destroyed under Customs supervision prior to liquidation of the entry, as provided in 19 U.S.C. 1304(f). The 10 percent additional duty is assessable for failure either to mark the article (or container) to indicate the English name of the country of origin of the article or to include words or symbols required to prevent deception or mistake.

"C" is the correct answer.

71. Articles not marked as required under 19 CFR 134 shall be subject to _____ additional duties on the final appraised value unless exported or destroyed under Customs supervision prior to liquidation of the entry.

A. 5 percent
B. 10 percent
C. 20 percent
D. 30 percent
E. No additional duties may be assessed

 As per 19 CFR 134.2:

§134.2 Additional duties.

Articles not marked as required by this part shall be subject to additional duties of 10 percent of the final appraised value unless exported or destroyed under Customs supervision prior to liquidation of the entry, as provided in 19 U.S.C. 1304(f). The 10 percent additional duty is assessable for failure either to mark the article (or container) to indicate the English name of the country of origin of the article or to include words or symbols required to prevent deception or mistake.

"B" is the correct answer.

Note: Yes, it certainly appears that the author of the exam inadvertently repeated essentially the same question in questions 70 & 71.

Section XII: Broker Compliance

72. John Doe took the Customs broker license exam in April 2009 at the Port of New York, and subsequently obtained his license through the port of Miami in October 2010. One month later, John was hired by Unknown Customs Brokers ("Unknown"), a national company employing 9 other licensed brokers. Unknown possesses a corporate broker's license. In August 2012, while perusing old Customs Bulletin notices, John realizes that Unknown did not file John's triennially-due status report ("triennial"), nor pay the associated fee. Moreover, John searches his records and finds a written notice sent by certified mail in March 2012, from the Miami Port Director, notifying him of the suspension of his license. John is determined to continue his career as a licensed broker. Which of the following courses of action should John take?

A.   Contact the port of Miami and submit his triennial report within 60 calendar days.

B.   Request that Unknown immediately file a triennial report on his behalf, including a statement acknowledging third party liability for the late filing, and pay the associated fee.

C.   Realize that his broker's license has been revoked by operation of law and file an application for a new license.

D.   Do nothing and continue to transact customs business as a licensed customs broker because Unknown filed a triennial report for the company's corporate broker's license. Therefore, John did not have to file a separate individual triennial report.

E.   Submit a well-formed appeal to CBP headquarters, citing third party liability. Then submit a copy of the appeal to the Port of Miami.

 As per 19 CFR 111.30(d)(4):

*(4) Failure to file timely. If a broker fails to file the report required under paragraph (d)(1) of this section by March 1 of the reporting year, the broker's license is suspended by operation of law on that date. By March 31 of the reporting year, the port director will transmit written notice of the suspension to the broker by certified mail, return receipt requested, at the address reflected in Customs records. If the broker files the required report and pays the required fee within 60 calendar days of the date of the notice of suspension, the license will be reinstated. **If the broker does not file the required report within that 60-day period, the broker's license is revoked by operation of law without prejudice to the filing of an application for a new license.** Notice of the revocation will be published in the Customs Bulletin.*

"C" is the correct answer.

73. A broker hires an employee on a full-time basis on March 1, 2012. The employee was working at the brokerage on a part-time basis since January 1, 2011. By which date is the broker required to inform the Port Director of this new employee?

A.   January 31, 2011
B.   February 10, 2011
C.   March 31, 2012
D.   April 10, 2012
E.   January 1, 2013

 As per 19 CFR 111.28(b)(1)(ii):

*(ii) New employees. In the case of a new employee, the broker must submit to the port director the written information required under paragraph (b)(1)(i) of this section **within 10 calendar days after the new employee has been employed by the broker for 30 consecutive days.***

Regardless of whether the employee is part-time or full-time status, the broker is required to inform the Port Director of the new employee as per above regulation. "B" is the correct answer.

74. A broker hires someone as an employee on March 15, 2013, whose broker license was revoked on February 5, 2002, with prejudice. Per CBP regulations, what is the next course of action?

A.   The broker (employer) should send a letter to the CBP Assistant Commissioner requesting authorization to employ the personnel.

B.   The employee should not accept employment until she sends a petition to the CBP Assistant Commissioner of the Office of International Trade requesting authorization to accept the employment with the broker, and the petition is approved.

C.   The broker should do nothing, as the license was revoked over 5 years ago.

D.   The broker may hire the employee, however, the employee must not receive a power of attorney to sign on behalf of the brokerage.

E.   The broker should submit written notification to the Port Director with required information under 19 CFR 111.28(b)(1)(i) within 5 calendar days after the new employee has been employed by the broker for 60 consecutive days.

 As per 19 CFR 111.42(a)(3):

(a) General. Except as otherwise provided in paragraph (b) of this section, a broker must not knowingly and directly or indirectly:

... ...

(3) Employ, or accept assistance in the furtherance of any customs business or transactions from, any person described in paragraph (a)(1) of this section, without the approval of the Assistant Commissioner (see §111.79);

AND as per 19 CFR 111.79:

§111.79   Employment of broker who has lost license.

Five years after the revocation or cancellation "with prejudice" of a license, the ex-broker may petition the Assistant Commissioner for authorization to assist, or accept employment with, a broker. *The petition will not be approved unless the Assistant Commissioner is satisfied that the petitioner has refrained from all activities described in §111.42 and that the petitioner's conduct has been exemplary during the period of disability. The Assistant Commissioner will also give consideration to the gravity of the misconduct which gave rise to the petitioner's disability. In any case in which the misconduct led to pecuniary loss to the Government or to any person, the Assistant Commissioner will also take into account whether the petitioner has made restitution of that loss.*

Accordingly, the petition for employment to the Assistant Commissioner must be submitted by the employee. "B" is the correct answer.

75. Payment of an annual user fee of $138 is required for each permit and the user fee must be paid by the due date as published annually in which of the following:

A.   In the Port Office where the fees are to be paid
B.   In the Help Section on the Customs and Border Protection web site under Trade Support/Broker
C.   In the CBP Compliance manual for brokers
D.   In the Federal Register
E.   In the revised editions of the Code of Federal Regulations

 As per 19 CFR 111.96(c):

*(c) User fee. Payment of an annual user fee of $138 is required for each permit, including a national permit under §111.19(f), granted to an individual, partnership, association, or corporate broker. The user fee is payable when an initial district permit is issued concurrently with a license under §111.19(a), or in connection with the filing of an application for a permit under §111.19 (b) or (f), and for each subsequent calendar year at the port through which the broker was granted the permit or at the port referred to in §111.19(c) in the case of a national permit. **The user fee must be paid by the due date as published annually in the Federal Register**, and ...*

"D" is the correct answer.

76. When must a Licensed Customs Broker file a written status report with CBP?

A.   January 1, 2014, and January 1, 2015
B.   January 1, 2014, and January 1, 2017
C.   February 1, 2014, and February 1, 2015
D.   January 1, 2015, and January 1, 2018
E.   February 1, 2015, and February 1, 2018

 As per 19 CFR 111.30(d):

*(d) Status report—(1) General. **Each broker must file a written status report with Customs on February 1, 1985, and on February 1 of each third year after that date**. The report must be accompanied by the fee prescribed in §111.96(d) and must be addressed to the director of the port through which the license was delivered to the licensee (see §111.15). A report received during the month of February will be considered filed timely. No form or particular format is required.*

Also known as the "Customs Broker Triennial Status Report." "E" is the correct answer.

77. When must an individual broker who is a qualifying member of a partnership provide written notice to the Assistant Commissioner of CBP, with copies of the written notice to the director of each port through which a permit has been granted, that his or her employment as a qualifying member has been terminated?

A.   Immediately
B.   As soon as possible after submitting a written waiver to the Port Director in the permitted district
C.   30 days after the termination of employment
D.   120 days after the termination of employment
E.   180 days after the termination of employment

 As per 19 CFR 111.28(c):

(c) Termination of qualifying member or officer. In the case of an individual broker who is a qualifying member of a partnership for purposes of §111.11(b) or who is a qualifying officer of an association or corporation for purposes of §111.11(c)(2), **that individual broker must immediately provide written notice to the Assistant Commissioner** *when his employment as a qualifying member or officer terminates and must send a copy of the written notice to the director of each port through which a permit has been granted to the partnership, association, or corporation.*

"A" is the correct answer.

78. Which of the following is a requirement for an individual customs broker license?

A.   Be in possession of a valid driver license
B.   Be an active member of the Customs Broker Association
C.   Test negative for drugs
D.   Attain a grade point average of 3.5 in college credit hours
E.   Be 21 years of age

 As per 19 CFR 111.11(a):

§111.11   Basic requirements for a license.

(a) Individual. In order to obtain a broker's license, an individual must:

(1) Be a citizen of the United States on the date of submission of the application referred to in §111.12(a) and not an officer or employee of the United States Government;

(2) **Attain the age of 21 prior to the date of submission of the application** *referred to in §111.12(a);*

(3) Be of good moral character; and

(4) Have established, by attaining a passing (75 percent or higher) grade on a written examination taken within the 3-year period before submission of the application referred to in §111.12(a), that he has sufficient knowledge of customs and related laws, regulations and procedures, bookkeeping, accounting, and all other appropriate matters to render valuable service to importers and exporters.

"E" is the correct answer.

79. Which of the following is NOT "Customs Business" as defined in the Code of Federal Regulations?

A. Payment of duties, taxes and fees
B. Corporate compliance activity
C. Determining the admissibility of merchandise
D. Determining the classification of merchandise
E. Preparation and filing of CBP Form 7501

 As per 19 CFR 111.1:

Customs business. "Customs business" means those activities involving transactions with CBP concerning the entry and admissibility of merchandise, its classification and valuation, the payment of duties, taxes, or other charges assessed or collected by CBP on merchandise by reason of its importation, and the refund, rebate, or drawback of those duties, taxes, or other charges. "Customs business" also includes the preparation, and activities relating to the preparation, of documents in any format and the electronic transmission of documents and parts of documents intended to be filed with CBP in furtherance of any other customs business activity, whether or not signed or filed by the preparer. **However, "customs business" does not include the mere electronic transmission of data received for transmission to CBP and does not include a corporate compliance activity.**

"B" is the correct answer.

80. A broker must submit new employee information to CBP within 10 calendar days after the broker has employed a new employee for 30 consecutive days. Which of the following data elements is not a requirement in this notification?

A. Name of employee
B. Social security number of employee
C. Date and place of birth of employee
D. Current home address
E. Last three prior home addresses

 As per 19 CFR 111.28(b)(1)(i) & (b)(1)(ii):

(b) Employee information—(1) Current employees—(i) General.
... ...

For each employee, the broker also **must provide the social security number, date and place of birth, current home address, last prior home address, and, if the employee has been employed by the broker for less than 3 years, the name and address of each former employer and dates of employment for the 3-year period preceding current employment with the broker.** *After the initial submission, an updated list, setting forth the name, social security number, date and place of birth, and current home address of each current employee, must be submitted with the status report required by §111.30(d).*

(ii) New employees. In the case of a new employee, the broker must submit to the port director the written information required under paragraph (b)(1)(i) of this section within 10 calendar days after the new employee has been employed by the broker for 30 consecutive days.

"E" is the correct answer.

Book 2 Introduction
How to Start Your Own CHB Business

Most customs brokers have thought to themselves at least once, "what it would be like run my own customs brokerage business?" Well, once you have a little experience under your belt, have concluded that the time has come to go out on your own, and have acquired some resources and potential clients, then this book will end up saving you much wasted time and frustration.

The reason I wrote this book is that when I first decided to start my own customs brokerage business, instructions on doing so from US Customs or the customs brokerage community were nowhere to be found. I resolved to methodically log and document all the steps that I actually took in setting up my own customs brokerage business from start to finish. I knew that doing so would prove to be an invaluable service for others following the same path.

$ Money Saving Tip $
Some regional banks offer free checking accounts with relatively high interest that might suit your new small business. ACH services may be extra, so shop around. www.checkingfinder.com

So, with this book, the reader is able to bypass the trial and error method that I used when setting up my own customs brokerage business. This guide systematically outlines, step-by-step, how to most efficiently open your own customs brokerage business—and how to do it on a budget.

You may have a long list of prospective customers that you can switch over to your new operation. You may few such contacts. Either way, your ambition to offer a service, superior to any other in your market, will, by itself, grow your business. Just use this book for direction, stick with your own creative marketing plan, be pro-active yet patient, and GROW YOUR BUSINESS.

Necessary Links

Customs website:
www.cbp.gov

Code of Federal Regulations (CFR) Online:
www.eCFR.gov

Harmonized Tariff Schedule (HTS) Online:
www.usitc.gov/tata/HTS/bychapter/index.htm

Customs Forms:
http://www.cbp.gov/xp/cgov/toolbox/forms/

IRS Small Business:
www.irs.gov/businesses/small/index.html

$ Money Saving Tip $

Have not yet been able to purchase your own 19 CFR or HTSUS? The online versions of these texts are easily searchable (e.g., use your computer's "find" function [Ctrl + F] to quickly locate item descriptions and HTS numbers within these PDF files) and are always up-to-date.

Start with Customs
Start Here

Customs Broker License

First, let's assume that you do have your customs broker license. If you don't, then let's get that first. Read part one of this book on how to become a licensed customs broker. If you're already studying for the exam, then keep it up and good luck—the international shipping industry needs more licensed brokers and you're nearly there.

To Operate Under a Trade Name

Some individual customs brokers operate under their own personal names (e.g. John Doe). Others choose to give their small business a name (e.g. John Doe, DBA Perfect Customs Brokerage). Either way will work, but if you choose to operate under an assumed business name or Doing Business As (DBA) trade name, then Customs requires that the individual customs broker first submit a proposal to operate under a trade name in the form of a letter (see sample letter on the following page, and also refer to 19 CFR 111.30 (c) to verify all information is up-to-date) to the Customs Broker Compliance Branch before proceeding with district permit application, filer code application, etc.

In your letter to Broker Compliance, refer to and attach evidence of your authority to use the trade name (usually in the form of your State's department of licensing confirmation letter or license). Also be sure to include your customs broker license number with this and all other such correspondence to Customs.

Customs will review your letter and will send back written approval to you within a couple weeks. They may be kind enough to email or fax confirmation back to you if politely asked to do so in your letter.

$ Money Saving Tip $
Need to courier docs overseas? Although no current US domestic service still exists, DHL, or an authorized reseller of DHL, can sometimes offer international rates at nearly half that of standard UPS and FedEx rates.

Sample: Proposal to operate under a trade name

John Doe
Perfect Customs Brokerage
3000 NE 309th Ave
Port City, WA 98682
Tel: 360-123-4567
johndoe@coldmail.com

(Date)

U.S. Customs and Border Protection
1300 Pennsylvania Ave., NW
Attn: 1400 L St., Broker Compliance Branch
Washington, DC 20229

Re: Proposal to operate under a trade name

Dear Sir or Madam,

Per 19 CFR 111.30 (c) I am submitting evidence of my authority to use the trade name (John Doe, DBA) **"Perfect Customs Brokerage"** per attached acknowledgement letter from the Washington State Department of Licensing (unified business identifier number 600000000).

Best Regards,

John Doe
License#12345

District Permit Request

A customs broker can only conduct customs business in the ports that he or she has permits for. The first permit that you will want to apply for is for the district in which you will initially be making customs entries.

A national permit can be applied for, yet only subsequently to receipt of the district permit. An individual customs broker may utilize remote location filing (RLF) if he or she has a national permit. RLF will allow you to make entry on regular informal or formal entry at any port even if you don't have an office at that port. At this point, however, RLF is just something to keep in mind and consider down the road. Just go to www.cbp.gov and search "remote location filing" for more information on the subject if you would like.

Include the following information in your **district** permit application (see sample letter on following page)...

1) Broker license number, date of issuance, and delivered through port (attach copy of license)

2) Your office address (attach copy of lease agreement or title)

3) Evidence of right to use assumed business name if applicable (attach approval from state)

4) Name of individual broker to exercise responsible supervision and control (usually your name)

5) List of other districts for which you have a permit (write "none" if none)

6) "Records retained at" address, and recordkeeping contact name

7) All other persons employed by applicant (write "none" if none)

8) Note $100.00 permit fee (attach check, and see 19 CFR 111.96 to verify amount is up-to-date).

9) Note $138.00 annual user fee (attach check, and see 19 CFR 111.96 to verify amount is up-to-date).

Be sure to make your checks out to "Customs and Border Protection". As of 2013, the 19 CFR still (at least in my opinion) incorrectly instructs payments to be made out to the "United States Customs Service". Also be sure to time stamp and keep a copy of all such correspondence with Customs for your records.

Sample: District Permit Request

John Doe
DBA Perfect Customs Brokerage
3000 NE 309th Ave
Port City, WA 98682
Tel: 360-123-4567
johndoe@coldmail.com

(Date)

Ms. Jane Smith, Port Director, CBP

Re: Application for District Permit for Port of Port City

Dear Ms. Smith,

Please accept this letter as application for a district permit to perform customs business in the port of Port City. Required information per CFR19, 111.19 (b) is as follows:

1) Broker License Number 12345, Date of issuance 4/22/05 (delivered through port of New Orleans, copy of license attached)
2) Office address: 3000 NE 309th Ave, Port City, WA 98682 Tel: 360-123-4567 (copy of lease attached)
3) Copy of document which reserves applicant's business name with the state of Washington (attached)
4) Individual broker to exercise responsible supervision and control: John Doe
5) Other districts for which I have a permit: None
6) Records retained at: 3000 NE 309th Ave, Port City, WA 98682. Recordkeeping contact: John Doe
7) All other persons employed by applicant: None
8) $100.00 permit fee (attached)
9) $138.00 annual user fee (attached)

Best Regards,

John Doe, **License#12345**

Filer Code Request

Each broker conducting business with Customs will be issued a three-letter code that will be notated with entry numbers for all customs entries. This three-letter code is called the "filer code". To obtain a filer code, submit in filer code request letter (separate from the district permit request), and include the following information (see sample letter on following page)...

1)   Full legal name of requestor (you)
2)   Business contact (probably you)
3)   Business address and telephone number
4)   Broker license number, date of issuance, and "delivered through" port.

$ Money Saving Tip $
Need inexpensive or free accounting software such as "Express Accounts Free Accounting Software"? Check out CNET's website for downloads and reviews. Search for business software>>accounting and billing software.
www.download.com

NOTE: The requests for district permit and filer code can be submitted together (verify with port director or equivalent just in case). They will provide you with a receipt for your checks, and will notify you of approval within about two to three weeks.

Sample: Filer Code Request

John Doe
DBA PERFECT Customs Brokerage
3000 NE 309th Ave
Port City, WA 98682
Tel: 360-123-4567
johndoe@coldmail.com

(Date)

Ms. Jane Smith
Port Director
Customs and Border Protection (Port of Port City)

Re: Filer Code Request

Dear Ms. Smith,

Please accept this letter as application for a filer code. Information required to process this application is as follows:

1) Full legal name of requestor: John Doe
2) Business contact (Individual broker to exercise responsible supervision and control): John Doe
3) Business address: 3000 NE 309th Ave, Port City, WA 98682   Tel: 360-123-4567
4) Broker License Number 12345, Date of issuance 4/22/05 (delivered through port of New Orleans)

Thank you very much for your consideration. Please feel free to contact me should you require further information.

Best Regards,

John Doe
License#12345

Type of Organization
Keep it simple

Legal Designation

While you're patiently waiting for Customs to get back to you on your district permit and filer code applications, it may be a good time to focus on the structure of the business. Many large freight forwarder and customs brokerage operations are incorporated. For your start-up business, however, it may be best to keep it simple. By that I mean that I mean consider registering your new business with your state as a sole proprietorship rather than an LLC or corporation.

I would not suggest a partnership for any type of business. A wise man once said "the partnership is the one ship that won't sail"? It's too difficult to make something work that equally involves the interests of more than one party, and hours worked and perceptions of contributions to the partnership will vary and eventually cause discontent and resentment.

As your business grows you can later decide to expand on your sole proprietorship by easily converting to an S-Corporation. You can also purchase liability and/or errors and omissions insurance from an insurance or surety bond company to help protect your company.

$ Money Saving Tip $
Some companies charge a substantial monthly fee to list your business in their publications. Note, however, that there are many free print directories, online directories, and search engines for you to register with.

Taxes

Taxes on your business will depend on several different factors, including legal designation, estimated income, and local tax code. It will be worth your time to consult with a trusted CPA in your area to try to gain a better understanding of your specific tax considerations. A consultation may cost you some money upfront (maybe about $100.00 a visit?), but will, without a doubt, give you peace of mind that is hard to put a price on.

One thing that every business owner must do, however, is to separate personal finances from business finances. This means setting up a separate bank account for your business. All business-related expenses come out of your business' account, and all business-related income goes into this account—no exceptions. Doing so will allow you to accurately compute your taxes, as well as let you know if your business is making a profit.

As a general rule of thumb, set aside about 1/4 of all withdrawn profits into yet another separate bank account (most may prefer a savings type account) for your business so that you will have these funds available for taxes. So, for example, if taking out $1,000.00 from your business' checking account, only $750.00 will go into your personal bank account, and the other $250.00 will go into and remain your business' savings account in preparation for your quarterlies and tax time. Again, consult with a good CPA for details that will be relevant to you own unique situation.

An EIN (employee identification number) is not absolutely necessary to run your sole-proprietor business (as opposed of other forms of business), but some of your vendors may require this ID number when applying for credit with them. You may obtain an EIN from the IRS if you wish by applying online at the following…

www.irs.gov/smallbiz

The IRS's small business website also ACTUALLY provides very informative online tutorials, among other useful tools. You can even sign up for a free newsletter to help keep you up-to-date on IRS-related regulations and tips.

$ Money Saving Tip $
Use the EFTPS method of paying your IRS taxes. It is the quickest, most accurate, and the cheapest method of all for a small business. Go to www.irs.gov/smallbiz to learn more regarding EFTPS.

Marketing Your CHB Business
Get the Word Out

Still waiting for your district permit and filer code? Now is a perfect time to start working on your marketing plan.

You do not have to spend a lot of money to advertise your business. Here are just a few of the best methods of getting your business' name out there. And, they're all free.

Customs Website

Ask your port director (or equivalent) if they can list your new business on CBP's list of brokers as soon as your filer code is created. All active brokers are listed by the port within they operate on the Customs website (www.cbp.gov), and importers often search and are shepherded here (by Customs, etc.) when looking for someone to clear their shipment. Getting listed may take a little patience and persistence, but the amount of exposure your company gets from this is well worth the wait.

Port Website

Most ports (e.g. The Port of Tacoma, The Port of Norfolk, etc.) have very business-friendly websites. Among the various port-related resources they often provide for the benefit of local commerce, is a directory of local warehouses, trucking companies, freight forwarders, and customs brokers. Contact your port (air, ocean, or both) and ask to be added to the list. This service should also be free, and is another great way to get a reference from a credible source.

Other Marketing Advice

I also recommend the book *Guerilla Marketing* by Jay Conrad Levinson. This book is just full of creative, yet proven ideas to advertise your on-a-budget business. It is extensive in its description of all different types of effective marketing techniques.

$ Money Saving Tip $
Making multiple trips to Customs, etc.? Deduct about 50¢ per mile as an expense. See www.irs.gov/smallbiz for the current rate.

ABI Vendor
Test Drive it for the Right Fit

Selecting an ABI Vendor

Finding an ABI provider is easy. Choosing the best ABI provider for your company takes some shopping around.

An initial one-time licensing fee will run anywhere from $10,000.00 to $2,000.00. After that, monthly maintenance fees for ABI providers can be as expensive as $1,000.00 per month or as low as $200.00 per month. Most offer a full array of ABI capabilities, but some may offer more accounting and other optional features than others. Some require you to buy an on-site server to run their software off of, while others allow you to do everything online thru the use of their server—as if you were creating and sending an email from your Hotmail or Gmail email account.

Feel free to compare the actual functionality of a couple different vendors with actual one-on-one demo's, either in-person or remotely online. Also, get a good feel for a company's culture. Your instincts should tell you whether they will offer excellent or below-average customer service for when you have a question or problem with their system. My best advice to you on the subject is to not only choose your ABI vendor based on their pricing, but also based on their technical and customer support expertise. We chose SmartBorder (http://www.smartborder.com/), after trying two other ABI vendors. They made ABI Certification a pain-free process. It is easy for me to endorse them because I know their product is one of the best in the industry. Their system is accessible from anywhere with an internet connection, and handles necessary Customs transactions such as: Entries (7501,3461), RLF, ISF, truck manifest, ocean manifest, electronic invoice, In-bond 7512, Exports, Reconciliation, Protests, OGA filing, 5106, Statement processing, and PMS.

A current listing of all ABI vendors, certified by US Customs, can be found at http://www.cbp.gov/document/guidance/abi-software-vendors-list

Reproducing Customs Forms

The Customs Forms Management Office (located in Washington, DC) requires all ABI providers to submit their versions of US Customs forms (3461, 7501, etc.) to their office for approval before the forms are printed by individual brokers (via their laser or inkjet printers). Customs is concerned that their forms be kept uniform, and Customs may request this letter of approval at anytime.

Interestingly enough, not all ABI providers seem to have this important letter of proof, so it is important to request that your prospective ABI provider provide a copy of this letter for your file before you commit to buying their product.

Letter of Intent

Once you have received your district permit and filer code from Customs, you will ask the ABI provider to provide a letter of intent template (see sample letter on following page, and see 19 CFR 143 to verify information is up-to-date) that you or your ABI provider can send to the Customs Office of Information and Technology (OIT). The only thing that you will need to add to the template should be your new filer code and a signature. Have the letter of intent mailed to the OIT or call them at (703) 650-3500 to ask if you can fax the letter in order to expedite the process. Make sure that your ABI provider also gets a copy of the submitted letter. Go to www.cbp.gov and type "getting started with ABI" for current instructions in detail or go to the following URL: http://www.cbp.gov/document/guidance/letter-intent-instructions

$ Money Saving Tip $
Thinking of printing your own business cards or promotional material? Outsource (instead of printing your own) to a local printing company? It's the most convenient and cost effective way.

Sample: ABI Letter of Intent

John Doe
Perfect Customs Brokerage
3000 NE 309th Ave
Port City, WA 98682
Tel: 360-123-4567
johndoe@coldmail.com

(Date)

Office of Information and Technology
Director of Client Representatives Branch
7501 Boston Blvd. 2nd Floor, Room 211
Springfield, VA 22153

RE: Letter of intent to participation in ACS/ABI.

Per 19 CFR 143.2, this letter of intent sets forth our commitment to develop, maintain and adhere to the performance requirements and operational standards of the ABI system in order to ensure the validity, integrity and confidentiality of the data transmitted.

1)   The following is a description of the computer hardware, communications and entry processing systems to be used and the estimated completion date of the programming: (*ABI provider will advise these details*).
2)   Our offices are located at: 3000 NE 309th Ave
     Port City, WA 98682. Contact: John Doe.
3)   The name of the participant's principal management and contact person regarding the system: John Doe
4)   The system is being developed by the following data processing company: PDQ Systems. Contact: Denise Richards
5)   Entry filer code: XYZ

Please feel free to contact us should you have any questions.

Best regards,

John Doe, LCB, License#12345

The letter of intent will be processed in about a week. Customs will assign an "ABI representative" (not to be confused with your "ABI vendor") to you. He or she will contact you to introduce themselves, and you can advise your ISA confirmation number (see next paragraph) at that time as well. Once an ABI rep is assigned, you will work closely with him or her and with your ABI provider to test your ABI transmissions. Ask your ABI provider to help you prepare for and walk you through this ABI testing period, which can be completed within a couple days (depending on your provider).

VPN Interconnection Security Agreement

The Trade Virtual Private Network (VPN) Interconnection Security Agreement (ISA) is how Customs informs the ABI applicant of the importance of keeping the connection between your computer and Customs' servers secure. Go to the following online form, read the agreement, and complete and submit the security agreement acceptance form.

https://apps.cbp.gov/tvpn/tvpn.asp

Once the VPN ISA has submitted you will receive a confirmation number via email. Simply reply to the confirmation email from Customs to complete the ISA acceptance process. Keep this confirmation number and provide it to your ABI representative when they contact you.

Selecting a Surety Company
That was Easy

The surety company that you choose will be able to issue single transaction bonds and continuous bonds to accompany your customs entries.

Before deciding on a surety company, check with your ABI provider to see if they integrate a specific company's bonds in their system. If they do, and if the surety's rates are reasonable, then use them.

Otherwise, selecting a surety company can still be much easier than selecting an ABI provider as prices seem to be relatively similar between competing companies. Ask for a few quotes to get a better idea of what's out there.

$ Money Saving Tip $
Want shipping industry news for free? Sign up for the Journal of Commerce's free newsletter at **www.joc.com**

However, I would recommend choosing a surety company that does not charge a minimum for your single transaction bonds, and one that has an easy-to-use bond application system. Some may let you get your single transaction bonds directly online (web-based), while others will have you download (stand-alone) software that will allow you to issue bonds directly from your desktop.

To get a current listing of Customs approved surety companies that can provide you with a quote go to www.cbp.gov and search for "surety names/codes". Or try typing the following URL http://www.cbp.gov/sites/default/files/documents/surety%20codes_1.pdf

Running Your CHB Business
Do it Differently

The day-to-day operations of your new customs brokerage business is entirely up to you. You can get as creative as you want. That's to your advantage, because most of the customs brokerage businesses out there appear to be doing the same thing. And some may have (just as any corporation is susceptible to) lost their soul.

Power of Attorney

A signed power of attorney (POA) from the importer is required in order for a customs broker to conduct customs business on behalf of that importer.

In regards to the POA, an individual customs broker can do one of two things. You can choose to purchase a boilerplate-type POA form in bulk from a specialty printing company. The National Customs Brokers & Freight Forwarders Association of America (NCBFFAA), for example, has published several different versions of the power of attorney for the transportation industry. They can be purchased at Apperson Print Management Services, located on the web at http://www.appersonprint.com/

One of your other options is to refer to Customs' example of the power of attorney (as written in 19 CFR 141.31) as a benchmark, and customize it to fit your company (see sample POA on following page). I recommend this method as it is FREE and less intimidating to customers than the long form published by the NCBFFAA.

And as you have your customer fill out the power of attorney, ask them to also complete and return what I call the "customers instructions to broker" (see sample following POA). The importer can use this form to describe their imported product, and clarify delivery and billing details. This lets your new client know that you care about their input, and provides up-front information in writing.

Sample: Customs Power of Attorney

Customs Power of Attorney

KNOW ALL MEN BY THESE PRESENTS, THAT

_____

(Full name of company or individual)

_____

(Legal designation, such as corp., individual, sole prop., LLC, or partnership)

located at

_____

(Business Address)

and doing business under the laws of the State of

_____, using EIN or SSN_____

hereby appoints the grantee, **John Doe, DBA Perfect Customs Brokerage** as a true and lawful agent and attorney of the principal named above with full power and authority to do and perform every lawful act and thing the said agent and attorney may deem requisite and necessary to be done for and on behalf of the said principal without limitation of any kind as fully as said principal could do if present and acting, and hereby ratify and confirm all that said agent and attorney shall lawfully do or cause to be done by virtue of these presents until written notice of revocation is delivered to the grantee. In the case of a partnership, this power of attorney will only be effective two years from the date below.

_____   _____

(Principal's signature)   *(Date)*

Sample: Customer Instructions to Broker

Customer Instructions to Broker

1) The product that I am importing can best be described as...

_____
(What is it? What is it made of?)

_____
(What is it used for? What is it used in conjunction with?)

2)   Please deliver to...

_____
(delivery address)

_____
(delivery location contact name and telephone#)

*This location **does / doesn't** have a loading dock. (Please circle one)*

3)   Please bill to...

_____
(billing address)

_____
(billing contact name and telephone#)

ACH Payment

Complete Customs Form 401 (ACH Credit Enrollment Application) and fax, email, or mail the completed application to the Customs Revenue Division. Upon receipt, they will send instructions to you on ACH payer procedures as well as show you how to send an ACH pre-note test (necessary test for ACH user approval) through your bank to Customs. Once approved, you can work with your ABI provider and bank to set everything else up. Until then, Customs will accept checks submitted with the entry or entry summary. Go to www.cbp.gov and type "signing up for ach" for details and current instructions. Or try going direct via the following URL: http://www.cbp.gov/trade/trade-community/automated/automated-systems/gs-automated-systems/ach/debit-details

Accounting Software

If you're not a seasoned CPA (like the rest of us), then keeping track of your company's finances may require accounting software that is easy to use. If your ABI provider offers accounting software that is integrated within their ABI software product, then feel free to use it as that may help simplify things.

If they do not offer integrated accounting software, then stand-along accounting software such as QuickBooks will work as well. Because of its widespread use, many ABI providers include functions in the ABI software that allow you to easily transfer data to and from QuickBooks.

Pricing

Be aware of your competitors' pricing. You may want to beat their pricing and/or offer importers a much more simplified version of the typical customs brokerage invoice. If you can boast about your great rates then feel free to compare yours to the "typical" customs broker on your website or via other methods of advertising.

Creativity can also enter into your method of pricing of your customs brokerage services. You might not have the cash on hand that a larger business has, so you could offer a substantial discount to an importer if he or she submits payment to you at the time of or before delivery of her shipment. This will help you to cash flow your business, and give you a chance to go out and meet your customers.

Truckers

Contact several different truckers and get an account setup with them before your first shipment. Most will require you to complete a credit check application, while others will ask for payment to be made on a COD basis for the first couple of shipments. Either way, it is nice to have a friend in your trucking company.

Necessary Office Equipment

In regards to necessary office equipment, a minimalist would only really need a computer, printer, telephone, and shredder (Customs requires all information-sensitive material to be shredded rather than put in the dumpster). Some ABI vendors may require you to purchase a stand-alone server in order to operate their software.

$ Money Saving Tip $
Cleared a small shipment and have some free time? Deliver using your own car or rent a truck (your car insurance co. may have weight restrictions). This is also a good chance to see your customer.

Recordkeeping

Customs requires brokers to keep records (either in paper or electronic form) of transaction for five years from the entry date. The IRS requires an individual or business to keep tax-related records for three years (though some recommend keeping longer).

However, there is no need to invest in a row of file cabinets if you're on a budget. Just go to Wal-Mart or Target and buy manila file folders, some hanging files to organize them in, and a few banker boxes to hang the hanging files in. Not only is this method more economical, but the banker boxes are easier to move around and store.

Working with Customs

Customs doesn't care whether the customs broker that is submitting an entry to them works for the largest freight forwarder in America, or whether he or she is working off a ten dollar coffee table in the corner of their apartment. Just do your best to build a reputation as an honest and straight-forward broker, and Customs will treat you fairly.

Also, be aware that Customs is a government institution and things take time (including their role in processing your before-mentioned applications).

In closing, I would simply like to wish you a sincere "keep your head up" on your customs brokerage business.

! Final Tip(s) !
Finally, I recommend that you try to avoid the use debt to finance your business. Have a long-term game plan and grow the business with a patient heart.

Book 3 Introduction

Import & Export Documentation Simplified:
A Handbook of Samples, Templates, & Tips

What this book IS...

- A cheat sheet-like, easy-to-read overview of each of the most popular types of import & export documents in use today
- Thorough yet concise dissection of a wide variety of the most prevalently used shipping docs and forms
- Formatted for a side-by-side comparison of all blank forms vs. all correctly completed forms
- A compilation of documents completed in a manner most commonly practiced
- A practitioner's (not theorist's) guide to real-world import & export documentation
- Easy to navigate from one form to the next
- International business simplified

What this book IS NOT...

- A collection of exhaustive ramblings on how a dictionary defines each document
- Inclusive of irrelevant documents and parts thereof so commonly used on documents
- Laced with outdated theory and terminology
- Solely for the experienced veteran of international documentation

Disclaimer:

This book is designed to provide expert guidance regarding the subject matter covered. This information is given with the understanding that neither the author nor the publisher is engaged in rendering legal, accounting, or other professional advice. Since the details of your situation are fact dependent, you should also seek the advice of a competent professional.

All samples and templates contained herein are at the complete disposal of the owner of this book. Some of the templates contained in this book may be replicated by making multiple facsimile copies of a form or forms for repetitive use, or by carefully detaching the 8.8" x 11" pages from their binding. Though the utmost care was put into the creation of each sample and template, some templates will not be directly suitable for use as official documents. For example, both the Bill of Lading and Cargo Insurance Certificate must be issued by the cargo carrier and insurance company respectively.

2

Air Waybill (AWB)

Arrival Notice (A/N)

Bill of Lading (BL)

Booking Request

Cargo Insurance Certificate (COI)

Certificate of Origin (COO)

Commercial Invoice (CI)

Declaration for Free Entry of Returned U.S. Goods (USGR)

Declaration of No Wood Packing Material (WPM)

Declaration of Non-Coniferous Wood Packing Material (WPM)

Entry Summary (Customs Form 7501)

Importer Security Filing Form (ISF)

Importer's Blanket Statement of Non-Reimbursement of
    Anti-Dumping Duties (AD/CVD)

Letter of Credit Application   (L/C)

Packing List (PL)

Power of Attorney (POA)

Pre-Shipment Inspection Certificate (PSIC)

Pro Forma Invoice

Purchase Order (PO)

Sales Order (SO)

Shipping Instructions (SI)

Telex Release Request (TLX)

Toxic Substances Control Act Statement (TSCA)

Air Waybill (AWB)

ALSO KNOWN AS:
AWB. Air Consignment Note.

REQUIRED FOR:
All Air Imports and Exports

NOT REQUIRED FOR:
N/A

ORIGINAL COPIES NORMALLY REQUIRED?:
No

IN SUMMARY:
The air waybill is issued by the shipping company to the shipper, and serves the following purposes...

- It confirms the shipping company's receipt of goods tendered to it by the shipper.
- It exists as a contract between the shipper and the shipping company outlining the agreement to deliver the freight as per the air waybill.
- It communicates information regarding the consignee and notify parties at destination, airline routing and flight details, and handling instructions as per the shipper's instructions.

USEFUL TIPS:
The International Air Transport Association (IATA) is the air cargo industry's trade group. It is comprised of international and domestic airline companies and it maintains the specifications and uniformity of international air transport tools such as the air waybill. More on the air waybill can be found on IATA's website.

https://www.iata.org/whatwedo/cargo/pages/air_waybill.aspx

WHAT TO REMEMBER:
Unlike the ocean bill of lading, the air waybill is always non-negotiable, meaning that the original copy does not constitute title of the shipped goods.

Shipper's Name and Address	Shipper's Account Number ( )	Air Waybill

<table>
<tr><td rowspan="2">Consignee's Name and Address</td><td rowspan="2">Consignee's Account Number
( )</td><td>Copies 1, 2 and 3 of this Air Waybill are originals and have the same validity</td></tr>
<tr><td>It is agreed that the goods described herein are accepted in apparent good order and condition (except as noted) for carriage SUBJECT TO THE CONDITIONS OF CONTRACT ON THE REVERSE HEREOF. ALL GOODS MAY BE CARRIED BY ANY OTHER MEANS INCLUDING ROAD OR ANY OTHER CARRIER UNLESS SPECIFIC CONTRARY INSTRUCTIONS ARE GIVEN HEREON BY THE SHIPPER, AND SHIPPER AGREES THAT THE SHIPMENT MAY BE CARRIED VIA INTERMEDIATE STOPPING PLACES WHICH THE CARRIER DEEMS APPROPRIATE. THE SHIPPER'S ATTENTION IS DRAWN TO THE NOTICE CONCERNING CARRIER'S LIMITATION OF LIABILITY. Shipper may increase such limitation of liability by declaring a higher value for carriage and paying a supplemental charge if required.</td></tr>
</table>

Issuing carrier's agent name and city	Accounting Information

Agent's IATA Code	Account No.	

Airport of Departure and Requested Routing	Reference Number

<table>
<tr><td>To</td><td>By First Carrier (Routing and Destination)</td><td>Currency</td><td>CHGS Code</td><td>PPD</td><td>COLL</td><td>Declared Value for Carriage</td><td>Declared Value for Customs</td></tr>
<tr><td colspan="2">Airport of Destination   Requested Flight/Date</td><td colspan="2">Amount of Insurance</td><td colspan="4">INSURANCE -- If carrier offers Insurance, and such Insurance is requested in accordance with the conditions thereof, Indicate amount to be insured in figures in box marked "Amount of Insurance".</td></tr>
</table>

Handling Information

No. of Pieces RCP	Gross Weight	kg lb	Rate Class	Commodity Item no.	Chargeable Weight	Rate/ Charge	Total	Nature and quantity of goods (Incl. dimensions or volume)

(Prepaid)	(Weight Charge)	(Collect)	Other Charges
	(Valuation Charge)		
	(Tax)		I hereby certify that the particulars on the face hereof are correct and that insofar as any part of the consignment contains dangerous goods, such part is properly described by name and is in proper condition for carriage by air according to the applicable Dangerous Goods Regulations.
	(Total Other Charges Due Agent)		
	(Total Other Charges Due Carrier)		Signature of Shipper or his Agent
(Total Prepaid)	(Total Collect)		
(Currency Conversion)	(CC Charges in Dest. Currency)		Executed on (Date) (Place) Signature of Issuing Carrier or Its Agent
For Carrier's Use only at Destination	(Charges at Destination)	(Total Collect Charges)	

(Sample)

000-0000 0000   000-0000 0000

Shipper's Name and Address ABC CO., INC. 1234 A ST. ANYTOWN, USA	Shipper's Account Number ( )	Air Waybill Issued by Joe's Shipping Co. JSC

Copies 1, 2 and 3 of this Air Waybill are originals and have the same validity

Consignee's Name and Address BEST SPORTS CO., LTD. 888 OMOTE-DORI, YOKOHAMA, JAPAN TEL: (XXX) XXX - XXXX FAX: (XXX) XXX - XXXX	Consignee's Account Number ( )	It is agreed that the goods described herein are accepted in apparent good order and condition (except as noted) for carriage SUBJECT TO THE CONDITIONS OF CONTRACT ON THE REVERSE HEREOF. ALL GOODS MAY BE CARRIED BY ANY OTHER MEANS INCLUDING ROAD OR ANY OTHER CARRIER UNLESS SPECIFIC CONTRARY INSTRUCTIONS ARE GIVEN HEREON BY THE SHIPPER, AND SHIPPER AGREES THAT THE SHIPMENT MAY BE CARRIED VIA INTERMEDIATE STOPPING PLACES WHICH THE CARRIER DEEMS APPROPRIATE. THE SHIPPER'S ATTENTION IS DRAWN TO THE NOTICE CONCERNING CARRIER'S LIMITATION OF LIABILITY. Shipper may increase such limitation of liability by declaring a higher value for carriage and paying a supplemental charge if required

Issuing carrier's agent name and city	Accounting Information

Agent's IATA Code	Account No.	

Airport of Departure and Requested Routing LOS ANGELES (LAX)	Reference Number PO 1234

To NRT	By First Carrier (Routing and Destination) JS	Currency USD	CHGS Code	PPD X	COLL	Declared Value for Carriage NVD	Declared Value for Customs $10,000.00 USD

Airport of Destination NARITA (NRT)	Requested Flight/Date JS123/01	Amount of Insurance NIL	INSURANCE – If carrier offers insurance, and such Insurance is requested in accordance with the conditions thereof. Indicate amount to be insured in figures in box marked "Amount of Insurance"

Handling Information
Please Notify Consignee to Pick up. These commodities, technology, or software were exported from the United States in accordance with the Export Administration Regulations. Diversion contrary to U.S. law prohibited.

No. of Pieces RCP	Gross Weight	kg lb	Rate Class	Commodity Item no.	Chargeable Weight	Rate/ Charge	Total	Nature and quantity of goods (Incl. dimensions or volume)
1000	204	K	K		309			SPORTS EQUIPMENT (BASKETBALLS & VOLLEYBALLS) DIMS: 1 @ 102X102X102 CM 1 @ 102X102X76 CM

(Prepaid) PREPAID	(Weight Charge)	(Collect)	Other Charges
	(Valuation Charge)		
	(Tax)		
	(Total Other Charges Due Agent)		I hereby certify that the particulars on the face hereof are correct and that insofar as any part of the consignment contains dangerous goods, such part is properly described by name and is in proper condition for carriage by air according to the applicable Dangerous Goods Regulations.
	(Total Other Charges Due Carrier)		Signature of Shipper or his Agent
(Total Prepaid) $900.00 USD	(Total Collect)		
(Currency Conversion)	(CC Charges in Dest. Currency)		Executed on (Date) (Place) Signature of Issuing Carrier or Its Agent
For Carrier's Use only at Destination	(Charges at Destination)	(Total Collect Charges)	

000-0000 0000

3

Air Waybill (AWB)

Arrival Notice (A/N)

Bill of Lading (BL)
Booking Request
Cargo Insurance Certificate (COI)
Certificate of Origin (COO)
Commercial Invoice (CI)
Declaration for Free Entry of Returned U.S. Goods (USGR)
Declaration of No Wood Packing Material (WPM)
Declaration of Non-Coniferous Wood Packing Material (WPM)
Entry Summary (Customs Form 7501)
Importer Security Filing Form (ISF)
Importer's Blanket Statement of Non-Reimbursement of
        Anti-Dumping Duties (AD/CVD)
Letter of Credit Application   (L/C)
Packing List (PL)
Power of Attorney (POA)
Pre-Shipment Inspection Certificate (PSIC)
Pro Forma Invoice
Purchase Order (PO)
Sales Order (SO)
Shipping Instructions (SI)
Telex Release Request (TLX)
Toxic Substances Control Act Statement (TSCA)

Arrival Notice (A/N)

ALSO KNOWN AS:
A/N. Notice of Arrival.

REQUIRED FOR:
All Imports

NOT REQUIRED FOR:
N/A

ORIGINAL COPIES NORMALLY REQUIRED?:
No.

IN SUMMARY:
Carriers will routinely and automatically send written notification of a shipment's upcoming importation in the form of an arrival notice. The arrival notice is emailed, faxed, and/or snail mailed to the "shipper" and "notify party" entities as listed on the bill of lading or air waybill.

USEFUL TIPS:
Ask your customer (the exporter/shipper) to email a copy of the bill of lading to you as soon as it is available from the carrier at origin. The bill of lading is normally available within a day or two from the date of departure from the foreign port of lading. With information from the bill of lading on hand, the importer can follow-up with the carrier to ensure that a timely arrival notice will be sent to the appropriate parties at destination.

WHAT TO REMEMBER:
The importer should take special note of the arrival notice's 1) cargo pickup location and 2) estimated arrival date at destination in order to prevent costly, yet avoidable, storage charges (also known as "demurrage") at the port of import. Demurrage begins to accrue on a daily basis immediately after the "last free day". The last free day at destination may or may not be included on the carrier's arrival notice, and can be confirmed by contacting the carrier as per their contact instructions as notated on the arrival notice.

ARRIVAL NOTICE

JSC JOE'S SHIPPING CO.

SHIPPER		BL NO. BOOKING NO.			
		EXPORT REFERENCES			
CONSIGNEE		MAIL NOTICE OF ARRIVAL TO			
NOTIFY		CARGO PICKUP LOCATION			

ETA AT PORT OF DISCHARGE	COMBINED TRANSPORT – PLACE OF RECEIPT
VESSEL AND VOYAGE	PORT OF LOADING
PORT OF DISCHARGE	COMBINED TRANSPORT – PLACE OF DELIVERY

MARKS AND NUMBERS	NO. OF PKGS.	DESCRIPTION OF GOODS	GRS WEIGHT	MEASUREMENT

FREIGHT & CHARGES	RATE	PER	AMOUNT	PREPAID	COLLECT	***CONTACT OFFICE***

(Sample)
ARRIVAL NOTICE

⚙ JSC JOE'S SHIPPING CO.

SHIPPER BEST SPORTS, LTD. 888 OMOTE-DORI, YOKOHAMA, JAPAN	BL NO. JSCU23456789 BOOKING NO. JSCU23456789
	EXPORT REFERENCES PO#5678
CONSIGNEE ABC CO., INC. 1234 A ST. ANYTOWN, USA	MAIL NOTICE OF ARRIVAL TO ABC CO., INC. 1234 A ST. ANYTOWN, USA ATTN: LOGISTICS DEPT.
NOTIFY SAME AS CONSIGNEE TEL: (XXX) XXX - XXXX FAX: (XXX) XXX - XXXX EMAIL: DEE@ABCSPORTY.COM	CARGO PICKUP LOCATION PIER XYZ 999 PORT BLVD., LOS ANGELES, CA TEL: (XXX) XXX - XXXX FAX: (XXX) XXX - XXXX

ETA AT PORT OF DISCHARGE 01/01/20XX 12:00 PM	COMBINED TRANSPORT – PLACE OF RECEIPT
VESSEL AND VOYAGE JOE EXPRESS V. 002E	PORT OF LOADING YOKOHAMA
PORT OF DISCHARGE LOS ANGELES	COMBINED TRANSPORT – PLACE OF DELIVERY

MARKS AND NUMBERS	NO. OF PKGS.	DESCRIPTION OF GOODS	GRS WEIGHT	MEASUREMENT
"BEST SPORTS JAPAN" CONTAINER NO. JSCU1234567 SEAL NO. 2468	1000 BOXES ON 2 PALLETS	SPORTS EQUIPMENT (BASEBALLS)	150.000 KGS	2 CBM

FREIGHT & CHARGES	RATE	PER	AMOUNT	PREPAID	COLLECT	***CONTACT OFFICE*** JOE'S SHIPPING CO. 888 OCEANSIDE ROAD LOS ANGELES, CA TEL: (XXX) XXX - XXXX FAX: (XXX) XXX - XXXX
OCEAN FREIGHT			AS ARRANGED	X		
ADDL. FEES ORIGIN			AS ARRANGED	X		
THC DESTINATION	50.00 USD	1	50.00 USD		X	

4

Air Waybill (AWB)
Arrival Notice (A/N)

Bill of Lading (BL)

Booking Request
Cargo Insurance Certificate (COI)
Certificate of Origin (COO)
Commercial Invoice (CI)
Declaration for Free Entry of Returned U.S. Goods (USGR)
Declaration of No Wood Packing Material (WPM)
Declaration of Non-Coniferous Wood Packing Material (WPM)
Entry Summary (Customs Form 7501)
Importer Security Filing Form (ISF)
Importer's Blanket Statement of Non-Reimbursement of
    Anti-Dumping Duties (AD/CVD)
Letter of Credit Application   (L/C)
Packing List (PL)
Power of Attorney (POA)
Pre-Shipment Inspection Certificate (PSIC)
Pro Forma Invoice
Purchase Order (PO)
Sales Order (SO)
Shipping Instructions (SI)
Telex Release Request (TLX)
Toxic Substances Control Act Statement (TSCA)

Bill of Lading (BL)

ALSO KNOWN AS:
Clean Bill of Lading. Non-negotiable or Negotiable Bill of Lading. BOL. BL.

REQUIRED FOR:
All Ocean Imports and Exports

NOT REQUIRED FOR:
N/A

ORIGINAL COPIES NORMALLY REQUIRED?:
The necessity of issuing Original Bills of Lading (OBL) depends on the method of transfer of ownership as agreed upon between shipper and consignee.

IN SUMMARY:
The bill of lading is issued by the shipping company to the shipper, and serves the following purposes...

- It confirms the shipping company's receipt of goods tendered to it by the shipper (usually once loaded on the vessel).
- It exists as a contract between the shipper and the shipping company outlining the agreement to deliver the freight as per the bill of lading.
- It reveals that the importer of record at destination is the consignee party unless otherwise specified.
- It can function as legal title to the merchandise.

USEFUL TIPS:
Confirm beforehand with your customer, the consignee as listed on the bill of lading, regarding what additional details they would like to have included on the BOL.

WHAT TO REMEMBER:
As with all contracts, it is important to explicitly and clearly communicate all of your instructions to the shipping company so that they may properly draft the bill of lading for you accordingly. See the section of this handbook titled "Shipping Instructions (SI)" on how to do so. Request a proof copy of the BOL within a day or two after the sailing of the vessel so that any discrepancies may be corrected prior to the closing of the carrier's manifest.

(VOID—Actual Bill of Lading Must Be From Issuing Carrier) **BILL OF LADING**

SHIPPER	BOOKING NO.
	EXPORT REFERENCES
CONSIGNEE	FORWARDING AGENT REFERENCES
NOTIFY	POINT AND COUNTRY OF ORIGIN

PIER/TERMINAL	COMBINED TRANSPORT - PLACE OF RECEIPT
VESSEL	PORT OF LOADING
PORT OF DISCHARGE	COMBINED TRANSPORT - PLACE OF DELIVERY

MARKS AND NUMBERS	NO. OF PKGS.	DESCRIPTION OF GOODS	GRS WEIGHT	MEASUREMENT

FREIGHT & CHARGES	RATE	PER	AMOUNT	PREPAID	COLLECT	LADEN ON BOARD DATE
						PLACE OF BL ISSUE
						DATE OF BL ISSUE
						BL NO.
						SIGNED BY

SHIPPER'S LOAD AND COUNT
THESE COMMODITIES, TECHNOLOGIES, OR SOFTWARE WERE EXPORTED FROM THE UNITED STATES IN ACCORDANCE WITH THE EXPORT ADMINISTRATION REGULATIONS. DIVERSION CONTRARY TO U.S. LAW IS PROHIBITED.
Received in external apparent good order and condition except as otherwise noted. The total number of the packages or units stuffed in the carrier's receipt, said to contain the goods described in the particulars furnished by the shipper to be transported to the port of discharge, or to such other place authorized or permitted herein, or so near thereto as the vessel can get, lie and leave without delay, and there to be delivered to consignee, or authorized receiver, or on carrier on payment of all charges due thereon. The description of the goods and the weights shown on this bill of lading are furnished by the merchants

JSC JOE'S SHIPPING CO.   (Sample) BILL OF LADING

SHIPPER ABC CO., INC. 1234 A ST. ANYTOWN, USA	BOOKING NO. JSCU12345678
	EXPORT REFERENCES PO#1234
CONSIGNEE BEST SPORTS, LTD. 888 OMOTE-DORI, YOKOHAMA, JAPAN	FORWARDING AGENT REFERENCES
NOTIFY SAME AS CONSIGNEE TEL: (XXX) XXX – XXXX FAX: (XXX) XXX – XXXX	POINT AND COUNTRY OF ORIGIN ANYTOWN, USA

PIER/TERMINAL	COMBINED TRANSPORT – PLACE OF RECEIPT
VESSEL AND VOYAGE JOE EXPRESS V. 001W	PORT OF LOADING LOS ANGELES
PORT OF DISCHARGE YOKOHAMA	COMBINED TRANSPORT – PLACE OF DELIVERY

MARKS AND NUMBERS	NO. OF PKGS.	DESCRIPTION OF GOODS	GRS WEIGHT	MEASUREMENT
"ABC CO., INC., U.S.A." CONTAINER NO. JSCU1234567 SEAL NO. 678	1000 BOXES ON 2 PALLETS	SPORTS EQUIPMENT (BASKETBALLS & VOLLEYBALLS)	204.000 KGS	2 CBM

FREIGHT & CHARGES	RATE	PER	AMOUNT	PREPAID	COLLECT	
						LADEN ON BOARD DATE JAN. 31ST 20XX
OCEAN FREIGHT	400 USD	1	400.00 USD	X		PLACE OF BL ISSUE LOS ANGELES
ADDL. FEES ORIGIN	100 USD	1	100.00 USD	X		DATE OF BL ISSUE JAN. 31ST 20XX
THC DESTINATION	5000 JPY	1	5000 JPY		X	BL NO. JSCU12345678
						SIGNED BY JOE E. SUCCESS

SHIPPER'S LOAD AND COUNT

THESE COMMODITIES, TECHNOLOGIES, OR SOFTWARE WERE EXPORTED FROM THE UNITED STATES IN ACCORDANCE WITH THE EXPORT ADMINISTRATION REGULATIONS. DIVERSION CONTRARY TO U.S. LAW IS PROHIBITED.

Received in external apparent good order and condition except as otherwise noted. The total number of the packages or units stuffed in the carrier's receipt, said to contain the goods described in the particulars furnished by the shipper to be transported to the port of discharge, or to such other place authorized or permitted herein, or so near thereto as the vessel can get, lie and leave without delay, and there to be delivered to consignee, or authorized receiver, or on carrier on payment of all charges due thereon. The description of the goods and the weights shown on this bill of lading are furnished by the merchants

5

Air Waybill (AWB)
Arrival Notice (A/N)
Bill of Lading (BL)

Booking Request

Cargo Insurance Certificate (COI)
Certificate of Origin (COO)
Commercial Invoice (CI)
Declaration for Free Entry of Returned U.S. Goods (USGR)
Declaration of No Wood Packing Material (WPM)
Declaration of Non-Coniferous Wood Packing Material (WPM)
Entry Summary (Customs Form 7501)
Importer Security Filing Form (ISF)
Importer's Blanket Statement of Non-Reimbursement of
      Anti-Dumping Duties (AD/CVD)
Letter of Credit Application   (L/C)
Packing List (PL)
Power of Attorney (POA)
Pre-Shipment Inspection Certificate (PSIC)
Pro Forma Invoice
Purchase Order (PO)
Sales Order (SO)
Shipping Instructions (SI)
Telex Release Request (TLX)
Toxic Substances Control Act Statement (TSCA)

Booking Request

ALSO KNOWN AS:
Cargo/Freight Booking Request. Cargo/Freight Pickup Request.

REQUIRED FOR:
Exports

NOT REQUIRED FOR:
N/A

ORIGINAL COPIES NORMALLY REQUIRED?:
No

IN SUMMARY:
A booking request is a request made by a shipper and addressed to a carrier for the purpose of reserving space on an upcoming vessel or flight.

USEFUL TIPS:
Securing just the right booking request can be a challenge. The following factors should be considered...

- When will the supplier have their material or shipment ready?
- By what date does the shipment need to be tendered to carrier in order to meet customer's deadline?
- Does the customer restrict the use of certain types or specific carriers?
- How many days or weeks out is the carrier booked?

WHAT TO REMEMBER:
A shipper's booking request to their carrier does not have to be a formal procedure. It can be as informal as a short email as long as all the main details pertinent to the shipment booking are effectively communicated.

Booking Request

Date:

To:

Shipper's Export Reference:
Air or Ocean:
If Ocean, Container Type:
Commodity:

Shipper:
Pickup Location:
Shipment Ready for Pickup (Date & Time):
Consignee:

Port of Loading--Door or CY:
Final Destination--Door or CY:
Special Routing Instructions?:

AES ITN#:
Hazardous Cargo?:
Ocean Freight & Origin Charges (Prepaid or Collect):
Destination Charges (Prepaid or Collect):
Cargo Insurance Required?:
Original Bills of Lading Required?:

Shipment Details:

Pallet	No. of Pkgs.	Pallet. Dims.	Grs. Wt.	Tare Wt.	Net Wt.

(Sample)

ABC Co., Inc.
1234 A St.
Anytown, USA

Booking Request

Date: 1/1/20XX

To: Joe's Shipping Co.

Shipper's Export Reference: PO#1234
Air or Ocean: Ocean
If Ocean, Container Type: Less than Container Load (LCL)
Commodity: Sports Equipment (Basketballs & Volleyballs)

Shipper: ABC Co., Inc. 1234 A St., Anytown, USA
Pickup Location: (same as above)
Shipment Ready for Pickup (Date & Time): On 01/01/20XX a.m. (8am to 12pm)
Consignee: Best Sports, Ltd. 888 Omote-Dori, Yokohama, JAPAN

Port of Loading--Door or CY: Los Angeles--Door
Final Destination--Door or CY: Yokohama--Door
Special Routing Instructions?: Please book on the vessel Joe Express v.001w

AES ITN#: Please submit AES ITN# on behalf of ABC Co., Inc.
Hazardous Cargo?: No
Ocean Freight & Origin Charges (Prepaid or Collect): All Prepaid
Destination Charges (Prepaid or Collect): All Collect
Cargo Insurance Required?: No.
Original Bills of Lading Required?: Yes.

Shipment Details:

Pallet	No. of Pkgs.	Pallet. Dims.	Grs. Wt.	Tare Wt.	Net Wt.
#1	500 Boxes	40"x40"x40"	250 Lbs	60 Lbs	190 Lbs
#2	500 Boxes	40"x40"x30"	200 Lbs	40 Lbs	160 Lbs
Totals	1000 Boxes	On 2 Pallets	450 Lbs	100 Lbs	350 Lbs

6

Air Waybill (AWB)
Arrival Notice (A/N)
Bill of Lading (BL)
Booking Request

Cargo Insurance Certificate (COI)

Certificate of Origin (COO)
Commercial Invoice (CI)
Declaration for Free Entry of Returned U.S. Goods (USGR)
Declaration of No Wood Packing Material (WPM)
Declaration of Non-Coniferous Wood Packing Material (WPM)
Entry Summary (Customs Form 7501)
Importer Security Filing Form (ISF)
Importer's Blanket Statement of Non-Reimbursement of
     Anti-Dumping Duties (AD/CVD)
Letter of Credit Application   (L/C)
Packing List (PL)
Power of Attorney (POA)
Pre-Shipment Inspection Certificate (PSIC)
Pro Forma Invoice
Purchase Order (PO)
Sales Order (SO)
Shipping Instructions (SI)
Telex Release Request (TLX)
Toxic Substances Control Act Statement (TSCA)

Cargo Insurance Certificate (COI)

ALSO KNOWN AS:
Certificate of Insurance. COI. Marine Insurance. Marine Insurance Policy.

REQUIRED FOR:
Recommended for All Imports and Exports

NOT REQUIRED FOR:
N/A

ORIGINAL COPIES NORMALLY REQUIRED?:
Yes

IN SUMMARY:
Marine insurance is like any other form of insurance in that the assured (i.e. the purchaser of the cargo insurance policy) pays a fee to the insurance/surety company in the form of a premium payment in order to protect assets (i.e. the in-transit cargo).

USEFUL TIPS:
A commonly accepted amount of coverage is 110% of the cargo value (as stated on the supplier's invoice). The average cost of coverage will vary somewhat between different insurance companies, though a rate at about 0.001 times the amount of coverage would be about average. So, for example, if an importer or exporter wanted to insure 110% of a shipment valued at $10,000.00 USD, then the amount of coverage (also known as insured value) would be $11,000.00. The cost of insurance would then be $11.00 ($11,000.00 x 0.001). Most insurance companies will allow their customers to issue their own cargo insurance certificates online via their website.

WHAT TO REMEMBER:
Generally speaking, the average marine insurance policy does not pay out under the following scenarios...

- Loss of market (i.e. a customer will not pay for the delivered goods)
- Damage or deterioration of goods arising from a prolonged shipment delay
- Loss of material due to the inherent nature of the product
- Strikes, riots, and wars (unless explicitly provided for or added to policy)

(VOID—Actual Certificate Must Be From Issuing Insurance Co.)

Cargo Insurance Certificate	
Insurance Company:	Date of Issuance: Place of Issuance: Date of Shipment:
Assured:	Policy#: Certificate#:
Vessel/Flight:	Insured Value:
Place of Origin: Port of Loading:	Final Destination: Port of Discharge:
Commodity Description: Marks & Numbers: Pieces & Weights:	
Notes:	
Claims Agent at Destination:	
Conditions:	

By: _____ Title: _____ Date_____
     (Signature of the Assured)

(Sample)

Cargo Insurance Certificate	
Insurance Company: Paco's Del Mar Marine & Casualty 1234 C St. Anytown, USA	**Date of Issuance:** 1/1/20XX **Place of Issuance:** Anytown, USA **Date of Shipment:** 1/1/20XX
Assured: ABC Co., Inc. 1234 A St., Anytown, USA	**Policy#:** 1234567 **Certificate#:** 1234567
Vessel/Flight: Joe Express v.001w	**Insured Value:** $11,000.00 USD
Place of Origin: Anytown, USA	**Final Destination:** Yokohama, Japan
Port of Loading: Los Angeles, USA	**Port of Discharge:** Yokohama, Japan

Commodity Description: Basketballs & Volleyballs

Marks & Numbers:
Container#JSCU1234567
"ABC Co, Inc., U.S.A."

Pieces & Weights:
1000 Boxes, 450 Lbs Grs.

Notes: Each claim for loss or damage shall include a deduction in the exact amount of the policy deductible.

Claims Agent at Destination: Kotatsu Marine & Casualty, LLC, 234 Harbor Way, Yokohama, Japan

Conditions: This insurance is subject to the latest American Institute Cargo Clauses Free of Particular Average—American Conditions (FPAAC) available at the time of shipment.

Additional terms and conditions of this certificate available at Paco's Del Mar's homepage.

By: _____ Title: _____ Date_____
    (Signature of the Assured)

7

Air Waybill (AWB)
Arrival Notice (A/N)
Bill of Lading (BL)
Booking Request
Cargo Insurance Certificate (COI)

Certificate of Origin (COO)

Commercial Invoice (CI)
Declaration for Free Entry of Returned U.S. Goods (USGR)
Declaration of No Wood Packing Material (WPM)
Declaration of Non-Coniferous Wood Packing Material (WPM)
Entry Summary (Customs Form 7501)
Importer Security Filing Form (ISF)
Importer's Blanket Statement of Non-Reimbursement of
        Anti-Dumping Duties (AD/CVD)
Letter of Credit Application   (L/C)
Packing List (PL)
Power of Attorney (POA)
Pre-Shipment Inspection Certificate (PSIC)
Pro Forma Invoice
Purchase Order (PO)
Sales Order (SO)
Shipping Instructions (SI)
Telex Release Request (TLX)
Toxic Substances Control Act Statement (TSCA)

Certificate of Origin (COO)

ALSO KNOWN AS:
COO.

REQUIRED FOR:
Some Imports and Exports

NOT REQUIRED FOR:
N/A

ORIGINAL COPIES NORMALLY REQUIRED?:
No

IN SUMMARY:
Although the commercial invoice will also usually contain a statement regarding the country of origin of the goods, the certificate of origin is a separate document by which the shipper or manufacturer certifies that the goods contained herein are products of their country. A local chamber of commerce can also separately provide a certificate of origin, and if required, a certificate of origin may also be notarized.

USEFUL TIPS:
In general, if a product consists of material or parts from more than one country, then the country of origin of the commodity is the material or part that imparts the essential character of the good. For example, if all the parts of a child's bicycle were produced in the USA except for the training wheels, then the finished product would still be considered as originating in the USA. For specific advice on this topic concerning your product, you may consult with your customs broker.

WHAT TO REMEMBER:
A certificate of origin may be required depending on the customer, country of import, and type of commodity. When in doubt whether a certificate of origin is required or not for your shipment, go ahead and include it with the rest of your documents.

Certificate of Origin

Date:
Certificate#:
Invoice#:

Sold To:
Ship To:

Name of Person Completing Certificate:
Name of Firm:
Actual Mfr:

Carrier:

Qty.	Unit	No. Pkg.	Grs. Wt.	Tare Wt.	Net Wt.	Description of Goods

Marks: "ABC Co., Inc., U.S.A."

I declare that I am the person named above, acting in the capacity indicated, that the description and other particulars of the merchandise as specified above are correct as set forth in this certificate, and that the said merchandise was produced or manufactured in the United States of America.

By: _____   Title: _____
       (signature)

(Sample)

ABC Co., Inc.
1234 A St.
Anytown, USA

Certificate of Origin

Date: 1/1/20XX
Certificate#: 1234ABC
Invoice#: 1234

Sold To: Best Sports, Ltd. 888 Omote-Dori, Yokohama, JAPAN
Ship To: (same as above)

Name of Person Completing Certificate: Jane Doe
Name of Firm: ABC Co., Inc.
Actual Mfr: ABC Co., Inc.

Carrier: Hyundai Merchant Marine

Qty.	Unit	No. Pkg.	Grs. Wt.	Tare Wt.	Net Wt.	Description of Goods
500	Each	500 Boxes	0.5 Lbs	0.1 Lbs	0.4 Lbs	Basketballs (rubber)
500	Each	500 Boxes	0.4 Lbs	0.1 Lbs	0.3 Lbs	Volleyballs (synth. leather)
		1000 Boxes	450 Lbs	100 Lbs	350 Lbs	**Packaging Totals**

Marks: "ABC Co., Inc., U.S.A."

I declare that I am the person named above, acting in the capacity indicated, that the description and other particulars of the merchandise as specified above are correct as set forth in this certificate, and that the said merchandise was produced or manufactured in the United States of America.

By: _____   Title: _____
   (signature)

8

Air Waybill (AWB)
Arrival Notice (A/N)
Bill of Lading (BL)
Booking Request
Cargo Insurance Certificate (COI)
Certificate of Origin (COO)

Commercial Invoice (CI)

Declaration for Free Entry of Returned U.S. Goods (USGR)
Declaration of No Wood Packing Material (WPM)
Declaration of Non-Coniferous Wood Packing Material (WPM)
Entry Summary (Customs Form 7501)
Importer Security Filing Form (ISF)
Importer's Blanket Statement of Non-Reimbursement of
    Anti-Dumping Duties (AD/CVD)
Letter of Credit Application   (L/C)
Packing List (PL)
Power of Attorney (POA)
Pre-Shipment Inspection Certificate (PSIC)
Pro Forma Invoice
Purchase Order (PO)
Sales Order (SO)
Shipping Instructions (SI)
Telex Release Request (TLX)
Toxic Substances Control Act Statement (TSCA)

Commercial Invoice (CI)

ALSO KNOWN AS:
CI. Invoice. Customs Invoice.

REQUIRED FOR:
All Imports and Exports

NOT REQUIRED FOR:
N/A

ORIGINAL COPIES NORMALLY REQUIRED?:
No

IN SUMMARY:
The commercial invoice officially documents the details of a business transaction between two parties, and is used by customs to accurately assess the true value of the shipment.

USEFUL TIPS:
Remember the acronym "PIT CAR FUD" as a reminder for the most important elements to include on the commercial invoice to help ensure trouble-free customs clearances.

P = Pieces (quantity and unit of measure)
I = Importer of Record (sold to party)
T = Terms of Sale (INCO Terms)
C = Country of Origin (country where the goods were produced)
A = Actual Manufacturer (name and address--if known)
R = Related Parties? (shipper and importer)
F = Freight Charges (estimated ocean or air freight charges)
U = USD (Currency)
D = Description (in as much detail as possible)

WHAT TO REMEMBER:
Additional information may be added to the commercial invoice, including but not limited to: purchase order number, letter of credit number, container and seal number, carrier vessel or flight details, estimated departure and arrival dates, harmonized tariff schedule number, as well as any other information pertinent to the order or shipment.

Commercial Invoice

Date:
Invoice#:

Sold To:
Ship To:

Terms of Sale:
Country of Origin and Export:
Actual Mfr:
Freight Charges:

Qty.	Unit of Measure	Unit Price	Description of Goods	Total Value (USD)
		Total		

I certify that these goods are of USA origin, and this invoice to be true and correct.

By: _____   Title: _____
      (signature)

(Sample)

ABC Co., Inc.
1234 A St.
Anytown, USA

Commercial Invoice

Date: 1/1/20XX
Invoice#: 1234

Sold To: Best Sports, Ltd. 888 Omote-Dori, Yokohama, JAPAN
Ship To: (same as above)

Terms of Sale: C&F Yokohama
Country of Origin and Export: USA
Actual Mfr: ABC Co., Inc.
Freight Charges: $500.00 USD

Qty.	Unit of Measure	Unit Price	Description of Goods	Total Value (USD)
500	Each	10.00	Basketballs (rubber)	$5,000.00
500	Each	10.00	Volleyballs (synth. leather)	$5,000.00
			Total	$10,000.00

I certify that these goods are of USA origin, and this invoice to be true and correct.

By: _____   Title: _____
　　　　　(signature)

9

Air Waybill (AWB)
Arrival Notice (A/N)
Bill of Lading (BL)
Booking Request
Cargo Insurance Certificate (COI)
Certificate of Origin (COO)
Commercial Invoice (CI)

Declaration for Free Entry of Returned U.S. Goods (USGR)

Declaration of No Wood Packing Material (WPM)
Declaration of Non-Coniferous Wood Packing Material (WPM)
Entry Summary (Customs Form 7501)
Importer Security Filing Form (ISF)
Importer's Blanket Statement of Non-Reimbursement of
        Anti-Dumping Duties (AD/CVD)
Letter of Credit Application   (L/C)
Packing List (PL)
Power of Attorney (POA)
Pre-Shipment Inspection Certificate (PSIC)
Pro Forma Invoice
Purchase Order (PO)
Sales Order (SO)
Shipping Instructions (SI)
Telex Release Request (TLX)
Toxic Substances Control Act Statement (TSCA)

Declaration for Free Entry of Returned U.S. Goods (USGR)

ALSO KNOWN AS:
USGR. U.S./American Goods Returned Declaration. AGR.

REQUIRED FOR:
Duty exemption for Imports that are of U.S. origin and being shipped back to the U.S.

NOT REQUIRED FOR:
N/A

ORIGINAL COPIES NORMALLY REQUIRED?:
No

IN SUMMARY:
The "declaration for free entry of returned U.S. goods" is an affidavit made by both the shipper and the importer stating that their imported product is of U.S. origin and has not been advanced in value abroad in order to allow it duty free entry to the United States.

USEFUL TIPS:
Per the United States Code of Federal Regulations, Title 19 (Customs Duties), in any case in which the value of the returned articles exceeds $2,500 and the articles are not clearly marked with the name and address of the U.S. manufacturer, the port director may require, in addition to the declaration, such as a statement from the U.S. manufacturer verifying that the articles were made in the U.S., a U.S. export invoice, bill of lading or airway bill evidencing the U.S. origin of the articles and/or the reason for the exportation of the articles.

WHAT TO REMEMBER:
Per the United States Code of Federal Regulations, Title 19 (Customs Duties), the declaration must be made by the owner, importer, consignee, or agent having knowledge of the facts regarding the claim for free entry. If the owner or ultimate consignee is a corporation, such declaration may be signed by the president, vice president, secretary, or treasurer of the corporation, or may be signed by any employee or agent of the corporation who holds a power of attorney and a certification by the corporation that such employee or other agent has or will have knowledge of the pertinent facts.

Declaration for Free Entry of Returned U.S. Goods

Shipper's Declaration:

I, _____ (printed name), declare that to the best of my knowledge and belief that the articles herein specified were exported from the United States, from the port of _____ on or about _____, 20___, and that they are returned without having been advanced in value or improved in condition by any process of manufacture or other means.

Marks	Number	Quantity	Description	Value, USD

Date: _____

Address: _____

Signature: _____

Capacity: _____

Importer's Declaration:

I, _____ (printed name), declare that the (above) declaration by the foreign shipper is true and correct to the best of my knowledge and belief, that the articles were manufactured by _____ (name of manufacturer) located in _____ (city and state), that the articles were not manufactured or produced in the United States under subheading 9813.00.05, HTSUS, and that the articles were exported from the United States without benefit of drawback.

Date: _____

Address: _____

Signature: _____

Capacity: _____

(Sample)
Declaration for Free Entry of Returned U.S. Goods

Shipper's Declaration:

I, __Deng Xiaoping__ (printed name), declare that to the best of my knowledge and belief that the articles herein specified were exported from the United States, from the port of __Seattle_ on or about __Jan. 1st__, 20XX, and that they are returned without having been advanced in value or improved in condition by any process of manufacture or other means.

Marks	Number	Quantity	Description	Value, USD

Date: _____

Address: _____

Signature: _____

Capacity: _____

Importer's Declaration:

I, __Howard Hughes_____ (printed name), declare that the (above) declaration by the foreign shipper is true and correct to the best of my knowledge and belief, that the articles were manufactured by __The Boeing Co.____ (name of manufacturer) located in _Seattle, WA_____ (city and state), that the articles were not manufactured or produced in the United States under subheading 9813.00.05, HTSUS, and that the articles were exported from the United States without benefit of drawback.

Date: _____

Address: _____

Signature: _____

Capacity: _____

10

Air Waybill (AWB)
Arrival Notice (A/N)
Bill of Lading (BL)
Booking Request
Cargo Insurance Certificate (COI)
Certificate of Origin (COO)
Commercial Invoice (CI)
Declaration for Free Entry of Returned U.S. Goods (USGR)

Declaration of No Wood Packing Material (WPM)

Declaration of Non-Coniferous Wood Packing Material (WPM)
Entry Summary (Customs Form 7501)
Importer Security Filing Form (ISF)
Importer's Blanket Statement of Non-Reimbursement of
        Anti-Dumping Duties (AD/CVD)
Letter of Credit Application   (L/C)
Packing List (PL)
Power of Attorney (POA)
Pre-Shipment Inspection Certificate (PSIC)
Pro Forma Invoice
Purchase Order (PO)
Sales Order (SO)
Shipping Instructions (SI)
Telex Release Request (TLX)
Toxic Substances Control Act Statement (TSCA)

Declaration of No Wood Packing Material (WPM)

ALSO KNOWN OR REFERRED TO AS:
No (Solid) Wood Packing Material Certificate/Statement. WPM. ISPM 15.

REQUIRED FOR:
Exports to China, for which the shipper wants to certify, do not contain any solid wood packing material such as crates, pallets, etc.

NOT REQUIRED FOR:
N/A

ORIGINAL COPIES NORMALLY REQUIRED?:
No

IN SUMMARY:
Most countries require all imported solid (i.e. raw and unprocessed) wood packing material (WPM) to be either heat treated or fumigated, and subsequently stamped certifying this.

XX - 000
YY

XX = Country of manufacture:
000 = Code traceable to the source (pallet manufacturer)
YY = Treatment Measure (HT or MB [fumigated])

In addition to this requirement, the China customs service requires documentation of at least one of the following...

- Declaration of no wood packing material
- Declaration of non-coniferous wood packing material
- Certificate of fumigation
- Certificate of heat treatment

USEFUL TIPS:
Information regarding both heat and fumigation treatment and certification of the same can be found on USDA's website...

http://www.aphis.usda.gov/import_export/plants/plant_exports/wpm/index.shtml

Declaration of No Wood Packing Material

To the services of China Entry & Exit Inspection and Quarantine: It is advised that this shipment does not contain any solid wood packing material.

Shipment# (BL#, AWB#, or Booking#):

Country of Origin and Export:

Qty.	Unit	No. Pkg.	Pkg. Dims.	Grs. Wt.	Tare Wt.	Net Wt.	Description of Goods
							Packaging Totals

Marks:

By: _____   Title: _____   Date_____
   (Exporter's signature)

(Sample)

ABC Co., Inc.
1234 A St.
Anytown, USA

Declaration of No Wood Packing Material

To the services of China Entry & Exit Inspection and Quarantine: It is advised that this shipment does not contain any solid wood packing material.

Shipment# (BL#, AWB#, or Booking#): BL# JSCU12345678
Country of Origin and Export: USA

Qty.	Unit	No. Pkg.	Pkg. Dims.	Grs. Wt.	Tare Wt.	Net Wt.	Description of Goods
500	Each	500 Boxes	7"x7"x7" (per box)	0.5 Lbs	0.1 Lbs	0.4 Lbs	Basketballs (rubber)
500	Each	500 Boxes	5"x5"x5" (per box)	0.4 Lbs	0.1 Lbs	0.3 Lbs	Volleyballs (synth. leather)
		1000 Boxes	(cardboard)	450 Lbs	100 Lbs	350 Lbs	Packaging Totals

Marks: "ABC Co., Inc., U.S.A."

By: _____   Title: _____   Date_____
        (Exporter's signature)

11

Air Waybill (AWB)
Arrival Notice (A/N)
Bill of Lading (BL)
Booking Request
Cargo Insurance Certificate (COI)
Certificate of Origin (COO)
Commercial Invoice (CI)
Declaration for Free Entry of Returned U.S. Goods (USGR)
Declaration of No Wood Packing Material (WPM)

Declaration of Non-Coniferous Wood Packing Material (WPM)

Entry Summary (Customs Form 7501)
Importer Security Filing Form (ISF)
Importer's Blanket Statement of Non-Reimbursement of
    Anti-Dumping Duties (AD/CVD)
Letter of Credit Application   (L/C)
Packing List (PL)
Power of Attorney (POA)
Pre-Shipment Inspection Certificate (PSIC)
Pro Forma Invoice
Purchase Order (PO)
Sales Order (SO)
Shipping Instructions (SI)
Telex Release Request (TLX)
Toxic Substances Control Act Statement (TSCA)

Declaration of Non-Coniferous Wood Packing Material (WPM)

ALSO KNOWN OR REFERRED TO AS:
Non-Coniferous Wood Packing Material Certificate/Statement. WPM. ISPM 15.

REQUIRED FOR:
Exports to China, for which the shipper wants to certify, do not contain any coniferous wood packing material such as crates, pallets, etc.

NOT REQUIRED FOR:
N/A

ORIGINAL COPIES NORMALLY REQUIRED?:
No

IN SUMMARY:
Most countries require all imported solid (i.e. raw and unprocessed) wood packing material (WPM) to be either heat treated or fumigated, and subsequently stamped certifying this.

XX - 000
YY
XX = Country of manufacture:
000 = Code traceable to the source (pallet manufacturer)
YY = Treatment Measure (HT or MB [fumigated])

In addition to this requirement, the China customs service requires documentation of at least one of the following...

- Declaration of no wood packing material
- Declaration of non-coniferous wood packing material
- Certificate of fumigation
- Certificate of heat treatment

USEFUL TIPS:
Information regarding both heat and fumigation treatment and certification of the same can be found on USDA's website...

http://www.aphis.usda.gov/import_export/plants/plant_exports/wpm/index.shtml

Declaration of Non-Coniferous Wood Packing Material

To the services of China Entry & Exit Inspection and Quarantine: It is advised that all wood packing materials in this shipment are made of non-coniferous trees.

Shipment# (BL#, AWB#, or Booking#):
Country of Origin and Export:

Qty.	Unit	No. Pkg.	Pkg. Dims.	Grs. Wt.	Tare Wt.	Net Wt.	Description of Goods
							Packaging Totals

Marks:

By: _____ Title: _____ Date_____
    (Exporter's signature)

(Sample)

ABC Co., Inc.
1234 A St.
Anytown, USA

Declaration of Non-Coniferous Wood Packing Material

To the services of China Entry & Exit Inspection and Quarantine: It is advised that all wood packing materials in this shipment are made of non-coniferous trees.

Shipment# (BL#, AWB#, or Booking#): BL# JSCU12345678
Country of Origin and Export: USA

Qty.	Unit	No. Pkg.	Pkg. Dims.	Grs. Wt.	Tare Wt.	Net Wt.	Description of Goods
500	Each	500 Boxes	7"x7"x7" (per box)	0.5 Lbs	0.1 Lbs	0.4 Lbs	Basketballs (rubber)
500	Each	500 Boxes	5"x5"x5" (per box)	0.4 Lbs	0.1 Lbs	0.3 Lbs	Volleyballs (synth. leather)
		1000 Boxes	(cardboard)	450 Lbs	100 Lbs	350 Lbs	Packaging Totals

Marks: "ABC Co., Inc., U.S.A."

By: _____   Title: _____   Date_____
     (Exporter's signature)

12

Air Waybill (AWB)

Arrival Notice (A/N)

Bill of Lading (BL)

Booking Request

Cargo Insurance Certificate (COI)

Certificate of Origin (COO)

Commercial Invoice (CI)

Declaration for Free Entry of Returned U.S. Goods (USGR)

Declaration of No Wood Packing Material (WPM)

Declaration of Non-Coniferous Wood Packing Material (WPM)

Entry Summary (Customs Form 7501)

Importer Security Filing Form (ISF)

Importer's Blanket Statement of Non-Reimbursement of
     Anti-Dumping Duties (AD/CVD)

Letter of Credit Application   (L/C)

Packing List (PL)

Power of Attorney (POA)

Pre-Shipment Inspection Certificate (PSIC)

Pro Forma Invoice

Purchase Order (PO)

Sales Order (SO)

Shipping Instructions (SI)

Telex Release Request (TLX)

Toxic Substances Control Act Statement (TSCA)

Entry Summary (Customs Form 7501)

ALSO KNOWN AS:
7501. CBP FORM 7501.

REQUIRED FOR:
Most U.S. Imports

NOT REQUIRED FOR:
Exports

ORIGINAL COPIES NORMALLY REQUIRED?:
No

IN SUMMARY:
The entry summary is just as its name suggests. It is a final detailed summary whereby the importer (or customs broker on importer's behalf) provides to U.S. Customs all of the details of their importation, including harmonized tariff schedule (HTSUS) classification, value of shipment, special program indicator (SPI) for the sake of duty reduction such as NAFTA, etc. if applicable, the resulting duties, as well as other necessary statistical information,

USEFUL TIPS:
The completion and filing of the importer's entry summary to Customs can be likened to the filing of an individual's income taxes to the IRS. On the entry summary, the importer makes truthful and well-informed declarations regarding classification, valuation, and possible duty exempt status of their shipment. U.S. Customs depends on the accuracy of this information in order to effectively collect duties and taxes. And, just as a certified public accountant (CPA) can complete IRS form 1040, etc. on behalf of a taxpayer, a licensed customs broker (LCB) can complete, compute, and file the Customs form 7501 as a service for the importer. Instructions for filling out this Customs form as well as other downloadable Customs forms can be found on Customs' website.

http://www.cbp.gov/xp/cgov/toolbox/forms/

WHAT TO REMEMBER:
Though most U.S. imports are granted conditional releases soon after the importer or customs broker submits an entry to Customs, the "entry summary" along with payment of estimated duties must be filed within 10 working days of the shipment's release date.

Form Approved OMB No. 1651-0022
EXP. 08-31-2014

DEPARTMENT OF HOMELAND SECURITY
U.S. Customs and Border Protection

ENTRY SUMMARY

1. Filer Code/Entry No.		2. Entry Type	3. Summary Date
4. Surety No.	5. Bond Type	6. Port Code	7. Entry Date

8. Importing Carrier	9. Mode of Transport	10. Country of Origin	11. Import Date
12. B/L or AWB No.	13. Manufacturer ID	14. Exporting Country	15. Export Date
16. I.T. No.	17. I.T. Date 18. Missing Docs	19. Foreign Port of Lading	20. U.S. Port of Unlading
21. Location of Goods/G.O. No.	22. Consignee No.	23. Importer No.	24. Reference No.

25. Ultimate Consignee Name and Address	26. Importer of Record Name and Address
City State Zip	City State Zip

27.	28. Description of Merchandise			32.	33.	34.
Line No.	29. A. HTSUS No. B. ADA/CVD No.	30. A. Grossweight B. Manifest Qty.	31. Net Quantity in HTSUS Units	A. Entered Value B. CHGS C. Relationship	A. HTSUS Rate B. ADA/CVD Rate C. IRC Rate D. Visa No.	Duty and I.R. Tax Dollars Cents

Other Fee Summary for Block 39	35. Total Entered Value	**CBP USE ONLY**		TOTALS
	$	A. LIQ CODE	B. Ascertained Duty	37. Duty
	Total Other Fees $	REASON CODE	C. Ascertained Tax	38. Tax

36. DECLARATION OF IMPORTER OF RECORD (OWNER OR PURCHASER) OR AUTHORIZED AGENT

	D. Ascertained Other	39. Other
	E. Ascertained Total	40. Total

I declare that I am the ☐ Importer of record and that the actual owner, purchaser, or consignee for CBP purposes is as shown above, **OR** ☐ owner or purchaser or agent thereof. I further declare that the merchandise ☐ was obtained pursuant to a purchase or agreement to purchase and that the prices set forth in the invoices are true, **OR** ☐ was not obtained pursuant to a purchase or agreement to purchase and the statements in the invoices as to value or price are true to the best of my knowledge and belief. I also declare that the statements in the documents herein filed fully disclose to the best of my knowledge and belief the true prices, values, quantities, rebates, drawbacks, fees, commissions, and royalties and are true and correct, and that all goods or services provided to the seller of the merchandise either free or at reduced cost are fully disclosed. I will immediately furnish to the appropriate CBP officer any information showing a different statement of facts.

41. DECLARANT NAME	TITLE	SIGNATURE	DATE
42. Broker/Filer Information (Name, address, phone number)		43. Broker/Importer File No.	

CBP Form 7501 (06/09)

Form Approved OMB No. 1651-0022
EXP. 08-31-2014

DEPARTMENT OF HOMELAND SECURITY
U.S. Customs and Border Protection

ENTRY SUMMARY

1. Filer Code/Entry No.		2. Entry Type	3. Summary Date
AAA-XXXXXXX-X		01 ABI/A	01/09/2013

4. Surety No.	5. Bond Type	6. Port Code	7. Entry Date
XXX	8	2704	01/01/2013

8. Importing Carrier	9. Mode of Transport	10. Country of Origin	11. Import Date
JOE EXPRESS V.002E	10	JP	01/01/2013

12. B/L or AWB No.	13. Manufacturer ID	14. Exporting Country	15. Export Date
JSCU12345678	JPBESSPO888YOK	JP	12/21/2012

16. I.T. No.	17. I.T. Date	18. Missing Docs	19. Foreign Port of Lading	20. U.S. Port of Unlading
			58895	2704

21. Location of Goods/G.O. No.	22. Consignee No.	23. Importer No.	24. Reference No.
AXXX	XX-XXXXXXX	XX-XXXXXXX	

25. Ultimate Consignee Name and Address

26. Importer of Record Name and Address

ABC CO., INC.
1234 A ST.

City   State CA Zip

City ANYTOWN   State CA Zip XXXXX

27. Line No.	28. Description of Merchandise			32. A. Entered Value / B. CHGS / C. Relationship	33. A. HTSUS Rate / B. ADA/CVD Rate / C. IRC Rate / D. Visa No.	34. Duty and I.R. Tax
	29. A. HTSUS No. / B. ADA/CVD No.	30. A. Grossweight / B. Manifest Qty.	31. Net Quantity in HTSUS Units			Dollars Cents
	150 KGS. 1000 BOXES BL#JSCU23456789			NOT RELATED		
001	BASEBALLS HTSUS 9506.69.2040 150 KGS.		1000 NO.	5000	FREE	0.00
				C 500		
	HARBOR MAINTENANCE FEE				0.125%	6.25
	MERCHANDISE PROCESSING FEE				0.3464%	17.32
	ENTERED VALUE USD 5000					

Other Fee Summary for Block 39	35. Total Entered Value	**CBP USE ONLY**		TOTALS
501 6.25	$ 5,000.00	A. LIQ CODE	B. Ascertained Duty	37. Duty
499 25.00				0.00
	Total Other Fees	REASON CODE	C. Ascertained Tax	38. Tax
	$ 31.25			0.00

36. DECLARATION OF IMPORTER OF RECORD (OWNER OR PURCHASER) OR AUTHORIZED AGENT

	D. Ascertained Other	39. Other
		31.25
	E. Ascertained Total	40. Total
		31.25

I declare that I am the ☐ Importer of record and that the actual owner, purchaser, or consignee for CBP purposes is as shown above, **OR** ☒ owner or purchaser or agent thereof. I further declare that the merchandise ☒ was obtained pursuant to a purchase or agreement to purchase and that the prices set forth in the invoices are true. **OR** ☐ was not obtained pursuant to a purchase or agreement to purchase and the statements in the invoices as to value or price are true to the best of my knowledge and belief. I also declare that the statements in the documents herein filed fully disclose to the best of my knowledge and belief the true prices, values, quantities, rebates, drawbacks, fees, commissions, and royalties and are true and correct, and that all goods or services provided to the seller of the merchandise either free or at reduced cost are fully disclosed.
I will immediately furnish to the appropriate CBP officer any information showing a different statement of facts.

41. DECLARANT NAME	TITLE	SIGNATURE	DATE
DAVE THOMAS	ATTY-IN-FACT		01/01/2013

42. Broker/Filer Information (Name, address, phone number)	43. Broker/Importer File No.
PERFECT CUSTOMS BROKERAGE, INC. 888 CIRCULAR DR., ANYTOWN, USA TEL: (XXX)XXX-XXXX	12345

CBP Form 7501 (06/09)

13

Air Waybill (AWB)

Arrival Notice (A/N)

Bill of Lading (BL)

Booking Request

Cargo Insurance Certificate (COI)

Certificate of Origin (COO)

Commercial Invoice (CI)

Declaration for Free Entry of Returned U.S. Goods (USGR)

Declaration of No Wood Packing Material (WPM)

Declaration of Non-Coniferous Wood Packing Material (WPM)

Entry Summary (Customs Form 7501)

Importer Security Filing Form (ISF)

Importer's Blanket Statement of Non-Reimbursement of
    Anti-Dumping Duties (AD/CVD)

Letter of Credit Application   (L/C)

Packing List (PL)

Power of Attorney (POA)

Pre-Shipment Inspection Certificate (PSIC)

Pro Forma Invoice

Purchase Order (PO)

Sales Order (SO)

Shipping Instructions (SI)

Telex Release Request (TLX)

Toxic Substances Control Act Statement (TSCA)

Importer Security Filing (ISF)

ALSO KNOWN AS:
ISF. 10 + 2.

REQUIRED FOR:
All containerized and break bulk ocean Imports (destined for the United States).

NOT REQUIRED FOR:
Air Imports or Exports

ORIGINAL COPIES NORMALLY REQUIRED?:
No

IN SUMMARY:
For national security purposes, US Customs and Border Protection (CBP) absolutely requires importers (or their agents on their behalf) to submit electronically to CBP, at least 24 – 48 hours prior to their shipment being loaded on a U.S. destined vessel, 10 specific data sets of their cargo. They include...

1) Importer of record ID# (IRS# or Customs ID#)
2) Consignee ID#
3) Buyer name and address
4) Ship-to location name and address
5) Seller name and address
6) Manufacturer (or supplier) name and address
7) Container stuffing location name and address
8) Container consolidator (stuffer) name and address
9) Country of origin
10) Harmonized Tariff Schedule (HTS) number/code (at least up to six-digit level)

USEFUL TIPS:
Importer compliance with ISF requirements is highly dependant on an open line of communication between the shipper (seller) and importer (buyer). The foreign seller must be well aware at the time of the order that they are obligated to furnish the buyer with the required ISF data elements in order to avoid costly US Customs penalties.

WHAT TO REMEMBER:
Whether the importer transmits their ISF by themselves or through the services of a freight forwarder or customs broker, the transmission of ISF information must at least be 24 – 48 hours prior to the loading of the ocean container onto the vessel. Non-compliance penalties can be as much as $5,000.00 USD per violation.

Importer Security Filing Form (ISF)

To:

Master BOL#:
House BOL# (if applicable):
Estimated Load Date:

Importer of Record (IOR):
IOR ID#:
Consignee ID#:
Buyer:
Ship To:

Seller Name & Address:
Manufacturer Name & Address:
Container Stuffing Name & Address:
Consolidator Name & Address:

Description of Goods	Country of Origin	Harmonized Code (HTS)

By: _____ Title: _____ Date_____
   (Importer's signature)

(Sample)

ABC Co., Inc.
1234 A St.
Anytown, USA

Importer Security Filing Form (ISF)

To: Perfect Customs Brokerage, Inc.

Master BOL#: JSCU23456789
House BOL# (if applicable): N/A
Estimated Load Date: 12/21/20XX

Importer of Record (IOR): ABC Co., Inc. 1234 A St. Anytown, USA
IOR ID#: XX-XXXXXXX
Consignee ID#: (same as above)
Buyer: (same as above)
Ship To: (same as above)

Seller Name & Address: Best Sports, Ltd. 888 Omote-Dori, Yokohama, JAPAN
Manufacturer Name & Address: (same as above)
Container Stuffing Name & Address: (same as above)
Consolidator Name & Address: (same as above)

Description of Goods	Country of Origin	Harmonized Code (HTS)
Baseballs (leather)	Japan	9506.69.2040
Soccer balls (rubber)	Japan	9506.62.4080

By: _____ Title: _____ Date_____
　　　　(Importer's signature)

14

Air Waybill (AWB)

Arrival Notice (A/N)

Bill of Lading (BL)

Booking Request

Cargo Insurance Certificate (COI)

Certificate of Origin (COO)

Commercial Invoice (CI)

Declaration for Free Entry of Returned U.S. Goods (USGR)

Declaration of No Wood Packing Material (WPM)

Declaration of Non-Coniferous Wood Packing Material (WPM)

Entry Summary (Customs Form 7501)

Importer Security Filing Form (ISF)

Importer's Blanket Statement of Non-Reimbursement of Anti-Dumping Duties (AD/CVD)

Letter of Credit Application   (L/C)

Packing List (PL)

Power of Attorney (POA)

Pre-Shipment Inspection Certificate (PSIC)

Pro Forma Invoice

Purchase Order (PO)

Sales Order (SO)

Shipping Instructions (SI)

Telex Release Request (TLX)

Toxic Substances Control Act Statement (TSCA)

Importer's Blanket Statement of Non-Reimbursement of Anti-Dumping Duties (AD/CVD)

ALSO KNOWN AS:
Blanket Statement/Certificate. Non-Reimbursement Statement/Certificate.

REQUIRED FOR:
Imports that contain a commodity that is subject to anti-dumping duties.

NOT REQUIRED FOR:
N/A

ORIGINAL COPIES NORMALLY REQUIRED?:
No

IN SUMMARY:
The "importer's blanket statement of non-reimbursement of anti-dumping duties" is essentially an affidavit signed by the importer of record stating that their supplier (i.e. the shipper) will not reimburse them for anti-dumping duties payable by the importer to U.S. Customs. The statement references a specific commodity and a defined period of time. Anti-dumping cases are determined by the U.S. government in response to country-specific imports deemed sold to U.S. importers at a price significantly lower than in the foreign/home country.

USEFUL TIPS:
A sample of U.S. initiated anti-dumping cases is as follows...

- Steel and steel products from various countries
- Polyethylene retail carrier bags various countries
- Various products from China (cased pencils, fresh garlic, steel nails, etc.)
- Pasta from Italy
- Certain lined paper from India

WHAT TO REMEMBER:
Go to www.usitc.gov and see a list of current antidumping cases on the U.S. International Trade Commission's (USITC) website.

Importer's Blanket Statement of Non-Reimbursement of Anti-Dumping Duties

Date:
Importer:
Manufacturer:
Anti-Dumping Case Number:

I hereby certify that I have not entered into any agreement or understanding for the payment or for the reimbursement to me, by the manufacturer, producer, seller or exporter of all or any part of the antidumping duties upon all shipments of:

Commodity: _____

Countries of Origin: _____

Which have been and/or will be imported by this company.

This blanket applies to importations from (date): _____to (date):_____
I further certify that the U.S. Customs and Border Protection will be notified if there is any reimbursement of antidumping duties by the manufacturer, producer, seller, or exporter to the importing company at any time in the future.

Information regarding any refund of antidumping duties must be sent immediately to the CBP Port Director where this certificate is filed.

Failure to file this certificate prior to liquidation will result in the presumption of reimbursement and the assessment of double the antidumping duties.

By: _____   Title: _____
    (signature of company officer)

(Sample)

ABC Co., Inc.
1234 A St.
Anytown, USA

Importer's Blanket Statement of Non-Reimbursement
of Anti-Dumping Duties

Date: 1/1/20XX
Importer: ABC Co., Inc.
Manufacturer: Best Sports, Ltd. 888 Omote-Dori, Yokohama, JAPAN
Anti-Dumping Case Number: AXXX-XXX-XXX

I hereby certify that I have not entered into any agreement or understanding for the payment or for the reimbursement to me, by the manufacturer, producer, seller or exporter of all or any part of the antidumping duties upon all shipments of:

Commodity: ____Steel Ball Bearings_____

Countries of Origin: _____Japan_____

Which have been and/or will be imported by this company.

This blanket applies to importations from (date): _1/1/20XX_____to (date):_1/1/20XX __
I further certify that the U.S. Customs and Border Protection will be notified if there is any reimbursement of antidumping duties by the manufacturer, producer, seller, or exporter to the importing company at any time in the future.

Information regarding any refund of antidumping duties must be sent immediately to the CBP Port Director where this certificate is filed.

Failure to file this certificate prior to liquidation will result in the presumption of reimbursement and the assessment of double the antidumping duties.

By: _____   Title: _____
     (signature of company officer)

15

Air Waybill (AWB)

Arrival Notice (A/N)

Bill of Lading (BL)

Booking Request

Cargo Insurance Certificate (COI)

Certificate of Origin (COO)

Commercial Invoice (CI)

Declaration for Free Entry of Returned U.S. Goods (USGR)

Declaration of No Wood Packing Material (WPM)

Declaration of Non-Coniferous Wood Packing Material (WPM)

Entry Summary (Customs Form 7501)

Importer Security Filing Form (ISF)

Importer's Blanket Statement of Non-Reimbursement of
        Anti-Dumping Duties (AD/CVD)

Letter of Credit Application (L/C)

Packing List (PL)

Power of Attorney (POA)

Pre-Shipment Inspection Certificate (PSIC)

Pro Forma Invoice

Purchase Order (PO)

Sales Order (SO)

Shipping Instructions (SI)

Telex Release Request (TLX)

Toxic Substances Control Act Statement (TSCA)

Letter of Credit Application (L/C)

ALSO KNOWN AS:
Request to Open L/C. Application for Documentary Letter of Credit.

REQUIRED FOR:
Imports or Exports for which the agreed-upon form of payment is via a letter of credit

NOT REQUIRED FOR:
N/A

ORIGINAL COPIES NORMALLY REQUIRED?:
No

IN SUMMARY:
A letter of credit is a widely used international trade instrument of payment whereby the importer's bank pays the exporter subject to the exporter shipping the order and subsequently providing shipping documents exactly as per the terms and conditions as specified on the letter of credit.

USEFUL TIPS:
Most letters of credit are of the type called "irrevocable letter of credit", which means that the importer/buyer cannot unilaterally revise or cancel the letter of credit without the consent of both the importer/buyer and the exporter/supplier. This form of the L/C is more expensive than the "revocable letter of credit", however, it helps to ensure that the exporter is rightfully paid assuming he or she adheres to the terms and conditions of the "irrevocable letter of credit".

WHAT TO REMEMBER:
Correct spelling (even misspellings) and punctuation on shipping documents should match verbatim as spelled out on the letter of credit. Any such discrepancies could result in non-payment or in a delay of payment. The following documents are usually included in the list of required documents as advised by the L/C issuing bank.

- Bill of Lading (BL)
- Commercial Invoice (CI)
- Packing List (PL)
- Marine Insurance Certificate (COI)

Letter of Credit Application (L/C)

Date:

To:

Applicant:
Applicant Reference#:
Beneficiary:
Beneficiary's Advising Bank:

Type of Credit:
Draft:
Expiry Date:

Price Term:
Commodity Description:
Quantity:
Unit Price:
Amount:

Loading Port:
Unlading Port:
Latest Shipping Date:
Partial Shipments:
Transshipment:

Documents:
-
-
-
-

Note:
-
-
-
-

(Sample)

ABC Co., Inc.
1234 A St.
Anytown, USA

Letter of Credit Application (L/C)

Date: 1/1/20XX

To: LA Bank of XYZ, Inc.

Applicant: ABC Co., Inc. 1234 A St., Anytown, USA
Applicant Reference#: PO#1234
Beneficiary: Best Sports, Ltd. 888 Omote-Dori, Yokohama, JAPAN
Beneficiary's Advising Bank: Toto Industrial Bank, 800 Ura-Dori, Yokohama, JAPAN

Type of Credit: Irrevocable
Draft: At Sight
Expiry Date: February 28th, 20XX

Price Term: CIF Port of Los Angeles
Commodity Description: Table Tennis (Ping Pong) Balls
Quantity: 250 Gross (144 count per gross)
Unit Price: USD $40.00 / Gross
Amount: USD $10,000.00

Loading Port: Any Japanese Port
Unlading Port: Los Angeles, USA
Latest Shipping Date: January 31, 20XX
Partial Shipments: Prohibited
Transshipment: Allowed

Documents:
- Full set of on board Bills of Lading marked "Prepaid" and "Notify Applicant"
- Commercial Invoice in triplicate
- Packing List in triplicate
- Marine Insurance Certificate original endorsed in blank for 110% of the invoice value and insurance must include Institute Cargo Clause (C)

Note:
- All banking charges outside the U.S. and remittance charges are for the account of the beneficiary.
- Documents must be presented within 21 days after shipment, but within expiry date.
- This letter of credit is subject to the latest version of the Uniform Customs and Practice for Documentary Credits International Chamber of Commerce (ICC).
- Multi-modal Bill of Lading acceptable.

16

Air Waybill (AWB)

Arrival Notice (A/N)

Bill of Lading (BL)

Booking Request

Cargo Insurance Certificate (COI)

Certificate of Origin (COO)

Commercial Invoice (CI)

Declaration for Free Entry of Returned U.S. Goods (USGR)

Declaration of No Wood Packing Material (WPM)

Declaration of Non-Coniferous Wood Packing Material (WPM)

Entry Summary (Customs Form 7501)

Importer Security Filing Form (ISF)

Importer's Blanket Statement of Non-Reimbursement of
      Anti-Dumping Duties (AD/CVD)

Letter of Credit Application   (L/C)

Packing List (PL)

Power of Attorney (POA)

Pre-Shipment Inspection Certificate (PSIC)

Pro Forma Invoice

Purchase Order (PO)

Sales Order (SO)

Shipping Instructions (SI)

Telex Release Request (TLX)

Toxic Substances Control Act Statement (TSCA)

Packing List (PL)

ALSO KNOWN AS:
Packing Slip. Weight List.

REQUIRED FOR:
All Imports and Exports

NOT REQUIRED FOR:
N/A

ORIGINAL COPIES NORMALLY REQUIRED?:
No

IN SUMMARY:
The packing list is a shipping document prepared by the shipper that describes the shipment's packaging and may include quantities, weights, dimensions, marks, numbering, and types of packaging.

USEFUL TIPS:
Most customers require an "itemized packing list", which is a packing list that advises the weights of all packaged units. For example, if an ocean container contains 12 pallets of a commodity, then the itemized packing list will show the gross weight (the weight of the entire pallet), the tare weight (the weight of just the pallet and packaging material), and the net weight (the weight of the commodity by itself). And, these three weights would be included on the packing list for all 12 pallets.

WHAT TO REMEMBER:
Information provided on the packing list can and usually will duplicate the information already provided on the commercial invoice for the same shipment. In general, however, the packing list does not normally show the pricing or value of the shipment, but instead provides more detail in regards to how the shipment is packaged.

Packing List

Date:
Invoice#:

Sold To:
Ship To:

Terms of Sale:
Country of Origin and Export:
Actual Mfr:
Freight Charges:

Qty.	Unit	No. Pkg.	Pkg. Dims.	Grs. Wt.	Tare Wt.	Net Wt.	Description of Goods
							Packaging Totals

Marks:

I certify this document to be true and correct.

By: _____   Title: _____
　　　　　　(signature)

(Sample)

ABC Co., Inc.
1234 A St.
Anytown, USA

Packing List

Date: 1/1/20XX
Invoice#: 1234

Sold To: Best Sports, Ltd. 888 Omote-Dori, Yokohama, JAPAN
Ship To: (same as above)

Terms of Sale: C&F Yokohama
Country of Origin and Export: USA
Actual Mfr: ABC Co., Inc.
Freight Charges: $1,000.00 USD

Qty.	Unit	No. Pkg.	Pkg. Dims.	Grs. Wt.	Tare Wt.	Net Wt.	Description of Goods
500	Each	500 Boxes	7"x7"x7" (per box)	0.5 Lbs	0.1 Lbs	0.4 Lbs	Basketballs (rubber)
500	Each	500 Boxes	5"x5"x5" (per box)	0.4 Lbs	0.1 Lbs	0.3 Lbs	Volleyballs (synth. leather)
		1000 Boxes		450 Lbs	100 Lbs	350 Lbs	Packaging Totals

Marks: "ABC Co., Inc., U.S.A."

I certify this document to be true and correct.

By: _____   Title: _____
          (signature)

17

Air Waybill (AWB)

Arrival Notice (A/N)

Bill of Lading (BL)

Booking Request

Cargo Insurance Certificate (COI)

Certificate of Origin (COO)

Commercial Invoice (CI)

Declaration for Free Entry of Returned U.S. Goods (USGR)

Declaration of No Wood Packing Material (WPM)

Declaration of Non-Coniferous Wood Packing Material (WPM)

Entry Summary (Customs Form 7501)

Importer Security Filing Form (ISF)

Importer's Blanket Statement of Non-Reimbursement of
     Anti-Dumping Duties (AD/CVD)

Letter of Credit Application   (L/C)

Packing List (PL)

Power of Attorney (POA)

Pre-Shipment Inspection Certificate (PSIC)

Pro Forma Invoice

Purchase Order (PO)

Sales Order (SO)

Shipping Instructions (SI)

Telex Release Request (TLX)

Toxic Substances Control Act Statement (TSCA)

Power of Attorney (POA)

ALSO KNOWN AS:

POA. Customs Power of Attorney. Import Power of Attorney.

REQUIRED FOR:

All Imports for which the customs clearance services of a customs broker are used.

NOT REQUIRED FOR:

Exports

ORIGINAL COPIES NORMALLY REQUIRED?:

Yes

IN SUMMARY:

The customs power of attorney is a legal document by which the importer (the principal) authorizes a customs broker (the agent/attorney) to perform customs-related business on behalf of the importer.

USEFUL TIPS:

The legal language included in the customs power of attorney will vary somewhat from one customs brokerage operation to the next. The importer may grant a power of attorney to one or several different customs brokerage companies, and it is up to the importer's own discretion to limit (or expand on) a power of attorney to imports at a specific US port, on a specific shipment, within a specified time frame, etc. It should not be necessary to have the POA witnessed or notarized.

WHAT TO REMEMBER:

The customs power of attorney is only to be signed by an individual authorized to sign for the company. The original signed copy of the POA must be mailed to the customs broker for their record keeping requirements. In the case of a partnership, the customs power of attorney will only be effective two years.

Customs Power of Attorney

KNOW ALL PERSONS BY THESE PRESENTS, THAT

_____

(Full name of company or individual)

_____

(Legal designation, such as corp., individual, sole prop., LLC, or partnership)

Located at

_____

(Business Address)

Using EIN or SSN _____ hereby appoints the agent, _____ as a true and lawful agent and attorney of the principal named above with full power and authority to do and perform every lawful act the said agent and attorney may deem necessary to be done for and on behalf of the said principal without limitation of any kind as fully as said principal could do if present and acting, and hereby ratify and confirm all that said agent and attorney shall lawfully do or cause to be done by virtue of these presents until written notice of revocation is delivered to the agent. In the case of a partnership, this power of attorney will only be effective two years from the date below.

By: _____ Title: _____ Date_____

    (Principal's signature)

(Sample)

Perfect Customs Brokerage, Inc.
1234 B St.
Anytown, USA

Customs Power of Attorney

KNOW ALL PERSONS BY THESE PRESENTS, THAT

ABC Co., Inc. _____
(Full name of company or individual)

Corporation _____
(Legal designation, such as corp., individual, sole prop., LLC, or partnership)

Located at

1234 A St., Anytown, USA_____
(Business Address)

Using EIN or SSN XX-XXXXXXX___ hereby appoints the agent, Perfect Customs Brokerage, Inc., as a true and lawful agent and attorney of the principal named above with full power and authority to do and perform every lawful act the said agent and attorney may deem necessary to be done for and on behalf of the said principal without limitation of any kind as fully as said principal could do if present and acting, and hereby ratify and confirm all that said agent and attorney shall lawfully do or cause to be done by virtue of these presents until written notice of revocation is delivered to the agent. In the case of a partnership, this power of attorney will only be effective two years from the date below.

By: _____   Title: _____   Date_____
    (Principal's signature)

18

Air Waybill (AWB)
Arrival Notice (A/N)
Bill of Lading (BL)
Booking Request
Cargo Insurance Certificate (COI)
Certificate of Origin (COO)
Commercial Invoice (CI)
Declaration for Free Entry of Returned U.S. Goods (USGR)
Declaration of No Wood Packing Material (WPM)
Declaration of Non-Coniferous Wood Packing Material (WPM)
Entry Summary (Customs Form 7501)
Importer Security Filing Form (ISF)
Importer's Blanket Statement of Non-Reimbursement of
      Anti-Dumping Duties (AD/CVD)
Letter of Credit Application   (L/C)
Packing List (PL)
Power of Attorney (POA)

Pre-Shipment Inspection Certificate (PSIC)

Pro Forma Invoice
Purchase Order (PO)
Sales Order (SO)
Shipping Instructions (SI)
Telex Release Request (TLX)
Toxic Substances Control Act Statement (TSCA)

Pre-Shipment Inspection Certificate (PSIC)

ALSO KNOWN AS:
PSIC. Final Random Inspection Certificate.

REQUIRED FOR:
Exports to certain (usually developing) countries

NOT REQUIRED FOR:
N/A

ORIGINAL COPIES NORMALLY REQUIRED?:
Yes

IN SUMMARY:
Pre-Shipment Inspections (PSI) are required by certain importing countries' governments and by some foreign importers in a attempt to best confirm 1) the type of commodity being loaded and shipped, 2) the grade or quality of that commodity, and 3) the resulting accurate valuation of the arranged shipment.

USEFUL TIPS:
Exporters can find details on which countries require pre-shipment inspections as well as a list of private companies normally qualified to conduct pre-shipment inspections at export.gov, a resource for the US trade community and managed by the U.S. Department of Commerce's International Trade Administration.

http://export.gov/logistics/eg_main_018120.asp

WHAT TO REMEMBER:

Exporters should verify with their customer at the time of the order if a pre-shipment inspection certificate (PSIC) is required or not. If an order is inadvertently exported from the seller's country without the necessary pre-shipment inspection, then the shipment will likely be denied by the customer and/or government of the country of importation. Some PSIC inspectors may simply confirm the existence and quality of the material or commodity at the supplier's or consolidator's address. Other inspectors may actually witness the loading process of the goods into the subsequently sealed shipping container or conveyance.

Pre-Shipment Inspection Certificate (PSIC)

Date:
Certificate No.:
Purchase Order No.:

Importer:

Country of Origin and Export:
Container No.:
Seal No.:
Packaging Unit:
Average Weight per Packaging Unit:
Further Details of Import:

Qty.	Unit of Measure	Unit Price	Description of Goods	Total Value (USD)
			Total	

Details of Tests Carried Out:

Declaration:

By: _____ Title: _____
　　　　　(signature)

(Sample)

IAG
It's All Good Inspection Services, Inc.
1212 Check St.
Anytown, USA

Pre-Shipment Inspection Certificate (PSIC)

Date: 1/1/20XX
Certificate No.: IAG1212
Purchase Order No.: 8675309

Importer: Global Sporting Goods, Inc., 123 Sudirman-Thamrin Ave., Jakarta, Indonesia

Country of Origin and Export: USA
Container No.: JSCU9101112
Seal No.: S1234
Packaging Unit: Individual Shoe Boxes
Average Weight per Packaging Unit: 2.0 lbs. net, 0.5 lbs. tare, 2.5 lbs. gross
Further Details of Import:

Qty.	Unit of Measure	Unit Price	Description of Goods	Total Value (USD)
500	Pairs	20.00	Basketball Shoes (size 8)	$10,000.00
500	Pairs	20.00	Basketball Shoes (size 9)	$10,000.00
			Total	$20,000.00

Details of Tests Carried Out: Random sampling and visual inspection at time of loading

Declaration:

The consignment as described herein was duly inspected by IAG, Inc. or its authorized agent at ABC Co., Inc. 1234 A St., Anytown, USA on January 1st 20XX. A thorough and random sampling of at least 5% by quantity of the consignment was performed with reasonable care confirming that the contents, quality, and quantity of the consignment are in conformance with the terms of the purchase order 8675309. I hereby certify that the statements made on this document to be true and correct.

By: _____   Title: _____
          (signature)

19

Air Waybill (AWB)

Arrival Notice (A/N)

Bill of Lading (BL)

Booking Request

Cargo Insurance Certificate (COI)

Certificate of Origin (COO)

Commercial Invoice (CI)

Declaration for Free Entry of Returned U.S. Goods (USGR)

Declaration of No Wood Packing Material (WPM)

Declaration of Non-Coniferous Wood Packing Material (WPM)

Entry Summary (Customs Form 7501)

Importer Security Filing Form (ISF)

Importer's Blanket Statement of Non-Reimbursement of
    Anti-Dumping Duties (AD/CVD)

Letter of Credit Application   (L/C)

Packing List (PL)

Power of Attorney (POA)

Pre-Shipment Inspection Certificate (PSIC)

Pro Forma Invoice

Purchase Order (PO)

Sales Order (SO)

Shipping Instructions (SI)

Telex Release Request (TLX)

Toxic Substances Control Act Statement (TSCA)

Pro Forma Invoice

ALSO KNOWN AS:
Proforma. Estimate. Dummy Invoice.

REQUIRED FOR:
Imports and Exports requiring a commercial invoice, but one is not yet available for whatever reason.

NOT REQUIRED FOR:
N/A

ORIGINAL COPIES NORMALLY REQUIRED?:
No

IN SUMMARY:
A pro forma invoice may serve two purposes. First, and most common, is temporarily in lieu of an actual commercial invoice for customs purposes (see the section of this handbook titled "Commercial Invoice (CI)". Second, it may be automatically issued by a supplier at the time of the order with the customer, and serve as a sort of sales order (see section titled "Sales Order (SO)".

USEFUL TIPS:
The pro forma invoice should include all of the essential elements of the anticipated commercial invoice such as pricing, quantity, and terms of sale (INCO Terms) in order for customs to accurately assess the actual value of the shipment.

WHAT TO REMEMBER:
Although the pro forma invoice may suffice for US Customs purposes at the time of customs entry, an official commercial invoice must also be obtained from the supplier and maintained on file for recordkeeping requirements.

Pro Forma Invoice

Date:
SO#:

Sold To:
Ship To:

Payment Terms:
Ship by Date:
Ship via:
Terms of Sale:
Country of Origin and Export:
Type of Packaging:

Qty.	Unit of Measure	Unit Price	Description of Goods	Total Value (USD)
			Total	

(Sample)

ABC Co., Inc.
1234 A St.
Anytown, USA

Pro Forma Invoice

Date: 1/1/20XX
SO#: 4321

Sold To: Best Sports, Ltd. 888 Omote-Dori, Yokohama, JAPAN
Ship To: (same as above)

Payment Terms: Documents Against Payment
Ship by Date: 1/31/20XX
Ship via: Ocean Freight
Terms of Sale: C&F Yokohama
Country of Origin and Export: USA
Type of Packaging: Individually boxed for retail sale

Qty.	Unit of Measure	Unit Price	Description of Goods	Total Value (USD)
500	Each	10.00	Basketballs (rubber)	$5,000.00
500	Each	10.00	Volleyballs (synth. leather)	$5,000.00
			Total	$10,000.00

20

Air Waybill (AWB)

Arrival Notice (A/N)

Bill of Lading (BL)

Booking Request

Cargo Insurance Certificate (COI)

Certificate of Origin (COO)

Commercial Invoice (CI)

Declaration for Free Entry of Returned U.S. Goods (USGR)

Declaration of No Wood Packing Material (WPM)

Declaration of Non-Coniferous Wood Packing Material (WPM)

Entry Summary (Customs Form 7501)

Importer Security Filing Form (ISF)

Importer's Blanket Statement of Non-Reimbursement of
        Anti-Dumping Duties (AD/CVD)

Letter of Credit Application   (L/C)

Packing List (PL)

Power of Attorney (POA)

Pre-Shipment Inspection Certificate (PSIC)

Pro Forma Invoice

Purchase Order (PO)

Sales Order (SO)

Shipping Instructions (SI)

Telex Release Request (TLX)

Toxic Substances Control Act Statement (TSCA)

Purchase Order (PO)

ALSO KNOWN AS:
PO. Purchase Agreement. International Purchase Agreement. Purchase Contract. PC.

REQUIRED FOR:
The origin of all Imports and Exports

NOT REQUIRED FOR:
N/A

ORIGINAL COPIES NORMALLY REQUIRED?:
No

IN SUMMARY:
The flip side of a sales order, a purchase order is a document issued by the buyer/customer to the seller/supplier outlining the specifics of a proposed transfer of a good and/or service.

USEFUL TIPS:
For the purpose of clarity and to avoid any potential misunderstandings, the purchase order can include as much detail as possible, including, but of course not limited to the international commercial terms (Incoterms), quantity and detailed description of the product, packaging, purchase price, payment terms, and any additional general terms and conditions of the transaction deemed necessary.

WHAT TO REMEMBER:
Although also known as a purchase contract, the purchase order is not a legally binding contract until it is signed by or otherwise accepted by the selling party. Also, even though most international transactions are confirmed in US dollars (USD), it is essential that both parties are in agreement on the remittance currency to be used.

Purchase Order

Date:
PO#:

Vendor Name:

Sold To:
Ship To:

Payment Terms:
Ship by Date:
Ship via:
Terms of Sale:
Country of Origin and Export:
Type of Packaging:

Qty.	Unit of Measure	Unit Price	Description of Goods	Total Value (USD)
		Total		

The undersigned seller hereby acknowledges and agrees to the foregoing offer in accordance with the terms and conditions specified above.

By: _____   Date: _____
    (signature of seller)

(Sample)

Best Sports, Ltd.
888 Omote-Dori,
Yokohama, JAPAN

Purchase Order

Date: 1/1/20XX
PO#: 1234

Vendor Name: ABC Co., Inc.

Sold To: Best Sports, Ltd. 888 Omote-Dori, Yokohama, JAPAN
Ship To: (same as above)

Payment Terms: Documents Against Payment
Ship by Date: 1/31/20XX
Ship via: Air Freight
Terms of Sale: C&F Yokohama
Country of Origin and Export: USA
Type of Packaging: Individually boxed for retail sale

Qty.	Unit of Measure	Unit Price	Description of Goods	Total Value (USD)
500	Each	10.00	Basketballs (rubber)	$5,000.00
500	Each	10.00	Volleyballs (synth. leather)	$5,000.00
			Total	$10,000.00

The undersigned seller hereby acknowledges and agrees to the foregoing offer in accordance with the terms and conditions specified above.

By: _____ Date: _____
    (signature of seller)

21

Air Waybill (AWB)

Arrival Notice (A/N)

Bill of Lading (BL)

Booking Request

Cargo Insurance Certificate (COI)

Certificate of Origin (COO)

Commercial Invoice (CI)

Declaration for Free Entry of Returned U.S. Goods (USGR)

Declaration of No Wood Packing Material (WPM)

Declaration of Non-Coniferous Wood Packing Material (WPM)

Entry Summary (Customs Form 7501)

Importer Security Filing Form (ISF)

Importer's Blanket Statement of Non-Reimbursement of
    Anti-Dumping Duties (AD/CVD)

Letter of Credit Application   (L/C)

Packing List (PL)

Power of Attorney (POA)

Pre-Shipment Inspection Certificate (PSIC)

Pro Forma Invoice

Purchase Order (PO)

Sales Order (SO)

Shipping Instructions (SI)

Telex Release Request (TLX)

Toxic Substances Control Act Statement (TSCA)

Sales Order (SO)

ALSO KNOWN AS:

SO. Sales Agreement. International Sales Agreement. Sales Contract. SC.

REQUIRED FOR:

The origin of all Imports and Exports

NOT REQUIRED FOR:

N/A

ORIGINAL COPIES NORMALLY REQUIRED?:

No

IN SUMMARY:

The flip side of a purchase order, a sales order is a document issued by the seller/supplier to the buyer/customer outlining the specifics of a proposed transfer of a good and/or service.

USEFUL TIPS:

For the purpose of clarity and to avoid any potential misunderstandings, the sales order can include as much detail as possible, including, but of course not limited to the international commercial terms (Incoterms), quantity and detailed description of the product, packaging, purchase price, payment terms, and any additional general terms and conditions of the transaction deemed necessary.

WHAT TO REMEMBER:

Although also known as a sales contract, the sales order is not a legally binding contract until it is signed by or otherwise accepted by the purchasing party. Also, even though most international transactions are confirmed in US dollars (USD), it is essential that both parties are in agreement on the remittance currency to be used.

Sales Order

Date:
SO#:

Sold To:
Ship To:

Payment Terms:
Ship by Date:
Ship via:
Terms of Sale:
Country of Origin and Export:
Type of Packaging:

Qty.	Unit of Measure	Unit Price	Description of Goods	Total Value (USD)
		Total		

The undersigned buyer hereby acknowledges and agrees to the foregoing offer in accordance with the terms and conditions specified above.

By: _____   Date: _____
        (signature of buyer)

(Sample)

ABC Co., Inc.
1234 A St.
Anytown, USA

Sales Order

Date: 1/1/20XX
SO#: 4321

Sold To: Best Sports, Ltd. 888 Omote-Dori, Yokohama, JAPAN
Ship To: (same as above)

Payment Terms: Documents Against Payment
Ship by Date: 1/31/20XX
Ship via: Ocean Freight
Terms of Sale: C&F Yokohama
Country of Origin and Export: USA
Type of Packaging: Individually boxed for retail sale

Qty.	Unit of Measure	Unit Price	Description of Goods	Total Value (USD)
500	Each	10.00	Basketballs (rubber)	$5,000.00
500	Each	10.00	Volleyballs (synth. leather)	$5,000.00
			Total	$10,000.00

The undersigned buyer hereby acknowledges and agrees to the foregoing offer in accordance with the terms and conditions specified above.

By: _____   Date: _____
      (signature of buyer)

22

Air Waybill (AWB)

Arrival Notice (A/N)

Bill of Lading (BL)

Booking Request

Cargo Insurance Certificate (COI)

Certificate of Origin (COO)

Commercial Invoice (CI)

Declaration for Free Entry of Returned U.S. Goods (USGR)

Declaration of No Wood Packing Material (WPM)

Declaration of Non-Coniferous Wood Packing Material (WPM)

Entry Summary (Customs Form 7501)

Importer Security Filing Form (ISF)

Importer's Blanket Statement of Non-Reimbursement of
        Anti-Dumping Duties (AD/CVD)

Letter of Credit Application   (L/C)

Packing List (PL)

Power of Attorney (POA)

Pre-Shipment Inspection Certificate (PSIC)

Pro Forma Invoice

Purchase Order (PO)

Sales Order (SO)

Shipping Instructions (SI)

Telex Release Request (TLX)

Toxic Substances Control Act Statement (TSCA)

Shipping Instructions (SI)

ALSO KNOWN AS:

S.I. BL Instructions. International Shipping Instructions. Shipper's Letter of Instructions. S.L.I.

REQUIRED FOR:

All Exports

NOT REQUIRED FOR:

Imports

ORIGINAL COPIES NORMALLY REQUIRED?:

No

IN SUMMARY:

Shipping instructions are detailed instructions that a shipper provides to their carrier in order for the carrier to accurately draft and issue an export's bill of lading. Information provided by the exporter includes shipper contact details, consignee details, the bill to party and whether freight charges will be prepaid or collect, description of goods, weights, packaging, etc.

USEFUL TIPS:

If a carrier requires shipping instructions before the exact details are known, the shipper may have to estimate some information such as weights, etc. for them (also known as "dummy instructions") and then provide the carrier the missing details as soon as possible afterwards.

WHAT TO REMEMBER:

At the time of booking your export with your carrier, verify the actual deadline (date and time) for the submittal of shipping instructions. If the S.I. is late, your shipment may not make the vessel or flight as scheduled. Also, confirm with your freight forwarder if they can submit an export declaration (also known as AES) on your behalf. If they cannot, or if you are not using the services of a freight forwarder, then an Internal Transaction Number (ITN) will also be a required element of your S.I. Go to https://aesdirect.census.gov/ and www.bis.doc.gov to learn more regarding certain export requirements.

Shipping Instructions

Date:

Booking#:
ITN#:

Shipper:
Shipper's Export Reference:
Consignee:
Notify Party:
Country of Origin:

Port of Loading:
Port of Discharge:
Final Destination:

Description of Goods:
Marks:
Container No.:
No. and Type of Packages:

Pallet	No. of Pkgs.	Pallet. Dims.	Grs. Wt.	Tare Wt.	Net Wt.
Totals					

Value of Shipment (USD):
Ocean Freight:
Destination Charges:
Cargo Insurance Required?:
Original Bills of Lading Required?:

(Sample)

ABC Co., Inc.
1234 A St.
Anytown, USA

Shipping Instructions

Date: 1/1/20XX

Booking#: JSCU12345678
ITN#: N/A

Shipper: ABC Co., Inc. 1234 A St., Anytown, USA
Shipper's Export Reference: PO#1234
Consignee: Best Sports, Ltd. 888 Omote-Dori, Yokohama, JAPAN
Notify Party: Same as Consignee
Country of Origin: USA

Port of Loading: Los Angeles
Port of Discharge: Yokohama
Final Destination: Yokohama

Description of Goods: Sports Equipment (Basketballs & Volleyballs)
Marks: "ABC Co., Inc., USA"
Container No.: JSCU1234567
No. and Type of Packages: 1000 Boxes on 2 Pallets (see below)

Pallet	No. of Pkgs.	Pallet. Dims.	Grs. Wt.	Tare Wt.	Net Wt.
#1	500 Boxes	40"x40"x40"	250 Lbs	60 Lbs	190 Lbs
#2	500 Boxes	40"x40"x30"	200 Lbs	40 Lbs	160 Lbs
Totals	1000 Boxes	On 2 Pallets	450 Lbs	100 Lbs	350 Lbs

Value of Shipment (USD): $10,000.00
Ocean Freight: Prepaid
Destination Charges: Collect
Cargo Insurance Required?: No.
Original Bills of Lading Required?: Yes.

23

Air Waybill (AWB)

Arrival Notice (A/N)

Bill of Lading (BL)

Booking Request

Cargo Insurance Certificate (COI)

Certificate of Origin (COO)

Commercial Invoice (CI)

Declaration for Free Entry of Returned U.S. Goods (USGR)

Declaration of No Wood Packing Material (WPM)

Declaration of Non-Coniferous Wood Packing Material (WPM)

Entry Summary (Customs Form 7501)

Importer Security Filing Form (ISF)

Importer's Blanket Statement of Non-Reimbursement of
    Anti-Dumping Duties (AD/CVD)

Letter of Credit Application   (L/C)

Packing List (PL)

Power of Attorney (POA)

Pre-Shipment Inspection Certificate (PSIC)

Pro Forma Invoice

Purchase Order (PO)

Sales Order (SO)

Shipping Instructions (SI)

Telex Release Request (TLX)

Toxic Substances Control Act Statement (TSCA)

Telex Release Request (TLX)

ALSO KNOWN OR REFERRED TO AS:
BL Surrender Request. Waybill Release Request. Express Release Request.

REQUIRED FOR:
Exports for which exporter/shipper has confirmed receipt of payment from the customer and is ready to surrender control and ownership of the cargo to their customer.

NOT REQUIRED FOR:
N/A

ORIGINAL COPIES NORMALLY REQUIRED?:
No

IN SUMMARY:
The telex release request is an official request by the shipper and addressed to the shipping company. It authorizes the shipping company to release the shipment to the consignee at destination as notated on the Bill of Lading.

USEFUL TIPS:
The telex release request is not actually sent via a telex machine (an antiquated form of international telegraphic correspondence). Acceptable formats of the telex release request from the shipper will differ somewhat from carrier to carrier. Some carriers may accept the telex release request via a brief email, while others may require the request to be typed up on a carrier-supplied letter template and then sent as an email attachment.

WHAT TO REMEMBER:
Some customers may request their supplier (the shipper) to telex release the cargo to them prior to the shipper actually receiving payment. This practice is very risky since the supplier no longer maintains control of the shipment once it has been released to the consignee. However, once payment has officially been received by the shipper from the overseas customer, the telex release is a quicker method of releasing the goods to the customer than physically couriering original bills of lading to their foreign office.

Telex Release Request (TLX)

To:

We, _____ confirm and hereby authorize the telex release of the below mentioned shipment for which we surrender full sets of original bills of lading. You are kindly requested to release this cargo accordingly to the below mentioned "release to" party. Please duly notify the appropriate parties at destination regarding this cargo release. Thank you for your cooperation.

Shipment# (BL#, AWB#, or Booking#):
Container#:
"Release To" Party:

Return receipt requested.

By: _____ Title: _____ Date_____
    (Shipper's signature)

(Sample)

ABC Co., Inc.
1234 A St.
Anytown, USA

Telex Release Request (TLX)

To: Joe's Shipping Co.

    We, <u>ABC Co., Inc.</u>   confirm and hereby authorize the telex release of the below mentioned shipment for which we surrender full sets of original bills of lading. You are kindly requested to release this cargo accordingly to the below mentioned "release to" party. Please duly notify the appropriate parties at destination regarding this cargo release. Thank you for your cooperation.

Shipment# (BL#, AWB#, or Booking#): BL# JSCU12345678
Container#: JSCU1234567
"Release To" Party: Best Sports, Ltd. 888 Omote-Dori, Yokohama, JAPAN

Return receipt requested.

By: _____   Title: _____   Date_____
        (Shipper's signature)

24

Air Waybill (AWB)

Arrival Notice (A/N)

Bill of Lading (BL)

Booking Request

Cargo Insurance Certificate (COI)

Certificate of Origin (COO)

Commercial Invoice (CI)

Declaration for Free Entry of Returned U.S. Goods (USGR)

Declaration of No Wood Packing Material (WPM)

Declaration of Non-Coniferous Wood Packing Material (WPM)

Entry Summary (Customs Form 7501)

Importer Security Filing Form (ISF)

Importer's Blanket Statement of Non-Reimbursement of
     Anti-Dumping Duties (AD/CVD)

Letter of Credit Application   (L/C)

Packing List (PL)

Power of Attorney (POA)

Pre-Shipment Inspection Certificate (PSIC)

Pro Forma Invoice

Purchase Order (PO)

Sales Order (SO)

Shipping Instructions (SI)

Telex Release Request (TLX)

Toxic Substances Control Act Statement (TSCA)

Toxic Substances Control Act Statement (TSCA)

ALSO KNOWN AS:
Toxic Substances Control Act of 1976. TSCA.

REQUIRED FOR:
Imports and Exports containing chemicals (see the EPA's website for details www.epa.gov).

NOT REQUIRED FOR:
Exempt items (see the EPA's website for details www.epa.gov).

ORIGINAL COPIES NORMALLY REQUIRED?:
No

IN SUMMARY:
TSCA is a US law that regulates, among other things, the importation and exportation of chemicals and chemical-related merchandise and is administered by the Environmental Protection Agency (EPA). As it relates to importers and exporters, the TSCA Statement or TSCA Certification is a document that the US seller or US buyer must complete by A) certifying that their shipment either complies with TSCA rules or B) by certifying that their shipment is not subject to TSCA.

USEFUL TIPS:
Listed below are examples of items that require a completed TSCA Statement...

- Pigments, dyes, and ink
- Plastics in primary forms
- Soaps
- Lubricants
- Waxes
- Paint
- Cleaners, detergents, and air fresheners

WHAT TO REMEMBER:
If you need assistance regarding the TSCA applicability of your shipment, contact the TSCA Hotline at (202) 554-1404 and/or consult with your customs broker.

Toxic Substances Control Act Statement (TSCA)

Check the box corresponding to the applicable statement below (check only one):

Positive Statement:

☐ I certify that all chemical substances in this shipment comply with all applicable rules or orders under TSCA and that I am not offering a chemical substance for entry in violation of TSCA or any applicable rule or order there under.

Negative Statement:

☐ I certify that all chemical substances in this shipment are not subject to TSCA.

Authorized Name (please print): _____

Authorized Signature: _____

Title: _____

Shipment Ref#: _____

(Sample)

ABC Co., Inc.
1234 A St.
Anytown, USA

Toxic Substances Control Act Statement (TSCA)

Check the box corresponding to the applicable statement below (check only one):

Positive Statement:

☐ I certify that all chemical substances in this shipment comply with all applicable rules or orders under TSCA and that I am not offering a chemical substance for entry in violation of TSCA or any applicable rule or order there under.

Negative Statement:

☑ I certify that all chemical substances in this shipment are not subject to TSCA.

Authorized Name (please print): _____

Authorized Signature: _____

Title: _____

Shipment Ref#: _____

References

AES Direct Home Page.
https://aesdirect.census.gov/
Web 2013.

American Institute of Marine Underwriters Home Page.
http://www.aimu.org/
Web 2013.

Export.gov Home Page.
http://export.gov/
Web 2013.

Hinkelman, Edward G., *Dictionary of International Trade*, World Trade Press, California, 1994.

International Air Transport Association Home Page.
https://www.iata.org/
Web 2013.

International Chamber of Commerce Home Page.
http://www.iccwbo.org/
Web 2013.

Manresa, Maritza, *How to Open & Operate a Financially Successful Import Export Business*, Atlantic Publishing Group, Inc., Florida, 2010.

Turner, Krista, *Start Your Own Import/Export Business*, Entrepreneur Media Inc., 2010.

United States Customs and Border Protection Home Page.
http://www.cbp.gov/
Web 2014.

United States Department of Agriculture Home Page.
Animal and Plant Health Inspection Service
http://www.aphis.usda.gov/
Web 2013.

United States Environment Protection Agency Home Page.
http://www.epa.gov/
Web 2013.

United States Government Printing Office Home Page.
Title 19 Electronic Code of Federal Regulations "Customs Duties"
http://www.ecfr.gov/
Web 2014.

United States International Trade Commission Home Page
"Harmonized Tariff Schedule of the United States"
http://www.usitc.gov/
Web 2014.

Made in the USA
Lexington, KY
29 October 2015